Coming Out
Of Darkness

Gary Sigler

ISBN:149595935X
ISBN-13:9781495959356

Coming Out of Darkness

Chapter 1

God Will Perfect His Will In Your Life

"This I say therefore, and testify in the Lord, that ye henceforth walk not as other Gentiles walk, in the vanity of their mind, having the understanding darkened, being alienated from the life of God through the ignorance that is in them, because of the blindness of their heart" (Eph. 4:17-18).

We are entering into an exciting time in our Christian experience, but right now there is so much darkness prevailing over our minds that it is very, very difficult to see what God is revealing to the His seekers. Some of what I am about to share with you may therefore seem to be contrary to the scriptures, but it only *seems* contrary. God now has us in a position where most of us are so fed up with what we know has not worked for us, that we are ready to receive some truth and some understanding which goes beyond what we have perceived in the past.

When Paul wrote this passage in Ephesians 4:17-18, he had already given the Ephesians an almost entire view of God's plan, His will, and His purposes for them, and that is why he used the word *"therefore."* "Because of all of this that I have shown you, *therefore* don't be like the gentiles. Don't be like the unbelievers." And most of us do not realize that we can be a believer for many years, and still in our mind and in our understanding be like an unbeliever! We can know everything there is to know, *we think,* about the Word of God. We have walked and sought after God for years, and because of that we do not realize that we are in this condition of being like a gentile, having the understanding darkened, being alienated from the life of God that is in us.

What does Paul mean by being "alienated from the life of God"? We need to have an understanding that there are only two sources of life in the universe. We receive our life source from our human carnal consciousness, which is separated from the life of God, or from Christ who is one with God. Most Christians still are receiving their life source unknowingly from the natural or carnal man. They have never learned how to contact and live by the Spirit of Christ within them. Being "alienated from the life" simply means that I do not have an understanding that my Father and I are One. I have been alienated; my mind is darkened to the understanding that God and man are One. ***Having their understanding darkened, being alienated . . .***

There is still much teaching prevailing in the Church today about "the great falling away". I hear it on TV; I hear it wherever I go. I hear about the "great falling away" and "the man of sin who is soon to be revealed." That teaching is part of the darkness, because there is no possible way that the Church of the Living God could be in any more darkness than it has been in for the last two thousand years—**it is impossible**. The "falling away" that the Apostle talked about began even in Paul's lifetime, but it took root in the second century and has gone deeper and deeper into darkness for the last two thousand years. The first ray of light that God used to recover His Church back to its original design, intent and purpose—one of the very first people we are aware of that God used to bring restoration to His Church—was a man called Martin Luther (I am sure there were others, but he is a name that is well-known in the Church.) That is when the recovery began to take place to bring the Church out of darkness, and most of us do not realize how dark the Church was in those days. At that time, what was known as the Church was persecuting and killing everyone who was a genuine Christian. They took the scriptures out of homes and said it was illegal for people even to read the them, and that it was only the priest who could properly understand the scriptures to tell you what to do.

In the beginning this was not so. If you go back to chapter 1 of Ephesians and read up to the point of the word *"therefore"* in chapter 4, you will see that Paul had revealed to them first of all that they were chosen in God. Most still do not realize that we are chosen in God. The religious Gospel has made that not God's choice, but man's choice, because the religious Gospel says, "You were chosen in Him before the foundation of the world, because He knew there would come a day when you would choose Him; therefore, because He foreknew that you were going to do that, He chose you." Well then, **whose choice is it?**

If God chose you before the foundation of the world, that you should be holy and without blame before Him in love, *that is his choice!* Oh, we must get the Church to see this! It is going to happen. You are going to come to a point in your experience where you will fully reveal and manifest to the world the glory of God. It is *guaranteed,* because *God chose it to be so.* And the reason that we do not experience it is because of the darkness, the alienation from the life of God that is in us because of the blindness of our heart.

We are all in darkness to an extent. We have been *taught ignorance* in the Church for two thousand years. The Gospel that Paul preached when he was alive has been almost totally annihilated from the Christian's mind, and we have been taught things exactly opposite from what he taught and believed. **Being alienated . . .** Think of that! Here we are. We are one with God. In the very essence of our being is the God of the Universe, yet in our minds we are alienated from that life that is in us, because of the blindness that is on our eyes and on our heart.

The good news is that we are in the dawning of the

new day. God is beginning to lift the veil and to bring His seekers out of darkness. And that is the thing that is upon my heart more than anything else. When I thought about this this morning, I just had to weep in intercession, because the blindness is so heavy over the people of God. How we need intercessors, because some of the things we have to share in these days are going to seem contrary to the scriptures. But believe me, it is only seemingly, because every question that you might have regarding what I have to share with you can be answered, even though these are not simple questions which can be answered in a few seconds.

Understanding God's Omnipresence

God has a plan for us. If only we would understand some of the theological expressions that the Church has. Doctrines like omnipresence and omnipotence and omniscience. Do you know what "omnipresence" means? I am sure you do, but let us look at it. Omnipresence means that God is *everywhere,* and there is *nowhere* that God is not. That is literally what the word means. If God is truly omnipresent, there is no space in the universe where God is not, because His presence is all-pervading. Now if that is true, what about that man on his death-bed who has never acknowledged Christ? If God is not in that man who is not acknowledging Him, then God is not omnipresent—there is one place in this universe where He is not, and that is in that man. The Church needs to examine some of the things they themselves have taught in the past. What that man needs is not someone trying to convince him that he needs God; he needs someone with the authority and the power of the spoken Word to speak to the seed of God that is in that man to cause it to rise up! You can pray to God for a hundred years for something, and you may never see it happen; but you can learn to speak the Word and see it happen in a few seconds!

Jesus said it: If you have faith as a grain of mustard seed—not if you fast for a hundred years, if you pray for twenty years, if you read ten chapters of the Bible a day—but if you have the faith of a grain of mustard seed, you can *say* to that mountain, "Be removed!" And yet we pray to Him continuously, "O God, do this, and O God, do that!" Because of the blindness that is on our hearts, we are alienated from the life of God that is in us, and we are all the time praying to Him to do something. But He said to the very first disciples He had, "All authority and power is given unto Me; *go ye therefore* and make disciples." You don't have to try to get people saved; you don't have to try to get God into someone; you need to speak to the core of their being, and you will stir the Spirit of the Living God that is dormant in most of creation.

Experiencing Heavenly Places

Paul said that we have been blessed with *all* spiritual blessings in heavenly places. He said you have been *seated with Christ* in heavenly places. Why do we not experience that? Do you think if I were experiencing all of the blessings of God, if I experienced being seated in heavenly places with Christ, that I could be in the condition I am in today? Why don't we experience that? It is because of the blindness. We have become alienated from the life of God that is within us. We don't even know where "heavenly places" are. We think there is a planet up there somewhere where our spirit might be connected somehow. But do you know what heavenly places are? Heavenly places means *a conscious awareness of the reality of being one with God.*

There are at least three levels of consciousness in this realm: one is body-conscious, one is soul-conscious, and one is spirit-conscious. Many people are merely body-conscious; many people are just soul-conscious; and a few of us are beginning to become spirit-conscious. That means that when our mind is unveiled, and when our eyes become unveiled to the reality of the revelation that Paul gave to the Church in its very beginning, we will walk in a conscious awareness of Christ living through us. We won't have to try to do it, either Christ will just flow from our innermost being. For that to happen we have to begin to have our concepts changed, because the God that has been presented to us in Christianity has been presented in a way that has given us a false concept of Him. And that is nothing new, because Jesus had to fight that same battle when He was here. He said, "It has been written in your very own law, *but I say to you . . .*"

Some may say, "Brother, I go by the Word; if the Word says it, that's it. And the law says 'an eye for an eye and a tooth for a tooth,' so if you kill someone, I am going to kill you." Jesus said, "It has been written. It is in your very own Word." There is something wrong with some of the concepts that we pick up from the scriptures. He said, "It has been written, *but I say to you,* love your enemies; do good to them who despitefully use you." ***Our concepts have to be changed.***

A Santa Claus God?

We have a concept of God in Christianity which I call a *"Santa Claus God."* We have a Santa Claus God, because we feel that if we pray enough, if we fast enough, if we please God enough, He is going to answer our prayers. But if we don't read our Bible, if we are not good, if we don't do what He says, He is not going to answer our prayers. So therefore, everything we get from God depends upon our conduct, not upon God's grace, not upon His working in our life. We need to think about these things! A Santa Claus God. I know a person who used to say, "I prayed for my son for twenty years, and God finally saved him." What that person was really saying was that God made him pray and pray and fast, and He made him wait twenty years, and then He saved his son.

Think about your own experience with God. How many times have you said (and I know this is a Bible principle, and I am not against it, but it is a concept we have to fight), "Maybe if we fast over this thing long enough; maybe if we get together and we pray long enough . . ." We feel that we have to do something that will influence God to make Him work on our behalf, or on the behalf of someone we love or are praying for. Santa Claus God. God has a will, and that will of God is for every human being on the earth. He has a will, and a plan, and a design and a purpose for everyone. What can you do to change that? Now, if you have the religious concept of God, there is a great deal that you can do to change it. But if God is God, then we are not God. If God says, "I have chosen you to present you to my Father holy, unblameable and irreprovable in His sight," I cannot nullify that will of God. *He is God!* He is going to perfect in me what He wants to do.

Walking In All the Counsel of God

Now, we do have choices to make, and those choices we make affect our lives and may prolong God's working in us, but our will will not stop God from working in us His good pleasure and His good will for our life. If you could see that, you would not have to struggle anymore. If you clean up your life, and you quit going to movies, and you quit doing all kinds of things because you think you shouldn't, *you are just being religious.* If you enjoy going to movies, you need to go to movies until God, by His Spirit rising up and quickening you, pulls your desires in another direction. *That is salvation.* I have experienced salvation. Not the poor, low Gospel that I received in religion, but I have been saved! To be saved means that God quickens you by His energizing Spirit and causes you to walk in another direction. Now you may not choose to do that, and you may fight and struggle against that, but eventually *you are going to walk in all the counsel of God.* Why? **Because that is His will.** That is His good will. The Gospel that was preached in the very beginning by the angels was, "Peace on earth, *good will* toward men."

Calvary has a much deeper meaning when you begin to understand the heart of God and the awesome events that took place there. Every one of us would say, "God died for me." Yes He did; we all know that. But we think that to preserve that which He did, we must be pretty "good." We have to do certain things. We have to live a certain way, or it will nullify what He did for us at Calvary. That is the religious concept, and you may not even have that consciously in your mind, but it is hidden in your consciousness that you have to do certain things and live a certain way to please God, so that the effects of Calvary will be yours. And those very concepts keep the reality that was given to you at Calvary from manifesting in your life. You may not even be conscious of this, but it is deeply embedded in your consciousness. We have inherited in this country two thousand years of religious teaching and tradition absolutely contrary to the Word of God, yet when somebody begins to speak truth, what they speak seemingly is contrary to what you have been taught. It is not contrary to the Word; it is contrary to what you *believe* is the Word.

An All-Powerful God

God is all-powerful. You show me a church or a group of people anywhere in this country who believes that God is all-powerful, and I'll show you a glorious, magnificent presence of God in a group of people. But show me a people who believe in two powers, and I'll show you a weak, defeated, struggling and striving group of people. God is not all-powerful in our Christian tradition and in our thinking. Our father according to the flesh, the devil, seems to get more credit than our Father God. We have devils that are much more powerful than God's leadership on the earth today because of wrong concepts, and because of wrong thinking and speaking.

Whatever is in your heart and you believe, you will speak from your mouth; and the words that you speak from your mouth which come from your heart *create* for you that which you speak. You are a product of what you have been receiving, thinking, believing and speaking all of your life. So if you are defeated, if you can't find victory, if you have no joy in your life, it is because you have been taught wrong, which has made you believe wrong, made you receive wrong, and made you speak wrong to create for you that which you are today. *That is the truth. As a man thinketh in his heart, so is he.*

"All powerful." I hate to use the words "if God," but for illustration, *if God* is all powerful, and we believe that, how could the so called devil do what he has done to this country and to God's people? How could he take the Church into darkness for two thousand years? He could do it because of their not heeding Paul's admonition at the very beginning: "Don't be like the other gentiles, walking in the vanity of their mind." That is a realm of consciousness. The vanity of the soulish mind—that is where we are. We have had teachings in the past about body, soul and spirit, and coming out of the flesh, coming out of Egypt, coming out of the world, coming through the wilderness and into the Promised Land. The Promised Land is a level of consciousness. Christians hate the word *"consciousness,"* because it is taught in almost all the religions of the world, but it is not taught in Christianity. I wonder why. If you never become conscious of God's quickening power energizing your life, you will always be soul-conscious and body-conscious, but never spirit-conscious.

Turning from Darkness to Light

God has so much for the Church. In Acts 26:18, Jesus told the Apostle Paul (this was right at his conversion) that He was sending him *"To open their eyes, and to turn them from darkness to light, and from the power of Satan unto God, that they may receive forgiveness of sins, and inheritance among them which are sanctified by faith that is in me."*

14

How we need people today who can turn people from darkness to light, and from the power of Satan unto the power of God. But that cannot happen with the concepts of God that we have today. We cannot believe the goodness of God; we cannot believe the miracle of the cross. We haven't been taught. 2 Corinthians 4:4-7 says, *"In whom the god of this world hath blinded the minds of them which believe not, . . ."* (Now listen, when we read something like this, right away we say, "That doesn't apply to me; I am a believer. Believe me, these words are spoken to us!) *"In whom the god of this world hath blinded the minds of them which believe not, lest the light of the glorious gospel of Christ, who is the image of God, should shine unto them. For we preach not ourselves, but Christ Jesus the Lord; and ourselves your servants for Jesus' sake. For God, who commanded the light to shine out of darkness, hath shined in our hearts, to give the light of the knowledge of the glory of God in the face of Jesus Christ. But we have this treasure in earthen vessels, that the excellency of the power may be of God, and not of us."*

"God Who commanded the light to shine out of darkness." I believe that is happening today. There is so much darkness within us. When I began to see some of these things, I could not believe the darkness and the blindness of my own eyes as a believer for many years. The blindness that was on my eyes! And again I have to make this clear, it is grace that is bringing the revealing.

I have not always been "a good Christian"; I don't deserve to have the revelation of God that has been given to me. I didn't do anything to deserve it. But God has a perfect plan, intent and purpose for my life and for your life, and He *will* bring you into that plan and purpose.

The End of Grace?

One of the big questions that comes up is, "Look at all the people who have died; *what happens if I die?"* We have a concept in our minds, taught to us by our forefathers, that when you die that is the end of grace for you. No more grace. Death is the end of grace. As long as you have breath in your lungs, as long as you have the ability to cry out and receive God, you have grace; but when you die, *look out!* Grace is gone. You have had your opportunity in this life, and there is no more grace.

I have to tell you that is **absolutely** not true! The only reason that we die physically before God has fulfilled His plan and purpose in our life is because of the darkness and the blindness that are put over our eyes, and because of the wrong choices that we make while we are here. *But that does not stop God's plan.* It doesn't stop God. God is God! You are God's *idea.* God brought you into existence in physical form. You are His idea, but like the Prodigal, many of us have gotten lost and are in great darkness, and have been caught up in the lusts of the flesh and the pride of life. God is still God! And God has a love that we have never understood. He will perfect His will in you. Jesus is ***The author and the finisher of*** *our faith"* (Romans 8:7-8). Can you believe *"It is God that works in you both to will and to do of His good pleasure?"*

When you came to this earth, you were lost to who you were. As we grew we became filled with the nature and the character of sin. Did you ask to be born that way? Did you say, "God, when I am born, please fill me full of the lusts of the flesh"? I don't think so *"As in Adam all die,"* Paul says. As a carnal man we have a consciousness that is both good and evil. Have you understood that yet? Some of us are very good, some of us are not so good, some of us are evil. But it is the same nature inherited from Adam through the Fall.

God loves His creation. That is why the scripture says that the Lamb of God was slain from before the foundation of the world! God knew everything, or He wouldn't be all knowing, all powerful, and omnipresent. Jesus was chosen before the foundation of the world to be the Lamb that would restore the creation back to the Father. So I come into this life, I am born, and I am in darkness. And I am born with this nature that is anti-Christ; I am born with this nature that matures in some of us to be full of lust, full of envy, full of greed, and I might live seventy years in this darkness and blindness. We may live seventy years totally alienated and separated in our mind from God, living a life of sin, and then we die and religion tells us that because we lived seventy years in a life of sin and unbelief and greed, we are going to burn eternally in hell in endless torment. **This concept is totally wrong!** Now this might seemingly appear to be anti-Word, but oh, if you only knew the deep Love and the heart of your Father God. As we go on in these writings you will understand that we have been terribly deceived by religious tradition.

Awakening to the Gospel that Paul Preached

"Because the carnal mind is enmity against God: for it is not subject to the law of God, neither indeed can be. So then they that are in the flesh cannot please God." Until you have a mind that is renewed, a mind that dwells in the conscious awareness of the presence of God filling you, you are walking, at least in a degree, in the flesh. You are still part carnal, and that is the part we have to deal with; that is where all the unbelief is.

Ephesians 5:14 says, *"Wherefore he saith, Awake thou that sleepest, and arise from the dead, and Christ shall give thee light."* Did you ever realize, that you are sleeping? Do you know the scripture refers to that word "awake," even in the Old Testament, over, and over? Awake! Awake! Awake! Do you remember Daniel's vision where the angel says to Daniel, "In that day many who sleep in the dust of the earth shall arise." Do you realize that you were made from the very dust of the ground? And the Word tells us over and over again to wake up, to rise, to shake yourself, O Zion, and arise. Wake up! **WAKE UP!**

"For since by man came death, by man came also the resurrection of the dead. For as in Adam all die, even so in Christ shall all be made alive. But every man in his own order" (I Cor. 15:21-23). Now let me ask you a question again: Did you choose to be in Adam? **Was it your choice?** Could the "all" in Adam be any greater than the "all" that is in Christ? Does it really mean **"all"** who died in Adam shall be made alive in Christ? Once again: Is the **"all"** that is in Adam any greater than the **"all"** that is in Christ? Well if you believe what we have been taught, it does mean that! But listen to what it says: *"As in Adam all die, even so in Christ shall all be made alive, but every man in his own order."* How many men? *All!* But we read it this way: *For as in Adam all die, even so those who have received Christ shall be made alive.* Don't we read it that way? I believe we do so because of what we have been taught and because of what the scripture *seemingly* teaches.

I have said this before, and you really need to examine this: The Apostle Paul was so much more advanced spiritually than any other man in the New Testament times, and he had a much deeper understanding and revelation of God than any other writer or believer in those times. And he even said that this is *my* Gospel. Nobody else preached the Gospel that Paul preaches. That is why some of the things in the scriptures seem to be contradictory. Two believers at different levels of faith can see the same verse and interpret it differently. It does not mean necessarily that one is right and one is wrong, they just see it differently.

Oh the world needs the Gospel! *We* need the Gospel! And you see, when you begin to understand the gospel that Paul preached, it is so much easier to preach the Gospel—in fact, you don't have to. Whenever you get around people, you can just plant a few seeds. Just a few words. "A man went forth to sow." That is what I am doing—sowing. The words that I speak are seeds, and I guarantee you that they will grow.

Wisdom is the Proper Use of Knowledge
I need the wisdom to present the truth that I have been given. (O God, give us expression and words!) If there is anything we as Christians need to keep in our hearts, it is the knowledge that we need wisdom, because wisdom is the ability to properly use the knowledge that you have. You can have a great deal of knowledge and come into a great understanding of the scriptures, but without the wisdom you will go forth to proclaim that Word and do damage. I often tell people who hear me speak, "Please don't go out and tell other people what I said, but if you want them to hear the message, give them a tape." It is the best thing you can do, because the *carnal mind* will absolutely try to destroy the seeds of the Word of God.

Do you notice I don't use the word "devil" too much? People say, "Brother, don't you believe in the devil?"

No, I believe in God. And I believe that the only place the devil has is that place *in my mind* that I give him. If I give him no place, then he has no place. I don't believe it is even worthy to mention the devil; I would rather use the phrase *carnal mind.* "Brother, are you saying the devil is my mind?" I am saying that that is the only place where the devil can use anything that he has, because whoever gets the mind gets the man. And the devil has captured and captivated the minds of God's people through the blindness and through the ignorance that has been taught from the pulpits across America. It was not done knowingly so. Men who have had good hearts, men who have loved God, men who have desired above everything else to please God, have sown darkness and blindness over the hearts of God's people, because they themselves were ignorant, being blinded and darkened to the life that was in them.

"This I say therefore, and testify in the Lord, that you henceforth walk not as other gentiles walk." I believe that many of the saints that Paul was speaking to in those days had this revelation and understanding. You remember Jesus Himself spent forty days with His disciples unveiling to them the Gospel of the Kingdom. They had an understanding. They knew who they were. And because of that, sometimes just the very presence of one of those men would cause healing to take place! They understood, and so Paul in his teaching was reminding them in the Book of Ephesians of all that had

been given to them by God. "You have been *chosen;* you have been *predestinated;* there is a predestinated seed in you that *will* come to maturity, *but every man in his own order.* You have been seated with Christ in heavenly places; you have been redeemed by the power and the blood of the Lamb. ***Therefore*** don't walk as an unbeliever, being alienated in your mind from the life of God, through the ignorance and the blindness of your heart."

God is so good. Sometimes we hear a word like this and we think, "God, that person must really be special." Oh, if you only knew! You see the thing of it is, the word has to come out, and then even I *have to learn* by that word which is spoken or written. It is not so much that someone who speaks to you and reveals new things to you has it all together, but that God is so gracious. And I have known these things, and have known the heart of God for twenty years, but I have been bottled up, knowing that I just could not give it. There is too much darkness, too much blindness; there was too much religious teaching which was contrary to what God wants to bring to his people. But the time is now right for this message.

I can testify to you that God is God, because I have been in some of the most wretched, miserable conditions for a Christian that anyone could ever be in, and *every time* God came to me and rescued me out of it. Every time! And I have been months in darkness; I have been months thinking God left me; I have been months thinking that I must really have offended God. You see our wrong choices cause things like that to happen, but *God is God.* He says, "Gary, you are going to be this way because I designed it, I planned for it, and it is for your best interest. And because I am your Father and I have your best interest at heart, I am going to perform My will in your life. Now you can fight that, you can oppose that, but I am your Father. Don't you realize that I brought you forth, I created you? You were My idea. I am responsible for you, because I created you and brought you into being. And because I am responsible for you, if I did not perfect that in you which I desire to do, I would be an irresponsible parent!"

Can you understand that? God is responsible for that which He created. Aren't you responsible for the children that you bring into this life? How much more so is God responsible! Yet religion tells us that because we are rebellious, because we are caught up in pornography, because we're selling our bodies as prostitutes, God cannot help us. Well if He can't, then He is not God. If it depends on what I can do or what I can't do, then I am god, and He is not God!

Coming Out of Darkness

Chapter 2

Calvary's Emancipation Proclamation

"This I say therefore, and testify in the Lord, that ye henceforth walk not as other gentiles walk, in the vanity of their mind, having the understanding darkened, being alienated from the life of God through the ignorance that is in them, because of the blindness of their heart" (Eph. 4:17-18).

Alienation from the life of God *in us* is a great problem in the Church. All of us are still, to one degree or another, alienated from that life we have within us. And the only thing that is going to bring us into more of an understanding of that life, and prepare us for what God is about to do on the earth, is to have most of our concepts of God which we have been taught in the past by our forefathers torn down. They have to be uprooted, because what God wants to bring to the earth through His people is the Gospel of reconciliation. This is the only Gospel that Paul ever told us we need to preach. The people of the earth must be told the magnitude of Calvary's victory.

Very few of God's people are aware of "Calvary's Emancipation Proclamation." I think probably most of us know what the Emancipation Proclamation was; it was the proclamation that freed the blacks from slavery. And oh, if we knew the benefits of Calvary's proclamation! That is the reason that we are not moving in the power of God. The Church has so little power today. I know there are a few men who are operating somewhat in the power of God, and that it is flowing through certain ones in the gifts of the Spirit. But we haven't seen anything yet, because when God by His Spirit comes to maturity within the Church, we will see the power of God such as never has been seen before.

In these days we must understand the heart of God. There is coming such an awesome power of God to the Church, that if you don't understand His heart, and walk in the love of God, you will take His power and bring judgment to His people. You will cause them damage and harm. God *is* bringing judgment to His people, but it is a righteous judgment. You have to know the heart of God. You have heard it said that the Apostolic and the prophetic anointing of the early Church is going to be restored to the Church, and there are many men of God today who are prophesying and teaching that the Church as we knew it in its beginning stages is going to be restored. But that Church didn't make it the first time! And I am not so sure that if the Apostolic anointing and power came back to the Church as it was in the early days, the same thing wouldn't just happen all over again, unless God's people begin to understand the heart of God. I don't think such restoration is the answer. I think the only answer today for God's people is to really understand, and have unveiled to them, the heart of God.

All Shall Be Made Alive

There is a passage which has become very controversial in the Church, and I want to pick up with that again. That is 1 Corinthians chapter 15, beginning at verse 20 and going through verse 23: *"But now is Christ risen from the dead, and become the firstfruits of them that slept. For since by man came death, by man also came the resurrection of the dead. For as in Adam all die, even so in Christ shall all be made alive. But every man in his own order: Christ the firstfruits, afterward they that are Christ's at his coming."*

You remember I asked the question, is the **"all"** in Christ any less than the **"all"** in Adam? Because if we can take that verse literally, just as it is spoken, *"as in Adam all die, even so in Christ shall all be made alive,"* the question is answered. And to understand how this could possibly be, how we all died in Adam, and are made alive in Christ, we need to go back to the very beginning of creation to see what God's original purpose was for creating man.

I know we have all heard this, but God's original design, intent and purpose was to create humanity to contain and express His life on the earth. That was His intention from the very beginning. "Let us make man in our image, and let them have dominion over the earth."

So man was created to have the very life, nature and character of God, and then to be a possessor and take dominion over the earth. But we all know what happened: *For as in Adam all died* . . . What caused Adam to die? Every one of you could tell me that when Adam chose the wrong source for his life, it brought to him death, and then that death passed to all mankind, because we all came out of Adam. That is what the scripture says.

Religion tells us that you are a free moral agent, and God has given to you a free will, therefore you have the capability to choose right or wrong; you have the capability to choose either God, or a life of self; you have the capability and the free will to choose. We do have the freedom to choose, but as we will see, our will is bound up in the fall of Adam.

The Knowledge of Good and Evil Brings Death

When I was a struggling Christian with many bondages in my life, I was told, "The devil doesn't make you do the things you do. You have a choice, and if you will choose to do what is right, then that will enable God by His Spirit to work in your life. But you have to make the right choices." And you know what? *I never made the right choices!* I often tried making the right choice, but I found that I seldom had the power to carry through with it. Now I know a lot of people do, but I didn't have the character, nor the strength. I wanted God, but I also wanted the life that I had which was not compatible with the Christian life. I know a lot of people live at that place where I was. But all I was told was, "Gary, it's up to you. You have the free will to make the right choice."

Romans 5:12 says, ***"Therefore just as sin entered the world through one man, and death through sin, so in this way death came to all men, because all sinned."*** Now I have to ask you again: What brought Adam into death? What in the world did he do that caused him to die and caused me to die with him? God placed him in a garden with various things to eat and gave him very few instructions. When God created Adam He didn't give him a rule book, He gave him just a couple of words. He said, "Of every tree in the garden you may freely eat. But the day you eat of the tree of the *knowledge of good and evil,* you are going to die." That is what brought death to humanity. I have been teaching this for years, and I still do not have the full realization of it; I still don't have the full experience of it. But I'll tell you this, that the *root* of the darkness, and the alienation in our minds from the life of God, is the fruit of this tree of the knowledge of good and evil.

Now consider: *"Knowledge of good and evil".* Think about the teachings of Christianity, or any religion in the world. What is the basis of their teaching, if it isn't based upon the knowledge of good and evil? I know of no religion in the world, including Christianity, that does not base almost everything it teaches on choosing the good over the evil. Yet God says, "The very day, Adam, that you begin to eat that fruit, the very day that you begin to discern the difference between good and evil, is the day that you will die."

Why did God call it a death? It is because when God created Adam, He breathed into him, and we know that the word "breath" is the same word as "spirit," so what God breathed into Adam was His very own life and His nature. It says there was a Tree of Life in the midst of that garden, which simply means that Adam could have chosen to depend wholly and solely upon the life of God that was in him, the life that God literally had breathed into him (and there is so much in that life of God!). The life that God breathed into Adam was simply everything that He was. He breathed into him His energizing, quickening life. He breathed into him His power, His authority. Adam was an example of everything that God wanted on the earth. And God said to him, *"Don't partake of the knowledge of good and evil, because the moment that you begin to eat of the fruit of that tree, you will die."* You will be cut off from My life. Your consciousness will be separated, and you will become in your consciousness separated from Me, as a separate entity. And you will begin, then, to live your life not by the knowledge of the life that I placed within you, for that will be cut off, and you will have nothing left but a knowledge of good and evil. You will struggle all of your life trying to discern and trying to choose the good over the evil, but you will be cut off from My life. And then you will take this nature that is separated from Me, and you will produce *sons in your own image."* That is what happened at the fall, and that is what the Bible says. Adam and Eve then produced sons after their image. They lost the image of God.

What was the very first thing that Jesus did on the day of resurrection? The Word says in John 20:22 that on the eve of His resurrection, He appeared. The doors were closed, but He appeared in the midst of the disciples, and the very first thing that He did, it says, is *He breathed on them* and said, **"Receive ye the Holy Ghost."** That act restored back to those men what Adam had lost in the garden! Jesus once again, as God did in the beginning, breathed His life into them. 1 Corinthians 15:45 says, **"Christ was made a Life-giving Spirit."** And that's why Jesus said, "I am the Bread of Life. Do you really want to live by God? Then you have to know how to eat of Me. Do you really want to live, do you really want life?" He said, "As the Father has sent Me, and I live by the Father, whosoever will eat of Me will live by Me." That is the promise—if you eat of Me, if you learn to assimilate My life, you will live by Me.

This is why Paul said, **"Don't be as the gentiles, walking in the vanity of their mind, having the understanding darkened, being alienated from the life of God."** To be alienated from the life of God means that you believe in your consciousness that you and God are two separate entities. To be in death simply means that you cannot possibly even imagine that you and God are not two entities, but one. But that is how it was in the beginning; Adam was a full replica of what God wanted in humanity. That is why he was called "the first Adam," and Jesus is called "the second Adam" and "the last man". Jesus fulfilled that which Adam failed to do. Jesus restored man back to the Tree of Life. Humanity can once again live by the life of God, instead of trying to choose the good over the evil.

Now, not only did Adam make a fatal choice, but here is where Christianity as a whole has made the same mistake. Very, very shortly, just within a few years—in fact even beginning within the lifetime of the Apostle Paul, men began to revert back to the knowledge of good and evil, rather than learning how to discern and live by that life that was breathed into them by the new birth. Religion tells us this: "God loved you so much that He sent His own Son to die for you on the cross." And we are told that for the joy that was set before Him, Jesus endured the cross. But the magnitude of that victory, in the Christian's eyes, *is so limited,* because we have been fed for two thousand years from the tree of the knowledge of good and evil. "If you are good, God will bless you; if you aren't good, God won't bless you." The magnitude of Calvary's victory, according to the religious eyes, is that, yes, Jesus died for the world; He suffered on the cross, but His victory is limited only to those who, first of all, receive Him as Savior, and then after that learn to live by His rule book.

The book of Ephesians talks about the eternal purpose of God. The eternal purpose of God is that man would live from the flowing of God's life within him. Paul mentions several times in the Book of Ephesians, especially in chapter 3, the "mystery" of the gospel. We all know that if something is a mystery, it is sometimes not that easy to figure out. The Gospel is a deep and hidden mystery, especially from religious eyes, especially from people who have been trained all of their lives to discern the difference between good and evil. Now I know that there is a verse in the Bible which says that some have exercised their senses to discern both good and evil. But it doesn't say that they have learned to discern the *difference* between good and evil. It says they have learned to discern good and evil, *yet both are from the same source!* It's not too hard to discern evil, but it is very, very difficult to discern the truth about good sometimes. The truth is that you can be very good, and still not have God's character and His substance formed in your life.

If what the scriptures teaches us is true, just as sin entered into the world by one man, and through that sin death passed to all men, then what passed to all men was that seed that Adam took into him from the tree of the knowledge of good and evil. I know this is a repeat, but we must hear this and clearly get an understanding of it. Before God's people can ever grasp fully the reconciliation that He wants to bring through them, they have to understand His heart, because if you don't understand the heart of God, and you do become filled with His authority and His power, you will use it to judge, and you will not judge righteously.

God is coming to judge the earth, but He is a righteous judge. God knew, and it wasn't a surprise to Him, that His creation was going to fall. Every man that was born after Adam was separated in his consciousness and his awareness from that life that was in his spirit, and every man was then left with nothing but the discernment to choose between good and evil. Man was cut off in his spirit from the knowledge and the life of God, and because of it he had nothing left but the knowledge of good and evil. Therefore some men would become very good, and other men would be very evil. The people of the world as a whole, looking only through eyes of good and evil, would see that there was a group of good people and there was a group of evil people, and they would imagine that all the evil people needed God, but all the good people were pretty much OK. But listen! In God's eyes, every man that is born, *is born in death*. He is alienated and separated in his mind from the life of God that is in his spirit. He is left only with a knowledge of good and evil.

John 1:9 says that Jesus was ***"the true light that lights every man that comes into the world."*** Proverbs calls the light of man, the spirit, "the candle of the Lord." So every man that comes into this world has a spirit, has hidden deeply in his being that candle, that spirit from the Lord which needs to be ignited. And we can go to men, and we can tell them about the Gospel; we can convert them, we can even get them to believe intellectually that Jesus is the Son of God. But then we begin to teach them how to live according to the Bible, to choose the good over the evil, and we have done the same thing that Adam did in the very beginning. Even within ourselves we try to choose the good over the evil, rather than learning how to contact and live by that Holy Spirit of God that has been placed within us.

Can't we all see that? That is what is happening! We do not have, especially in the Church in America, many godly people who are manifesting the life and the character of God to a lost and dying world. We have many good people. And most of them think that because they are good, they are OK, and they are always trying to convince the one who is evil to change his ways so that God can help him—not realizing that good and evil are the same tree. We need the light of God to see this! Whether you are very good, or whether you are very evil, it is the same source of life that is cut off from the life of God.

Look again at Ephesians 4:17-18. *"This I say therefore, and testify in the Lord, that you walk not as other gentiles walk, in the vanity of their minds, having their understanding darkened, being alienated from the life of God through the ignorance that is in them, because of the blindness of their heart."* This is the situation today. We have people all over the earth who have been regenerated by the Spirit of the Living God, who have never learned other than to discern the difference between good and evil.

Let's go back and take another look at Calvary. God realized that because of Adam, the whole human race would be raised with a concept of knowing only the good over the evil. And He knew that it was absolutely hopeless. Paul told the Ephesians that before Christ, they were alienated. They were not members of the same family. But through the cross, God put into one both Jew and Gentile. Now one has to understand the mindset in those days, which was that the Jew was very "godly," and the gentile was the "ungodly." So Paul says that God by one offering put both the Jew and the Gentile into one body, thus bringing peace. The Word says Jesus was "the Lamb of God slain from before the foundation of the world." The question we have to ask —and this is a hard one to fight, this religious concept—is this: IS THE MAGNITUDE OF CALVARY'S VICTORY LIMITED ONLY TO THOSE WHO ARE ABLE TO CHOOSE THE GOOD OVER THE EVIL?

I questioned God about this for years, before I came into the understanding that I am sharing with you. I used to question God, because I was so full of the lust of the flesh, as a young person, and even as a Christian! I loved

God. I used to cry at night over my condition. But I wanted the things of the world. I wanted everything that you are not supposed to want. And I went through hell on earth as a man living to the full extent the experience of Romans, chapter 7. And the only reason we go through that is because of having the understanding darkened, being alienated from the life of God that is in us because of the blindness that is on our hearts. We have to realize the magnitude of Calvary's victory. The Emancipation Proclamation from the cross of Calvary was that *you are not guilty.*

You are living your life by the knowledge of good and evil if you are not one who has the ability and who has learned how to exercise your spiritual being so that you can live by God's life. It makes no difference how good you are, or how evil you are, your life source is still coming from the wrong place. In God's eyes, there is no difference. In the man or woman who is not living by the life of God, there is no difference between the good and the evil. *It is all from the wrong tree.* And all we have had for two thousand years, in Christianity, is religious teachings, trying to teach us how to be godly, trying to teach us and warn us to *choose the good over the evil.*

We need to read again Romans 5:12-21. You see, God understands our condition; we don't. Because of our religious traditions, we think that we deserve all the guilt, we deserve all the shame. But I didn't ask to be born having all the lust and wanting all the wrong things.

I didn't ask for it; *that was Adam's gift to me.* And so because Adam made a mistake, religion tells me that I came into this world constituted and filled with the character and the nature that loves to sin, or maybe I'm fortunate and I have been born with a character which is good. But religion will tell me that because I inherited a life that loves to sin, and loves to do all the things that I'm not supposed to do, I somewhere have to find within myself the power to put that down and to choose to live right, so that God can bless me and I can someday die and go to heaven. Yet the very first thing that was said of Jesus by John was, "Behold the Lamb of God who *takes away the sin of the world!*" I can testify that if you cannot overcome sin no matter how hard you try, if you will continue to seek after God, He will eventually grow within you, **and you will overcome!** The Christian life is not a matter of *will power,* but a matter of the Spirit of God flooding every area of your being, and that takes time. We are as "newborn babes" and it takes some of us many years to be transformed.

Church isn't a happy place today. Why? Because we are under so much guilt and condemnation. When we get together, there are times when we break through and we touch the Spirit of God, and there is some rejoicing, but it is so limited! It's so limited, because when you have the slightest—and I mean the *slightest*—bit of guilt in your consciousness, it separates you, and you can't break through to the Spirit of God. The very first thing John said was, "Behold the Lamb of God that *takes away* the sin of the world!" Did He do that? If you are religious, you will say He did, but you won't believe it, because your religious concept says, "Yes, He took away the sin of the world, but only for those who say, 'Jesus I receive You,' or only for those who learn to live and choose the good over the evil." Calvary is only beneficial to those who learn to make the right choices—that's what religion teaches us! And so we have multitudes of people all over the world who genuinely have been regenerated by the Spirit of God, but they never have been taught how to live by that life of God that is in them. All they are ever taught is how to choose the good over the evil. And when you do that, it alienates you from the life of God in you, and you become like an unbeliever, having your eyes blinded.

You see, an unbeliever has no consciousness, no awareness at all that they have the Spirit of God in them. But if you have been regenerated, you do have that consciousness. At times you will experience the flowing of God, but because of your concepts, when you sin it will cause a blockage, for *guilt cannot enter into the presence of God!* The only people who enter into the presence of God and live there are people who know how *not to be guilty.* As long as you are in the flesh, I can guarantee you every day of your life you are going to err and miss God. Since 1969 I have avidly, every day of my life, sought after and hungered after God. In 1969, when

I had the experience of being caught up into the heavenly realms and of experiencing God flooding me, I became extremely hungry for God. And I have spent literally hundreds and hundreds of hours on my face and in the scriptures hungering and seeking after God. I have been one of the most hungry-after-God people, yet I still make mistakes every day. It is because I have not learned how to live fully by the life of God within me. And, in fact, it is not even a matter of learning. It is a matter of God's life growing, it is a matter of the Spirit of God maturing within me. It is a matter of my seeking, every day of my life, not after something which is in a distant heaven, but that which is within—learning how to contact the reality of the Spirit, the energizing, quickening spirit of God, so that every day I can enter into His presence, and I can feast upon the spiritual manna. From that experience, I am energized and quickened and enabled a little more to walk in the life of God. But when I begin in my consciousness to choose the good over the evil, I am separated in my consciousness from God, alienated from that life. And I am left as Adam was again, to struggle around in darkness trying to choose the good over the evil, trying to whip my flesh into line.

Jesus did say, "If any man will come after Me, let him deny himself, and take up his cross and follow Me." But that has been so misunderstood in the Church, because there is no way that Adam, your carnal man, can put himself to death. **IT CANNOT BE DONE!** And that is why the Apostle Paul said in Romans chapter 8 that if you through the *spirit* put to death the deeds of the flesh, you will live. The Christian life is totally a life of learning how, through the *spirit,* to live godly. You will never do it in your own strength. You will not live long enough to learn how to live godly. All you will be is condemned because you can't make it. The flesh cannot live godly.

You simply need to behold the *Lamb* that takes away the sin of the world! You have absolutely no problem with God except in your religious mind. God's people have a hard time believing the goodness and the loveliness of God, because we feel that we have to be justified in His sight by what *we* do, rather than by what He has done. Yet I can go to anyone on the street, I can go to a prostitute in the gutter, and I can say to her, "Lady, you have absolutely no problems with God, absolutely none." And I can guarantee you that when I begin to speak this way, the words that flow out of me will begin to generate in her. I will say to her, "Little lady, **there will** come a day in your life when you will fully reveal and manifest to the world the glory of God." *There will come that day!*

Another verse we need to look at says that the last enemy to be destroyed is death. What is God's concept of death? It is living not by His life, but by a life of good and evil. God's concept of death is having the consciousness of being separated from Him. If you are separated from God, then you are in death; so for the last enemy, death, to be destroyed would mean that there would not be anything, anywhere, in any place that was not reconciled to Him—for if there were any place, anywhere in the universe, that was not reconciled to God, then it would be in death.

Coming Out of Hell

You all are going to have to bear with me on what follows, because it may take a long while to teach and to reveal all of the misconceptions in the doctrines that we have learned. And I am just going to touch on one of them now, the subject of hell. I will cover this in more detail as we go on in this work. There are many other authors who have covered this subject in the true light of God's nature, and I would be happy to recommend them to you.

The biggest question in people's minds is the question of hell and the seeming teaching in Revelation about the eternal torment of hell. Let me just give you a little concept of what hell is. Hell is a literal place. Hell is a place that probably most of the world, and even probably most Christians, are going to experience at one time or another. Let me give you an example of hell. Do you remember a few years ago when the man heading the biggest ministry the world has ever seen confessed publicly, before the whole world, his sin? That man went through hell. Not only did he go through hell because he was caught and had to publicly confess, but he also suffered under the opinions of others—especially

Christians. And I want you know that when I first heard about that, God revealed to me the heart of Jimmy Swaggart. He showed me a man who was not a hypocrite, as the world and as most Christians assumed, but he was a man caught in the web of the knowledge of good and evil. He had the largest ministry the world had ever known, and had probably spoken to more people than any other man at the time, but his message was very judgmental and critical. If you ever heard Jimmy preach, you know that he was a hell-fire and brimstone preacher. Why? Not because he was a hypocrite, but because he hated so much his carnal life style, and he struggled so desperately with that thing. He didn't want anybody else to ever have to suffer what he suffered; and he did not understand, nor did he know, the extent of the love of God.

There is a book I wrote called *Coming Out of Condemnation.* Right after this happened to Jimmy, God revealed to me that he needed intercession. I wept and I groaned and I travailed for that man. I felt his suffering. I felt his agony. And God said, "It is time that My people understood that they don't need to feel condemnation." (I wrote the book, and please get one—not because I wrote it, but because I can guarantee that you, too, suffer under condemnation, and you need to read that book.) And God said, "Write that book, and send it to Jimmy Swaggart." And of course you know how we all think. I thought, "Well, you know, he has this big ministry, and he's in the middle of this; how can I even give it to him?" But I just addressed it: "Jimmy Swaggart, Baton Rouge, Louisiana," and I sent it off. Within a few days, I got a letter from Jimmy thanking me for sending it.

I'll tell you, Christian, you just haven't been caught. Now I realize that in Adam, in our natural character, there are some who are very strong-willed, and they are able by their self-effort to be very good people. However, they will condemn you something fierce, because you are not able to do what they can do. And they will preach hell-fire and brimstone to you and have your ears smoking. Yet God has men and women positioned all over the earth today who understand what I am telling you. Judgment *is* coming, and I believe it is coming quickly. Hell is coming to the earth. The fiery indignation is coming to the earth in a fully righteous judgment. The fires of God are coming, and the Word says that *our God is a consuming fire.* I have been judged by that fire many times. Do you think that Jimmy Swaggart didn't go through a burning? Can you imagine what it would be like if you had your deepest sins revealed to the world? How about even to your family? (Now I know this is not still true for all of us. Right now I don't have a problem like that, but years ago I did. I would have been absolutely humiliated to have the world exposed to my sin.)

Yet you know that Revelation says that there is a day coming when we shall stand before God and the books will be opened. Do you know what that book is? Paul says that you are living epistles, written not with ink, but with the Spirit of the Living God. Each of us is a book. There is coming a day for everyone when their book will be opened. But let me tell you something: the fire of God, the judgments of God are never vindictive! We are taught a doctrine of eternal punishment. I will provide more detail later, how the concept of eternal punishment all happened. I will tell you now that it began basically with the Roman Church. It began by men, leadership in the Church, who wanted to instill fear into the hearts of God's people. We know that the Bible says that perfect love casts out all fear, but yet the churches, almost everywhere in all denominations and in all sects, have within their Gospel and their teaching, *fear.* If we need to fear anything, it is the carnal self-life that keeps us separated in our mind from the life of God in our spirit.

You have heard this expression: "If you really do love someone or something, let it go." Let it go, because if you try to hold onto it, if you keep it in bondage, there can be no genuine love flowing. God's people today need to be set free. *Behold the Lamb of God that takes away the sin of the world!* If the religious concept is true, the victory at Calvary was a very, very small and a very, limited victory. If the religious concept is true, when this thing all winds up, there are going to be a few on God's side, but the devil is going to have the masses of humanity. That is not a great victory. Even common sense tells us that.

God knew that when He brought you forth into this life you were going to be separated and alienated in your mind from His life, and there are people who live seventy or a hundred years, and for one reason or another, they never, *never,* hear someone preach the true Gospel to them. Oh, they hear the religious gospel. But they don't want that. They don't want to hear, "You've got to change your life. If you want to be used by God, you can't do that! Do you want the blessings of God? You can't do that!" They don't want to hear that, because they are just like you, they are selfish. Self wants what self wants. But when God regenerates your spirit, then you begin to want the things of God.

If people begin to realize the extent of God's love, they will flock to Him. Can you imagine what it would be like for a prostitute to walk into a church where everybody knows she is a prostitute, yet they would love her, they would minister to her, and they would draw her into worship? Can you imagine how long she would be a prostitute? (And even if she was, that's God's business and not yours.) Do you have enough conviction in your knowledge of God and in the words that you speak to believe that you could speak *life* into her? Because if you can't, she doesn't need your church. If she only hears how she needs to change her life and clean herself up, it is useless. She can't. She doesn't need to hear that. If you will love her and minister life to her and not the letter of the law, she will begin to grow and change.

Let's go to Romans 5:12-21. *"Therefore just as sin entered into the world through one man, and death through sin, and in this way death came to all men because all sinned. For before the Law was given, sin was in the world, but sin is not taken into account where there is no law. Nevertheless, death reigned from the time of Adam to the time of Moses, even over those who did not sin by the breaking of a commandment.* (These verses are so plain!) *As did Adam who was a pattern of the one to come. But the gift is not like the trespass, for if the many died by the trespass of one man* (and we know "the many" was the whole world) *how much more does God's grace, and the gift that came by grace of the one man Jesus Christ overflow to the many* (Again, the gift of God is not like the result of the one man's sin.) *for judgment followed one sin and brought condemnation, but the gift followed many trespasses and brought justification.* (That doesn't compute in our minds!) *For if by the trespass of the one man, death reigned through that one man, how much more will those who receive God's abundant provision of grace and the gift of righteousness reign in life through the one man Jesus Christ.* (The next is a key verse:) *Consequently just as the result of the one trespass was condemnation for all men, so also the result of the act of righteousness was justification that brings life for all men."*

How can we separate those two? How can we say "in Adam they all die, but in Christ they are not all going to be made alive"? We would rather read it that "condemnation was for all men, so the result of the one act of righteousness was justification to those who receive Jesus and begin to walk in obedience to His commands." It doesn't say that. And I know that sounds right. What am I saying? Do I have the liberty to live any way I want to live? Are you telling me that I can do anything that I want to do, and that eventually I'm still going to be OK? If your attitude is, "If what you are telling me is true, then I am going to go live it up," then my answer to you is this: you do not know God, and you desperately need to be saved. But I will tell you this, *you do not have a free will.* Adam took care of that for you, and he bound up the human race into the will of the flesh. You do not have a free will. We can obtain freedom in our will only by learning how to contact and fellowship with God in our spirit. By spending time in God's presence, and learning to live there, His Spirit will flow into our natural will and transform it into His will.

The Pentecostals love to say, "We are filled with the Holy Ghost." Well, let me tell you something: If you are really filled with the Holy Ghost, you will be a holy person. But you cannot be that way by trying to be that way. *Trying to do the right thing doesn't work.* If you are full of the Holy Spirit, you will be controlled, moved and motivated by that Holy Spirit. But you can't work for it. You can't "live right" for it. You can't try to choose the good over the evil for it, because that puts you into the works of the flesh. Trying with your carnality to choose the good over the evil puts you in that category of being alienated in your mind from that life that is in your spirit. You can't make it that way.

"As the result of the one trespass was condemnation for all men, so the result of one act of righteousness was justification that brings life to all men." So, can you live any way you want to? Yes. But here is the problem. You're going to go through hell one way or another. God had a plan in the very beginning for every human being that was ever born, and that is why I have shared so often that the scripture says we have been chosen in Him before the foundation of the world that we should be holy and without blame before Him in love. That is God's design; that is His plan, and that is His purpose, and your little will cannot stop God's purpose for your life. Absolutely impossible! I have done everything in my life but curse God. I have told Him, "Leave me alone! I can't do it anymore. I can't make it any more." God would just say, "Too bad, it's too late for you. You consecrated yourself to me and there is no turning back."

You see, the teaching of religion has gotten confused between the "will" and the "choice." Your will is bound up in carnality, and you are not a free moral agent. You are bound up to that will of the flesh. But you can choose to do what is right. Now again, this sounds like the man in Romans 7, which it is. He chooses to do that which is right, but he finds in his members another law, warring and bringing him into the bondage of the flesh. We will go through that struggle. That is what happens when you choose to live by the knowledge of good and evil.

Another way to look at this is through the law of sowing and reaping. God's magnitude at Calvary took away the sin of the world, so you have no problems with God, but if you sow to the flesh, you will of the flesh reap corruption. If you are in the flesh, and you have been reaping the flesh, the answer for you is not to try to change and to choose the good over the evil; the answer for you is to *learn how to feed upon spiritual food.* Again as Jesus said, "If you will learn to eat of Me, you will live by Me." He was even so bold as to make a further statement that very few have been able to understand. He said, "If you will eat the food that I give you, you will never die," and He wasn't talking about spiritual death. He said, "Your fathers ate manna in the wilderness, and they died," and He obviously was talking about physical death. But he said, "If you will eat the Bread of Life, *you will never die."* You may say, "I haven't seen any examples of that." I'll tell you, there are men and women all over this earth—and you probably never met any of them—who have learned to eat the Bread of Life and have never died.

God has people on the earth who have learned how, and are learning how, to eat the Bread of Life. *They shall never die!* They are about to be loosed to all of creation, and they are about to begin to bring reconciliation and restoration to all of God's creation. And the sad, sad, thing is that all of Christianity is going to be in an uproar over a group of people manifesting the loveliness of God and the attributes of forgiveness and reconciliation.

Do you know what the Church is looking for? It is looking for the restoration of the Apostolic Church, saying, "You better be careful, saints, because the days of Ananias and Saphira are coming back to the Church." How many times have you heard that? If you are motivated to serve God out of fear, you will find yourself in the tree of the knowledge of good and evil. I have questioned God so much, and I wish God's people would learn to do this. (Don't be afraid to question God. Don't be afraid to question scriptures. We are taught in Christianity, "Oh, don't question! Just take what the man of God says. Don't question God." Please, I beg of you, you need to challenge God! He loves to reveal to you His secrets.) But all of us need our concept of God drastically changed. Our country, America, has not rejected God; they have rejected a Christianity which has given them such a low concept of Who God is. That is what they are rejecting. I rejected that God many years ago. I have not had the "Christian" concept of God in many years. I am a Christian, but that concept will kill you. How could you be a reconciler if you feel that people have to choose the good over the evil? How can you help someone who is constantly choosing evil? You can't help them unless you understand the heart of God, and can be a reconciler.

God's reconcilers are all over the earth. He is soon going to loose them, and they will go into churches, they will go into bushes, they will go everywhere, bringing reconciliation and revealing to God's people the heart of God. That day will come and hopefully soon! But whether it is this Fall or next year, I do know it is coming very quickly. It has to be happening soon, because there is so much revelation, and there is so much coming to the Church that is revealing much of God's heart.

All that has been written above can be summarized very simply: God truly does love humanity, and He does not expect you to choose the good over the evil, because He knows that you cannot. What you need is to discover the treasure of His life that is within, and to learn to live by that life. *"For God, who commanded the light to shine out of darkness, hath shined in our hearts, to give the light of the knowledge of the glory of God in the face of Jesus Christ. But we have this treasure in earthen vessels, that the excellency of the power may be of God, and not of us"* (2 Cor. 4:6-7).

Coming Out of Darkness

Chapter 3

Transformation, Not Condemnation

I believe with all my heart that the Church today needs a word to make us realize that *God is God!*. We have not realized in the Church the depths of what Jesus said from the cross: "Father, forgive them; they don't know what they are doing." Many of God's people suffer continually under condemnation for things in their lives over which they can't seem to reach victory. These things have to be transformed by the infiltration of the Spirit of God into our soul-life. We all have God in us, but what we need is for Him to grow in us and to transform us into His image and likeness. We need never be condemned for the condition of our natural life; we just need to keep hungering after God and seeking Him until He comes fully alive within us. This will take care of our faults. We also need to realize that this is a process that takes time as Jesus, who is the author and the finisher of our faith, works in us to bring us fully into His plan and purpose.

Religion, by contrast, tells us that when we come to God, we know what we should do, that we must do only those things we know we should do, and that this then allows God to be able to bless us so that we can grow spiritually. But oh, I am telling you, we are so ignorant, and we are so out of the way, because we do not understand that today, as surely as God is upon the throne, He is saying, *"Not guilty."* You are not guilty. God would never bring you before Himself and remind you of your sin. I am sure you are familiar with verses that say such things as, *"As far as the east is from the west, so far have I removed the transgressions of My people. Their sins and their iniquities will I remember no more"* (Psalm 103:12; Hebrews 8:12). Thank God that His people are beginning to get the message that they are not guilty! You are not guilty. You do not need condemnation; *you need transformation.*

Let's look again at Ephesians 4:17-18. *"This I say therefore, and testify in the Lord, that ye henceforth walk not as other Gentiles walk, in the vanity of their mind, having the understanding darkened, being alienated from the life of God through the ignorance that is in them, because of the blindness of their heart."*

I can assure you that we all fall somewhat into this category. If the Church was not blinded and alienated from the life of God received at the new birth, there is no way that the Church which we see with our physical eyes could be in its present condition. It is in that condition because for two thousand years the results of the work God accomplished at the cross have not been understood!

I have made the statement that there are men and women all over the earth today who are about to be loosed upon the Church. For the most part, they are men and women who have been totally outside of the system of today's so-called Christianity and are therefore unknown to many of God's people. But, thank God, the Church is beginning to open to them. If we are honest, we have to look at the situation today and say of the two thousand years of Gospel preaching, "What has it produced? *Not a whole lot!"* Yes, people are saved and people are blessed, but God's full purpose has never been fulfilled by the institutional church. God's purpose is to fill the Church with Himself and to build us up together into a habitation of God. *"In whom all the building fitly framed together groweth unto an holy temple in the Lord: in whom ye also are builded together for an habitation of God through the Spirit"* (Ephesians 2:21-22).

One of the saints whom God has raised up to reveal His purpose for the Church is J. Preston Eby. He is one of those lights shining in the darkness. (Write to him; he will put you on his mailing list, and he does not charge for his materials. You will find his address in the back of this booklet.) I feel that every one of God's seekers needs to hear what this man is saying to the Church. The following is an excerpt from one of his monthly newsletters.

Jesus came into the world in the time of the Roman Empire. He was crucified on a Roman cross, pierced with a Roman spear, and sealed in His sepulcher under a Roman seal. But praise God! He burst the bands of death, shattered the seal of mighty Rome, and arose the conquering Christ. And not only that, He ascended victor over all the powers of darkness. Having brought to naught the prince of this world, having brought in eternal redemption for a lost world and redeemed all back unto Himself, He sat down at the right hand of the Majesty on High and poured out on the first few citizens of his Kingdom the gift of the Holy Ghost. The Kingdom of God was birthed and gathered from Jew and Gentile alike a vast multitude into its bosom. What a flood of light and glory and power fell upon the world in the ministry of the humble followers of the Lamb! And oh what glorious days those were. How God blessed His Gospel. Mighty signs and wonders were performed as God confirmed His word with signs following. The word of God, anointed by the Holy Spirit, swept the world like a prairie fire. It encircled the mountains and crossed the oceans. It made kings to tremble and tyrants to fear. It was said of those early Christians that they had turned the world upside-down. So powerful was their message and spirit, in spite of persecution, in spite of untold thousands of saints impaled upon crosses, burned at the stake, and fed to hungry lions to the thunderous applause of wild spectators, the word grew and multiplied. For God dwelt mightily in the midst of His people. The knowledge of the glory of the Lord covered the earth as the waters cover the sea. Paganism fell. The mighty Roman Empire shut up its idol temples, sheathed its persecuting sword, and sat down as disciples at the feet of Christ and His apostles.

Oh, but there was another spirit at work also. A spirit and system set in among the saints of the Lord, and the manna of yesterday began to breed worms and stink. Refusing to follow on to know the Lord, they began instituting rules and regulations, laying down laws and formulating creeds, observing days and ordaining sacraments and ordinances, elevating human government, becoming disciples of Paul, of Apollos, of Cephas and many others. Before too many years had passed, men began to set themselves up as bishops and lords over God's heritage in place of the leadership of the Spirit. Instead of conquering by the power of the Spirit and

truth, men began to substitute their ideas and their
methods. Soon the glory and the power, the presence and
the word of God in the morning-time Church began to be
eclipsed, and the power of carnal-minded men gradually
took the place of the awesome presence of God.
Consequently, man's carnal understanding was put upon
the Scriptures, and as the Spirit of Christ fled from their
midst, men established a vast and elaborate system of
substitutes to take His place. The festivals of the Church
were created along the lines of pagan celebrations. Costly
and ornate edifices were constructed for worship. The
services became ceremonialized and elaborate. Relics of
saints and martyrs were cherished as sacred possessions.
The Church, with its array of godly-bedecked clergy and
its imposing ceremonies, assumed much of the stateliness
and visible splendor that belonged to the heathen system
that it had once supplanted. Christianity was now a
pageant, a ritualism, a vain philosophy, a superstition, a
social club, indeed an antichrist, a pot full of manna
infested with the worms of carnality and death, a
putrefying stench in the nostrils of God.

The Gospel preached by the nominal Church will never
get the job done. It will never bring the Kingdom of God
in power to deliver mankind from sin and death and
restore all things to God. The Church world is using
worldly means and soulish methods to promote its
programs today. It is conformed into the world's way of
doing things. This is true not only of the historic
denominations, but also of the Pentecostals, the
Charismatics, and, alas, some groups who profess to be
deeper life, Kingdom, or sonship people. Churches
compete against one another, who can have the most in

Sunday School, who can build the biggest building, who can win the most souls, which evangelist can draw the largest crowds, each one pointing to the success of their ministry, glorying in the size of their outreach or work, stressing how much could be accomplished with more money, and, to hear them tell it, just about the whole world is being brought to the feet of Jesus through their efforts. The Church world today is totally conformed to the world's way of doing things. Because of that, it is really no better off than the world it is trying so desperately to save. Because the average Christian today has been brought up with a certain "other" than Christ, he is totally unable to think except in terms of established orders, sects, denominations, credentials, creeds, assemblies, Church ceremonies, Church buildings, doctrines, meetings, communions, baptisms, programs, campaigns, crusades, choirs, pastors, rituals, ceremonies, vestments, offerings, conferences, Board meetings, committees, elections, Sunday schools, theological seminaries, fellowship halls, stained glass windows, platforms, special members, numbers and a thousand other things. Take all these things away from them and they would be spiritually destitute, totally incapable of doing the work of the Lord. But after they have spent a whole lifetime of this feverish Church activity, how many people are there who have ever taken the time to wait on God long enough to hear Him speak and divulge His will to their seeking hearts?

I declare to you of a truth that any man or woman who will take the time to seek God and God alone, hungering and thirsting after God's mind and God's will, that man will find himself drifting away from all the aforementioned things, and from them on to the mind of Christ. And lest any think that we are being brash or heretical to even suggest a departure from those things listed above, I invite you to carefully examine that list to determine which one of them Jesus Christ had used or even needed in His wonderful sonship ministry. It is astonishing to realize that Jesus knew absolutely nothing of any of it, yet He more effectively ministered the life of God, the power of God, the glory of God and the Kingdom of God than any man who has graced this planet. And, I do not hesitate to add, strip all of these away from a son of God, and what he will have left is Christ, only Christ. End quote

I tell you, God has men and women all over the earth with the message for the Church. Will you open to them? Because they are not religious, they will not condemn you, but they will minister life to you and cause you to grow up into Him. I am thankful that many of God's people are willing to listen to a message that will set them free, because to be set free, it takes the Spirit and the light and the word of God to break loose our mindset from religious tradition. And I know that every one of us likes to think that we are not religious. Almost every pastor I know who has a church says, "My church is not religious." Yet in every church I enter, without exception, I hear the sounds of bondage and religion.

"I beseech you therefore, brethren, by the mercies of God, that ye present your bodies a living sacrifice, holy, acceptable unto God, which is your reasonable service. And be not conformed to this world: but be ye transformed by the renewing of your mind, that ye may

prove what is that good, and acceptable, and perfect, will of God" (Romans 12:1-2).

How many times have we heard that passage preached as a call to consecration and dedication -- preached in the messages across America on holiness and right living? And if we have the religious mindset, we'll hear this or read this and we'll say, "Oh my, yes! Lord, I present my body to You," but then we will have brought up into our consciousness all those things in our life that we know should not be there. And after all, this word does say, *"Present your bodies a living sacrifice, holy . . ."* I used to say, "Oh God! I would love to do that." Oh how I would have loved to be able to go before God and say, "Father, I present my body to you, *holy, unblemished and undefiled."* I wanted so desperately to know the reality of the Scriptures. I wanted to be able to experience the heart-throb of God! Yet every time I would go into the Lord's presence, the light of God would begin to expose me, I would see all of those things in my life that should not be there and I would fall under guilt and condemnation.

You see, most of us haven't been taught about these things. We haven't been warned that there is no way that you can enter into the presence of God and not have the light of God expose you! If you move into the presence of God and you *don't* feel your weakness, if you *don't* sense your inabilities, if you're *not* aware of the sin and the habits in your life, then you haven't entered into His presence. But just because the light of God exposes all those things it doesn't mean that we should fall into condemnation. The light of God does what it is supposed to do; it exposes all the hidden areas of your heart. You'll begin to see things in your life that even you did not know were there. *But it is not for condemnation; it is for transformation.* God will never condemn you. He has paid the penalty for every transgression and disobedience.

We need to spend time in God's presence to have Him reveal His heart to us. He said from the cross, "Father, forgive them; they don't know what they are doing." They had just nailed Him to the cross! He was bleeding, He was dying, and He said, "Father, forgive them!" Could He possibly have asked anything in that moment which would not have been granted to Him? The very men who pierced His side and hung Him on a cross will one day bow the knee before the throne of God, and they will give glory to God. They put Him on a cross, but because they did that, the price for their redemption and ours was paid. Even though they did the most criminal act in the universe, they acted under the plan of an awesome, almighty, all-knowing God, who works all things after the counsel of His own will. And that is why He could say, "Father, forgive them; *they don't know.*"

And oh Christian, I can tell you that *you* don't know, either. If you have sin in your life, if you have habits that you haven't overcome, and you fall under condemnation, you don't know the depths of God's love! But how you need to know. And because of the condition of the system calling itself Christianity, there is not much forgiveness in the Church either, unless you have a strong will and a strong character which is able to put down those things in your life that shouldn't be there.

Christianity as we know it today is only "the survival of the fittest". Those who are out of the way, those who have habits and things in their lives which they cannot overcome are not even welcome in many churches.

We Christians do not understand that we inherited a sinful nature. We are taught it, but then we are condemned for acting like it. Those of us who have been regenerated **do** have a new nature. The Apostle Paul says in Romans 7:22-23, *"For I delight in the law of God after the inward man: but I see another law in my members, warring against the law of my mind, and bringing me into captivity to the law of sin which is in my members."* We are regenerated in our *inner man,* but that life in us must grow until it overcomes the law of sin and death. We have never been exposed to the truth that to stop sinning is a matter of growth and transformation. You can *will* to do what is right all you want, and you should, but until the Spirit of God grows up in you, you will continue to fall into sin.

Paul also says in Romans 7:18-20, *"For I know that in me (that is, in my flesh,) dwelleth no good thing: for to will is present with me; but how to perform that which is good I find not. For the good that I would I do not: but the evil which I would not, that I do. Now if I do that I would not, it is no more I that do it, but sin that dwelleth in me."*

The flesh is the carnal man. As long as we are living out from our carnal man we will always be brought into captivity to sin and death. Overcoming sin is not a matter of exercising our natural will. We must hunger and thirst after God. We must spend time in His presence every day so that His life may flow into our soul life and transform every area. Paul says here very plainly that if you are sinning, and you have a desire to please God, then it is not you that sins (not your new nature) but the sin principle that is still operating in your carnal man. The natural man will never improve: he must be put to death by your learning how to live in the Spirit. There are no "How to" books when it comes to living in the Spirit. You must spend time in the presence of God to be enabled to live according to His life.

When we were born, when we were brought into the world, every one of us inherited a nature from Adam. *Adam sold you into sin and death!* And it took me years to find this out. I used to go before God, and I would say almost continually, "God, I didn't ask to be born this way! God, I am just so eaten up with this stuff! I didn't ask to have the lusts of the flesh. Why?" I prayed every day. I would get up early every morning, and I would go out and seek God, and sometimes I would cry and say, "God, it's not fair!" I'd see Christians in church all around me, and they seemed to be so happy, and they seemed to be so free. (What little did I know!) But a lot of you can identify with this: If you are born on that side of the Tree of the Knowledge of Good and Evil that has a nature tending to do evil, and you want to be a Christian, the so-called "Christian" community will kill you. You don't have a chance as things stand today. But our churches are going to become hospitals.

There is absolutely no hope for you outside of finding the reality of Christ within you. You can love God and still be a failure at living the Christian life. Let me tell you something: One of the most miserable conditions you can ever be in (and many of you, again, can identify with this) is to have the love of God in your heart, yet basically you experience Romans 7:22-23, "I delight in the Law of God, but there is another law in my members bringing me into captivity to sin and death." I tell you, that when I met God in 1969, oh, I delighted in Him! And I had no knowledge of what I should and shouldn't do, I just delighted in God. And for a time after I was saved, in the evenings I used to open my Bible, and I would just read and cry -- and I would have a cigarette in my hand! I did that until someone told me, "You can't do that and be in God's presence. You are being deceived. You are getting a false spirit, a false sense of peace; you cannot enter into the presence of God with a cigarette. You can't do it."

What a terrible thing, to tell someone they can't get to God unless they clean up their life! We were born with a nature that is both good and evil. *That is why Jesus went to the cross.* We are ignorant and out of the way. We don't understand. We don't know why we act as we do. I didn't know why I acted the way I did. I wanted God, but I wanted what I wanted. I couldn't help it.

Have you ever been addicted to something, but, no matter how hard you tried, you experienced Romans 7: "I find another law in my members that brings me into captivity to the law of sin and death"? If someone has that natural characteristic in them which loves the things they shouldn't, they cannot be a member in good standing in many churches that I know today. But if they are on the "good" side of the Tree of the Knowledge of Good and Evil, then they are accepted. We really don't understand that what has been raised up out there calling itself "the Church" is *absolutely antichrist*. I'm not talking about people; I'm talking about *the system,* and the way that system has been set up is antichrist. A homosexual cannot be a member of such a church, a prostitute cannot be a member of such a church -- unless they change and clean their lives up. Someone might say, "Brother, don't you know that Paul said that you shouldn't even eat with someone who is in adultery?" Well, there is one thing I know in these days: I know the heart of God. I know what people need is not condemnation, I know what they need is not adjustment, I know what they need is not laws and regulations. What they need is *to understand the love and the heart of God,* because at Calvary the debt for sin was paid. God's people have been in bondage too long, thinking that there is something wrong with them, thinking that they don't really want God or they would be able to quit this habit or that habit. It just goes on and on and on.

"Present your bodies a living sacrifice and holy." In God's eyes, every one of you is most holy! How can we say that? We can say it because ***"Your sins and your iniquities will I remember no more."*** And, ***"As far as the east is from the west, so far have I removed the transgression of my people."*** And you say, "But, . . . but I'm still sinning, and I'm still doing things I shouldn't!" It doesn't matter, because when you understand God's concept of sin and His concept of Calvary, it will free you up from the guilt of just simply being who you are, and will then allow you the access into His presence

64

which will bring to you transformation. I have been speaking this for years -- if the Spirit of the living God is never formed in you, so that He begins to grow up in you and be expressed in you, *you will never change inwardly!* And if you only change outwardly, it doesn't help you anyway, because outward conduct and outward change do not produce anything but a better outward person. But what God needs is for His people to understand that because they are the way they are, because they inherited that nature from Adam, they need to feel no shame, no guilt, and no condemnation. I inherited all of those things that I was in the natural from my father Adam.

There are a number of physical weaknesses in the human race which can be inherited, yet if somebody develops a disease, we don't condemn them, do we? Of course we don't. And I tell you, *sin is a disease,* and you can't help it. Can I help it if an illness develops in my body? (I'm speaking here in natural terms.) Can I help it, and am I condemned for it? When I go to pray, am I reminded of this disease and do I say, "Oh my God, I shouldn't have this!" and then fall under condemnation? But that is what we do with sin, not realizing that it is just the natural man. *"I delight in the law of God, but I find another law at work in my members bringing me into captivity to the law of sin and death."* And you say, "But Brother, do we always have to live there?" No. Transformation is the only thing that will cure the sin disease in your body. It is the only thing.

You can pray all day, you can read the Bible all day, you can do anything you want to do, and if it is simply done in the natural, if there is no contact with the living, energizing Spirit of God, there will be no transformation. Do you remember that years ago, before Jesus came, there were priests in the temple praying 24 hours a day for the Messiah to come? Yet when He walked among them, they didn't recognize Him. Prayer doesn't always help you. There is only one hope for you, and that is that you *have a heart for God.* That is the *only* thing that is going to help you. And if you don't have a heart for God, it is very easy to obtain. If you get around people who love God, you will just find yourself having a heart for God. (We need to learn the power of transference. Many of us who have been in the deliverance ministry have been taught in the past about the "transference of spirits". Well, let me tell you something: we need to learn about the transference of the Holy Spirit!)

When we begin to grow up into God, and transformation begins to take place as the Spirit of God begins to flow into all areas of our lives and bring transformation, it becomes very easy to live godly. It becomes very easy to believe God. Why? Well, Paul tells you, ***"Be renewed in the spirit of your mind, that you may prove what is that good, and acceptable, and perfect, will of God."*** The good, the acceptable and the perfect will of God. We take a verse like that, and we can break it down and preach doctrines forever on it. But the key is to have a renewed mind to see that at the cross, because of the sacrifice, *you were made a holy person.* God would never look upon sin, and He need not, because He took the sins of humanity to the cross and into death, *and they are no longer there.*

Many people say, "That sounds like Christian Science. Are you saying there is no sin?" I am saying that **God took it away,** but merely seeing that there is no sin won't really help you. What will help you is simply to realize that *you need God.* And if you realize that your sin does not keep you and separate you from getting to God for the help that you need, that is "Christian sense", not Christian Science. In God's eyes there is no sin, and there is coming a day when we are going to realize that and begin to walk in it -- and then there won't be sin for us either. It was dealt with. *"Be transformed by the renewing of your mind"* (the Greek word is *metamorphoo,* which means an actual transformation; it's the same word that we would use for a caterpillar that is transformed into a butterfly). Right now we might look pretty ugly, but there is a work going on. I can look back now, and I can actually thank God for those things in my life that caused me to seek Him. I don't care how bad the sin was; I don't care how deep the lust, or whatever it was that was in my life; those things were used by God to drive me to Him. There are multitudes of Christians on the scrap heap because they have never understood that they don't have to be any certain kind of person to get to God.

Let's look at 2 Corinthians 3, beginning at verse 2: *"Ye are our epistle written in our hearts, known and read of all men: forasmuch as ye are manifestly declared to be the epistle of Christ ministered by us, written not with ink, but with the Spirit of the living God; not in tables of stone, but in fleshy tables of the heart."*

Now let's go on to verse 6: ***"Who also hath made us able ministers of the new testament; not of the letter, but of the spirit: for the letter killeth, but the spirit giveth life."*** I have heard many, many messages on that verse, yet some of the very pastors who spoke that verse could not help me when I went to them for help for my condition. ***"Who also hath made us able ministers of the new testament; not of the letter."*** Listen. He said, "able ministers of the *new* testament." Most of God's servants today would say, "Oh, I don't minister by the letter." If we would just stop and think sometimes what is meant by these words, we would see that whenever you are ministering by the letter of the word you are ministering by the law.

One of the big bondages in the Christian system is tithing. For years, my wife and I have not followed a set rule or principle of tithing. God told me many years ago, "Don't try to walk in the spirit by the letter of the law, because the minute you try to put laws upon the people, the very thing that you're trying to get them to do, they will not do." They won't do it, and that is natural, because with the knowledge of the Law comes the bondage to keep you from performing the Law (Romans 7). But religion has made it sound so nice: It's a shame that pastors even have to talk and teach about tithing; it's a shame! Why can't we teach people, "I hear God and you can hear God also." And what is He saying to *you?* Is He saying to you to tithe? Then by all means tithe.

My wife and I, if I may use us for an example again, have given away our rent money. We have given away our cars. At times, we have given way beyond the tithe. But if you put people under the law, some of them are going to fulfill the law. They are going to pay their tithe and then think that everything else they have is theirs to do with as they want. *Not so!* You need to do what He says. "For God has made us able ministers of the New Covenant -- *not of the letter."* Pastor, you should not be teaching people how to tithe; you should be teaching people how to enter into the presence of the Living God. You should be telling people, "Don't come to me and ask what you should do. Don't come to me and ask if you should tithe; come to me and let us worship together. Come to me and let me help you enter into the presence where He is, and then *do what He says."*

I used to walk into churches and hear forty-five minutes of teaching on giving, sometimes in every service. Then, when I ask the pastor, "Why are you doing that?" he will say, "Well, the people just aren't giving; they need to be taught how to give." Let me tell you something, pastors: If you are pastoring a church and your people aren't giving, the problem is not your people. We pastored at Fall Creek, Oregon, for three-and-a-half years, and I never asked people for money. I was still in the church system at that time, and I still went by some of the rules of the system, because I was still a lot more ignorant than I am today. But you know, I've always had that heart to give. And God sat me down for about four years recently, and I didn't minister anywhere to anyone, except on an individual basis, and He said when He released me to minister, "Always remember: I gave My very best. Therefore when you go into a church, when you go into a home, wherever you go, go *to give.* Try to give even more than you can receive."

God does have leadership on the earth today who will give. People tell me all the time, "Brother, it costs you money to make those tapes; and besides, if you would sell them, it would enable you to have the finances to fulfill God's will in your life." And I say, "Read Revelation, chapters 17 & 18, please," because the principles of Babylon, the principles of the world, the principles of our so-called Christianity are those of *buying and selling,* and the principles of the Kingdom are *giving and receiving.* I never tell anyone, "I won't receive from you." If you want to write me a check for a million dollars, I'll say, "Thank you, brother!" and I'll cry, and I'll thank God. But if you try to buy something from me, I won't sell it to you. It's not according to the principles of the Kingdom. Hear me, Church! Our churches have to be brought into Kingdom awareness and Kingdom living. If our churches were *giving* churches, rather than *taking* churches, we would fill them! We couldn't hold all the people! God gave His very best. So, Pastor, if your people aren't giving, don't blame the people.

If God wants to shut me down, all He has to do is to pull my finances away from me, and I can't minister, because I don't have anything to sell, I don't have any way to support my ministry outside of working physically. The most my wife and I can do together is to put about $200 a month into our ministry account to go toward producing the books and the tapes, but that is almost nothing.) So if I get crossways with God and He wants to shut me down, He can just pull the finances, and I can't minister. I would challenge every pastor and every minister: Let God do that in your life!

One of the key things that God needs to reveal to us is that the benefits of Calvary are ours regardless of our condition. I cannot emphasize this enough! If you are a prostitute, gay, if you are full of lust, envy, pride, jealousy -- whatever it is, *all you need is to learn how to touch God.* But yet, because of our Christian teaching, we have thought that to be impossible. We can't be a prostitute and touch God! We can't be full of lust; we can't commit adultery and touch God! But the truth is, if you are an adulterer or prostitute, and you never touch God, you will never change!

It sometimes takes years for transformation to take place in our lives. The Apostle Paul says, ***"For which cause we faint not; but though our outward man perish, yet the inward man is renewed day by day"*** (2 Corinthians 4:6). The word "renewed" is *anakainoo* (Strong's 341: to cause to grow up, new, to make new). Thayer's says this means that:

A) new strength and vigor is given to one
B) to be changed into a new kind of life as opposed to the former corrupt state.

This renewing is a process, not an instant change. No matter how carnal you think you are, if you will keep hungering after God, you will be renewed day by day. Everything in life takes time. First you have a seed, then a small blade, and eventually a full ear of corn. We are the seed of God. His seed is growing in the midst of our carnality, and eventually that seed of His life will grow and consume everything in us that is not of God. This is a work of grace, not a matter of self-effort or natural willing. *"It is not of him that wills, nor of him that runs, but of God that shows mercy"* (Romans 9:16).

As mentioned earlier, we have inherited habit patterns from our forefathers. The sins of the forefathers are visited upon the children for generations, and it's not a spiritual thing, it's a natural thing. Those things have to be transformed. (Grant you, in some cases it can be a spirit and be cast out, and you can be set free.) But in most of the cases, it is habit patterns which have developed, sometimes for generations, that you inherit. That's why I was full of lust; I inherited it just like a disease. And you know, we cannot receive anything from God except through the eyes of faith. If you are under condemnation and guilt, it's impossible for you to receive from God, because you feel that you *deserve* what you have. And again, nominal Christianity will teach you, "You deserve what you have -- look at what you are doing! You call yourself a Christian, and you are out there drinking and smoking and going to movies and doing all of those things." But you need *transformation, not condemnation.*

One of the first things that will help you is to have the revelation that God and man are one. And I want to explain to you just a little bit about what I mean when I say this, because I have been getting letters recently from people (and these people are not critical; they are people who love me and haven't known me very long, but who have come to love the ministry that I have). They tell me things like this: "You should never say God and man are one, because the New Age people and the New Age movement, and this one-world religious thing that is going on out there are saying some of the same things that you are saying. So therefore, if you use this terminology, you have to be careful, because it's New Age." But if New Age people are proclaiming the truth, if a Buddhist monk is speaking some truth, then do I *not* speak that truth because somebody will think that I am a monk, or a Hindu, or a Buddhist, or a New Ager? I have to speak it, because it is true! God and man *are* one. This is all through the Scripture, but let's look at just a few verses (these are all very familiar verses, but again, we have not had revelation on just basic, Scriptural, practical things).

In John 15:5, Jesus said, ***"I am the vine, ye are the branches."*** Picture that in your mind. Look at a vine that has branches. Are the branches and the vine two separate entities? I don't think so; they are one. Now that does not make the branch the vine, but it is a part of it, and the same life flows through both the vine and the branches. That is why I say over and over again that I believe with all my heart that I and my Father are one. But I am not my Father. *I'm not God!* However, I inherited God traits from my Father, just as I inherited natural traits from my natural father, and I am a human because I have a human life. If indeed Jesus lives in me -- and as the Apostle Peter and others have told us in the New Testament, the Divine life and nature of God are in me -- then how could I not be one with God?

The problem is that we identify with the human side, because we are in that fallen, darkened state, having our eyes darkened, being alienated from the life of God that is in us. That is the only problem. Jesus said we must be

73

born again, because there is a natural birth and there is a spiritual birth. And as the natural birth is earthy, the tendency of that natural birth is to always be dragging you downward back into the earth. But he that is born of the Spirit is spirit, which means that that part of you which is regenerated and born again is the spirit in you, and the spirit is always ascending and rising above. This is where the conflict comes in! The natural human life is always drawing down toward the earth, trying to pull you down, but your spirit is always wanting to ascend.

Another thing we haven't understood is that when you are born again you are as a little baby. I don't care if you are a hundred years old when you are born again, it is a spiritual birth just like a natural birth. But we take spiritual babies and we try to make them act like Father God! And they are just babies. Babies need only a few things: They need to be fed and properly taken care of. You cannot teach a baby about tithing, but you can feed him, and if you feed him properly, if you nourish your children properly, they may never understand the principle of tithing, but they will *be givers* -- oh they will be givers!

"And now I am no more in the world, but these are in the world, and I come to thee. Holy Father, keep through thine own name those whom thou hast given me, that they may be one, as we are" (John 17:11). How are Jesus and the Father one? The Apostle Paul tells us that the fullness of the triune God, the fullness of everything that God is, dwelt in a bodily form in the Man Jesus. Then Jesus has the audacity to pray, "Father, just as we are one, they are one." You see, if you have this

revelation, your problems are over, but the biggest tool of the enemy today in Christian circles is *fear;* because, brethren, in the last days there are seducing spirits and doctrines of devils. If you are in that church system today and you are entrenched in that system, you have been seduced -- terribly seduced -- and you don't even know it. The deception and seducing came in even before the Apostles died.

"Neither pray I for these alone, but for them also which shall believe on me through their word; That they all may be one; as thou, Father, art in me, and I in thee [Note that it is the same way!] ***that they also may be one in us: that the world may believe that thou hast sent me"*** (John 17:20-21). Now we can't believe these words, because we look with our eyes at what's out there in the system of Christianity. There is no oneness! You may say, "Brother, I'm not in darkness," but are you a Baptist, and are you entrenched in the Baptist tradition? Are you a Lutheran, entrenched in the Lutheran tradition? Are you a Pentecostal, entrenched in that religious tradition? Then you are in darkness! Pentecost is over, and people don't even know it. What is being produced out there by that name for the most part is a sham. "Prophets" are coming through and revealing to almost everyone in the church things about their lives, and because the people are in darkness, they don't realize that this is a *natural* capability. For anyone who becomes spiritual, discernment is a natural thing. You can't be in my presence very long before I can discern you. But for me to take the discernment that I have of you and prophesy it back to you is not right. Now I realize that there are many prophets in the land, and that there are some who have

75

maturity and some really do have a word from the Lord. But for the most part, it's a sham.

And we have heard another thing, which sounds so humble. I was taught as a young Christian, "Brother, be careful, be careful. Don't you ever touch the glory of the Lord. Don't you touch that." And one day I read, *"The glory which you gave Me, I have given to them, that they may be one"* (John 17:22). What is the glory? Most people don't know what it is. The glory of God is *the expression of God.* Wherever God is expressed, there is His glory. He said, *"I have given to them My glory,"* and the same Spirit that was in the Lord Jesus is now in you and me! But we don't know it. Oh, we are taught it, but we don't *know* it. Our preachers wouldn't even want us really to understand it, because if we did, most of them would be out of a job! Do you know what my job is as a minister? If I am a leader, my main function should be to teach you and raise you up in your awareness and abilities of God so that you no longer need my services, and I can go do it elsewhere Where are the anointed men and women of God who are able to minister not by the letter but by the Spirit of the Living God, to write upon your heart and cause you to rise up and minister to one another? Most of God's people have never had a proper vision of the Church. All we have seen is this in Revelation 17 (go read it, please): Mystery, Babylon the great, *the Mother of harlots!* And you say, "But Brother, there are precious, precious saints out there!" Yes, there are, and it says in Revelation 17 that Mystery, Babylon, that Mother of harlots, is decked *with gold and silver and precious stones,* which simply means that those are the characteristics of God. Gold is the Divine life and nature;

silver is the redemption; precious stones means the transforming power of God. Yes, there are precious saints out there, but they have never had anyone to bring them out of the darkness and bring them into full liberty and liberation in the power of the Spirit. We haven't had many men in this age and generation to raise up the saints of God to minister to one another.

There is no condemnation in what I say here, but if you have been going to the same church for twenty years, ten years, five years, and you are still sitting in the chair listening to the same man preach, *you are in darkness!* And I don't care how much light that man has, because if we are able ministers, not by the letter but by the spirit, people *cannot* stay the same. Some of these big ministries have had the same people sitting in the pews for years listening to the same man teach the same message. If a man or woman is ministering by the Spirit they will be bringing fresh manna. A word of the Lord ministered by the Spirit will enter into your heart, and if you are hungry for God, it will nourish you and build you up. If, on the other hand, all you are receiving is head knowledge, you will think you are progressing, but your life will not change. Paul said to the Corinthians, ***"Forasmuch as ye are manifestly declared to be the epistle of Christ ministered by us, written not with ink, but with the Spirit of the living God; not in tables of stone, but in fleshy tables of the heart"*** (2 Corin. 3:3).

When we ministered to the Church in Fall Creek, I used to tell people, "I don't care what your problem is; please come and be a part. Sit down and watch your life change. And if your life doesn't change, I will never condemn you. I will never come to you and say you cannot be gay, but you know what I will do? I will minister to you; I will pray for you; I will cry with you, and *you will be delivered.* You will be transformed by the Spirit of the Living God!"

Another concept keeps cropping up out there, the concept the church world has that God is again going to raise up the Apostolic Church. Men are setting themselves up in authority, saying, "You'd better be wary, saints, because the days of Ananias and Saphira are coming back!" They want you to fear their authority. It is an absolute disgrace to the Kingdom of God for a man to exercise authority over you as a believer. One who has true spiritual authority would never exercise that authority over another believer. ***"The anointing which you have received abides in you. And you don't need any man to teach you, but that same anointing will teach you of all things"*** (1 John 2:27). That's the truth. Even if every word that I'm speaking to you is truth, you won't hear it unless you hear *Him* speak to you! You have to realize that *within you* is the anointing, *within you* is the moving, *within you* is the resurrected Spirit of the Living God, and *He will speak to you!* It doesn't matter what your condition in life is, whether you are a king or a prostitute, God will speak to you, and *in His speaking is the transforming power to change you into a son or a daughter of God.*

"Oh foolish Christians, who has bewitched you that you should not obey the truth, before whose eyes Jesus Christ has been evidently set forth crucified among you" (Galatians 3:1). Paul is saying, "Don't you realize that Jesus Christ has been set forth crucified among you? Don't you realize that there is *absolutely nothing* that you need to do?" Now someone may say, "Well, Brother, I preach Jesus Christ and Him crucified." My reply would be, "Yes, but along with that you bring all your rules and regulations, and your shoulds and your shouldn'ts. Jesus Christ crucified is the end of the message! There is not one thing that you can add to that to make it any better; that's the end of the message." Jesus Christ crucified, buried and resurrected, that is the Gospel, and that is what will change you and bring you life.

"This only would I learn of you: did you receive the spirit by the works of the law or by the hearing of faith? Are you so foolish? Having begun in the spirit, are you now made perfect by the flesh?" (Galatians 3:2-3). Have you suffered so many things? Have you suffered for so long in this bondage? Has it all been in vain? *"He that ministers to you the spirit and works miracles among you, does he do it by the works of the Law or by the hearing of faith?"* (Galatians 3:4). Listen. If I had to minister to you because of meeting the standard of the law, I wouldn't have a chance! If the qualification to minister is to be one who is fully transformed and in the likeness of God, I fail miserably. That is not it. It is because I have *seen something of God,* and because I have seen something of God, I have had that contact with the Spirit of the Living God that has energized me and brought some transformation in my life. That's what qualifies me to minister! It's not the result of going to a bible school. William Law said many years ago that Christianity runs the Bible schools, thinking that they can put off Adam and put on Christ. That's not what happens

in a Bible school. You go into a Bible school full of the Spirit of God, and you'll come out systematized. You'll be taught how to teach people to do everything but contact God, because the teachers don't know how to do that themselves. You will know how to do everything just as you should do it, but you won't know how to contact God in reality and in spirit. (Again, I have made a blanket statement; I am sure there are schools of the Spirit that are wonderful.)

"Know ye therefore that they which are of faith, the same are the children of Abraham. And the Scripture, foreseeing that God would justify the heathen through faith, preached before the Gospel unto Abraham saying, In thee shall all nations be blessed. So then they which are of faith are blessed with faithful Abraham. For as many as are of the works of the Law are under the curse [Hear that! As many as are under the works of the law are under the curse.], *for it is written, Cursed is everyone that continues not in all the things which are written in the book of the law to do them. But that no man is justified by the law"* (Galatians 3:7-11). You see, Christian, if you can quit smoking, if you can quit all your lust, if you can quit doing everything that you think you shouldn't be doing, you will be no better off, if you don't have the substance and the reality of God formed in your life. *"The Law is not of faith, but the man that doeth them shall live in them"* (Gal. 3:12).

Notice this: *"Christ has redeemed us from the curse of the law"* (Galatians 3:13). I'm sure all of you could tell me what the curse of the law was. Basically, it was poverty, sickness, and death. Now why did the curse of the law come on you? How did you come under the curse of the law in the first place? By not walking according to the law! Because the law says that if you do all this, you will be blessed, but if you fail to do this or that, you will be cursed. The law was the best thing that God could bring to man at the time, because Jesus had not yet come and the Holy Spirit had not yet been given. Man had to have a guide in his natural life to show him the difference between godliness and ungodliness. It was a spiritual law, but we are natural, sold into sin by Adam. The Law was to bring in the awareness of sin, not to condemn you, but to make you realize that it is impossible to keep the law. It says in Deuteronomy 28:15 that if you don't keep the whole law, if you don't keep all the words of this covenant, all of these curses will come upon you -- all of the plagues, all of the poverty, all of the diseases, all of the sicknesses will come upon you.

Then Paul says in the New Testament, "Brothers and Sisters, Christ has redeemed us from the curse of the law." Well what does that mean? That means that if I break the law because I am ignorant, I don't suffer the curse, because He redeemed me from it. He said, "Your sins, your iniquities will I remove. I won't even remember them." You can say, "Wait a minute. You are not ignorant if you are saved." Oh yes you are! Let me tell you something: If you are not somewhat in ignorance, if you are not in some blindness, you will not be living a life according to the flesh, and you will not have these habits and hang-ups in your life. If they are there, it is because you are in ignorance. Ignorance just means you don't know. Christ redeemed us from the curse of the law.

You say, "Brother, you are teaching a liberation Gospel." And I say, Hallelujah! Why are things like "Christ has redeemed you from the curse" in the Word? If we were walking perfectly according to the law, we wouldn't have to worry about the curse anyway. Paul says He has redeemed you from that curse, because if there are things in your life that shouldn't be there, if you have problems and hang-ups and lusts, whatever you are struggling with, Christ has redeemed you from receiving the curse of the law. Such are the people that need it, not the righteous. (I have never heard this Gospel preached in church -- never.)

"Tell me, you that desire to be under the law, don't you hear the law? For it is written that Abraham had two sons, the one by a bondmaid, the other by a free woman. He that was of the bondwoman was born after the flesh [the natural carnal person:] *but he that is of the free woman, born of the promise, which things are an allegory. For these are the two covenants, the one from Mount Sinai which gendereth to bondage . . .* [Listen, and please remember this: Anytime you hear a man, and I don't care what his intentions are, who begins to teach to you the principles of the law, you have just left the Gospel and gone into bondage.] *. . . for this Hagar is Mount Sinai in Arabia and answers to Jerusalem which now is and is in bondage with her children. But the Jerusalem which is above is free, which is the mother of us all"* (Gal. 4:21-26).

The Church of the firstborn is those who have been regenerated and birthed into the Spirit of the Living God. There is no law for you -- none! The only law that we need is *the law of the Spirit of life in Christ Jesus!* As we have seen, the natural birth is always pulling you down; it is the law of that life, the law of the human life, that generates to bondage. The law of the religious system generates unto bondage, because they try to get you to live godly by telling you how to do it, and what you should do. But the Spirit of the Living God that is within each and every one of us is free from the bondage of the law. You are free to be who you are! And I'm going to say it: If you are a homosexual, you are free to be who you are. And if I were pastoring a church and you wanted to come to my church, I would say, "Please come!" The only requirement that I would ask of you is that you have a heart that you want to be transformed into His likeness.

Scripture says in verse 30 of Galatians 4, *"Cast out the bondwoman and her son, for the son of the bondwoman shall not be an heir with the son of the free woman."* Cast out the bondwoman. That is why Judgment is coming. Judgment is already beginning. You are going to begin to see that mystery harlot -- that Mystery Babylon, the mother of harlots -- begin to fall, because God has raised up men and women now who understand His heart and can bring righteous judgment to His people.

Remember what I shared with you before: "Our God is a consuming fire." There is a verse that says, "Who can abide in the day of His appearing, for He is like a refiner's fire and fuller's soap" (Malachi 3:2). And when God begins to shine upon you, the fire of His Holy Spirit will begin to burn within your being.

(Prophecy) *And I say unto you that I will ignite within you the Spirit of the Living God, and everything that is in your natural character, everything that is antichrist, everything that would hinder you, when you by the Spirit of the Living God enter into My presence, will be consumed. I will release from the innermost being of My people the fire of the Living God. And I say unto you, that fire shall ascend, and shall burn every area, every avenue of your thought and brain, and that fire of my Spirit shall burn and burn and burn and burn. My Spirit shall burn out all of the dross. For you see, if you are cast into the fire of My presence, nothing will come out of that fire but the pure gold and silver and the transformation of the inner man. So I say to you My people, come unto Me. Come unto Me without any sense of fear or inferiority or condemnation. But I would say to you, come into Me, come into My presence. Realize that there is no condemnation, for on the cross of Calvary the debt for every sin and every disobedience was completely wiped out and annihilated, and today the God of the Universe would say unto you that you are not guilty, but you are set free. You are not set free to live according to the flesh; You are not set free to live according to the flesh; you are not set free to continue in your bondage; but you are set free to enter into My presence without any sense of fear, guilt or inferiority, because I have shed the blood. The blood of the Lamb that was slain from before the foundation of the world has paid the price for every disobedience.*

Coming Out of Darkness

Chapter 4

The Kingdom Within

"But in the last days it shall come to pass, that the mountain of the house of the LORD shall be established in the top of the mountains, and it shall be exalted above the hills; and people shall flow unto it. And many nations shall come, and say, Come, and let us go up to the mountain of the LORD, and to the house of the God of Jacob; and he will teach us of his ways, and we will walk in his paths: for the law shall go forth of Zion, and the word of the LORD from Jerusalem. And he shall judge among many people, and rebuke strong nations afar off; and they shall beat their swords into plowshares, and their spears into pruninghooks: nation shall not lift up a sword against nation, neither shall they learn war any more" (Micah 4:1-3).

"But the saints of the most High shall take the kingdom, and possess the kingdom for ever, even for ever and ever" (Daniel 7:18).

"And the kingdom and dominion, and the greatness of the kingdom under the whole heaven, shall be given to the people of the saints of the most High, whose kingdom is an everlasting kingdom, and all

85

dominions shall serve and obey him" (Daniel 7:27).

I believe that we are beginning to enter into the experience of becoming the city of God. "The mountain of the Lord" speaks of a high revelation, an unveiling of our mind, to enable us to walk in the high realms of the Spirit. However, to receive this truth we must be willing to change. I do not mean only a change in outward conduct. If you are not walking in the reality of Christ in you, if God Himself is not coming alive in you, if His nature and character are not being formed in you, then either you are not regenerated, or your concept of God is definitely wrong.

Whenever the Bible mentions the last days, we always think of some far off future event. This is one reason we need our concepts changed. We have been in the last days ever since the resurrection of Jesus from among the dead. God needs a people who will give themselves totally to Him, mixing faith with His Word, arising in His resurrection power, and becoming the saviors spoken of in Obadiah 21 -- a people who will deliver all of creation from the bondage of corruption. I believe that those days are now upon us. God is now ready and waiting for a people to take hold of His reality in their lives, and to begin to reconcile all creation back to Himself. God is wanting to bring full salvation to the Church in these days, and If we will be open to hear His voice. *not harden our hearts.* Salvation is deliverance from the fall of Adam. We have been redeemed and restored back to the Tree of Life. Salvation is deliverance from poverty, sickness and death. Paul told Timothy that Jesus *"has abolished death and brought life and immortality to light through the gospel"* (2 Tim. 1:10). It is very difficult to find even a few who believe these words. There are many who believe in a prosperity and health gospel, but where are the people who are overcoming death? Jesus said that He is the Bread of Life, and that a man may eat of Him and *never die* (John 6:35).

The time is now right for a people to begin to rise and take the kingdom and possess the kingdom. The Jews, many years ago, were waiting for the Messiah to come and destroy their enemies and set up His kingdom. Today it is not much different. The majority of Christians are waiting once again for Jesus to come back, destroy all their enemies, and set up His kingdom. This concept was wrong for the Jews and it is also wrong for the Christians. God is a reconciler, not a destroyer. The only destruction He will bring is to your carnal man. Your selfish, carnal desires are going to be burned away so that your spirit will rise up in you to take possession of you. As long as we are passively waiting, there will be no manifestation of the Son of God in us.

One of the wrong concepts that some Christians have is in thinking that they have to wait for a corporate experience. They think that the sons of God will all be changed and manifested at the same time. I, too, believe that there will be a corporate experience, but according to God's timetable for each person. Every experience of God that you read of in the Word can be obtained by you as an individual. In fact, until we as individuals realize we can obtain the fullness of God and begin to seek Him for it, the corporate body will not do so. It was proven a long time ago by Enoch and Elijah that it is possible to overcome death. We do not have to wait for everyone. We as individuals must seek God for His reality in us, and then our lives will be affected and we can affect those around us.

The concept of God that we have been taught in the system of Christianity is, for the most part, a wrong concept. We have been taught that God is "way out there" somewhere in another realm called heaven, and that if we accept Jesus and do the best we can, God will bless us and we will go to heaven when we die. We are not taught how to live by the Spirit of God that is within us.

The religious system has taught us always to seek God in an outward way for our needs. This has given us a false concept of God. This has caused us to seek everything of God as though it were outside of us. We think that by all kinds of religious activity, what we need will come into us and bless us, or heal us, or prosper us. In actuality, *everything that God is* is already within us, waiting for us to discover the truth that God in us is sufficient to meet every need.

We have a "Santa Claus God". God does not withhold His blessings from anyone at any time. He makes His rain to fall on the just and the unjust. Whenever we ask God to heal us or prosper us, we have a wrong concept. What we are saying is, "God, You have all these good things and are withholding them from me." If you do not think God has all these things that He is not giving you, why would you ask Him for them? If it *were true* that God was withholding something from you, you could not get Him to change His mind by begging, crying or pleading. We cannot bribe God by our Bible reading, praying, crying, fasting, our goodness -- or anything else that we might try. The only hope we have is in discovering the truth of what Jesus taught: ***"The Kingdom of God is within you"*** (Luke 17:21). Jesus said in John 7:38, ***"He that believes in me, out of his innermost being will flow rivers of living water."*** In John 4:14, He said, ***"He that drinks of the water that I give him, it shall be in him a well of water springing up into eternal life."***

To have a proper concept of these things, we must realize who and where Christ is. The word *Christ* means "God's anointed". Jesus was called the Christ. As the Christ, He was the fullness of God. Colossians 2:9 says, in the Amplified version, *"For in Him the whole fullness of Deity (the Godhead) continues to dwell in bodily form -- giving complete expression to the Divine nature."* I don't think any of us would have a problem believing that, but we have never been taught the next verse: *"And you are in Him, made full and have come to fullness of life -- in Christ you too are filled with the Godhead: Father, Son and Holy Spirit, and reach full spiritual stature."* Ephesians 1:23 (Amplified) speaks of the Church, *"Which is His body, the fullness of Him Who fills all in all -- for in that body lives the full measure of Him who makes everything complete, and Who fills everything everywhere [with Himself]."*

After meditating and praying over these verses for some time, we will begin to have some understanding of how to fellowship with God. We will have our concept changed about how we are to pray. When we go to God, we won't ask for so many things. We will begin to realize that Christ is the fullness of God, and Christ in all His fullness is now being poured out from within us. God is at all times pouring His Spirit out, filling everything everywhere with Himself. When we see someone in lack or in need, instead of asking and begging God to meet that need, we realize that in us dwells the fullness of God to meet that need. We turn to the Spirit of God within us and we realize that *"I and my Father are one"* (John 10:30), and *"He that is joined to the Lord is one Spirit with the Lord"* (1 Cor. 6:17). So from within me, from within my spirit, I release the ability of God to go forth and do His will. My prayer then becomes not an asking of God, but a realizing of His ability within me to meet the needs of others.

God's desire is not that we ask Him to heal the sick and bless with finances or supply whatever the need, but that we yield our bodies to Him. He desires to fill us and flow through us to meet the needs of humanity. God's desire is to flow through a many-membered body with all of His riches in glory. There is no greater joy in all the earth than being filled with God's presence and then sensing that presence flow out of you and into someone else, meeting their need. Paul told the Ephesians that *the Church is His body, of His flesh and of His bones* (Eph. 5:29-30). God fills us with Himself so that we become channels of blessing to the whole world. When you pray, seek after God and His wisdom. Seek Him for His light and glory to be revealed in you. Hunger and thirst after His presence, so that you may experience His resurrection power coming alive in you, enabling you to do the works of God.

What a joy it is when you begin to understand that

everything of God that you have been seeking is on the inside of you, just waiting to be revealed. Then is fulfilled those words of old, ***"Arise and shine; for your light is come, and the glory of the Lord has risen upon you"*** (Isaiah 60:1).

As I was sitting in the quiet one day, the Lord spoke this to me: *"I am not withholding anything from anyone at any time. I am always pouring forth My Life, love, healing and blessings. I am your life, your healing, blessing, or whatever you need. When you are set free from something or healed, it is not because I have suddenly changed toward you and decided to bless you. It is because you have changed toward Me, or opened to Me and come into My light. It is that which has allowed My Life to flow out from your innermost being to meet your need. Everything that you need is in My Spirit dwelling within you. You need not reach out to Me in an outward way, but turn within and contact My Spirit within you; then I will flow from your innermost being to meet your need. He that believes in Me, out of his innermost being will flow living water that will bring healing and deliverance wherever it flows. There is nothing in this universe that can hinder you except your belief in another power to do so. I am God, and besides Me there is no God who can hinder you, no other power able to op you. I am constantly filling everything everywhere with Myself. Open to the flowing of My Spirit within you, and I will flow into your mind and renew it into My mind. I will flow into your will and subdue it, and make it altogether pliable to do My will. I will flow into your emotion, so that My Love will flow out of you. Stop having faith in the power of evil to hinder you. I do not withhold from one and give to another. I am always so available, so rich, and so free -- just like the air that you breathe. Come to Me and I will rest you. I live and move and have My being within you."*

Many people are hungry today to see God. The Word teaches us that we are the visible expression of the invisible God. You or I may be the only expression of God that people see. We need to seek God until we can say with the Apostle Paul, ***"I live; yet not I, but Christ lives within me, and the life I now live in the flesh I live by the faith of the Son of God"*** (Gal. 2:20). God is a Spirit, and by consecrating our bodies to Him, He is localized within us and can flow to the world.

Many today seek to see Jesus in His physical form. However, if you were to see Jesus without coming to realize that you too are to be a son of God, then seeing Him might not help you all that much in a practical way. Romans 8:29 says that ***Jesus was the firstborn among many brethren.***

Knowledge vs. Experience

Let's look again at Ephesians 4:17-18. ***"This I say***

therefore, and testify in the Lord, that ye henceforth walk not as other Gentiles walk, in the vanity of their mind, having the understanding darkened, being alienated from the life of God through the ignorance that is in them, because of the blindness of their heart."

This is where most of the Church has been for two thousand years. A great mistake we have made is in being satisfied with good teaching alone. We think that because we know something of God intellectually, we have it. I *know* that God is in me; I *know* that Jesus lives in me; I *know* that I am the visible expression of the invisible God. Because we know these things, most of the time we settle for that knowledge without having the experience of it being made real in our lives. We *must* begin to enter into the experience of being the visible expression of the invisible God. We fail to seek for these things because of wrong concepts. I was taught as a young Christian that I should not seek for experience, that I should just accept everything without accompanying feeling. Now, I realize that natural feelings can get us into trouble, but to not feel and experience spiritual things means that you do not have real faith. Faith will produce feelings. If we know something only intellectually, without the experience, it does not do us much good. The Word of God tells us of many wonderful things that belong to the one who has received God. If we never experience them, then what good are they? Paul says that *we are seated with Christ in heavenly places* (Eph. 2:6). We should hunger after God until we walk in the reality of this, and not think that we have it just because we know it.

Our knowledge of the Word must become experiential. There is nothing wrong with knowledge. To know that Jesus lives in us is wonderful. To know that we are filled with His Spirit is also wonderful. The problem comes when we settle for only the knowledge, instead of seeking God for the reality. The Apostle Paul told the Corinthians, *"Knowledge puffs up, but Love builds up"* (1 Cor. 8:1). Knowledge in itself can be very satisfying. Many Christians today are very satisfied with their knowledge of God. Some have great knowledge of the Word, and have become teachers without the experience. William Law said many years ago, in his book "The Power of the Spirit", that we are foolish to think that we can go to Bible School and learn how to put off Adam and put on Christ. You cannot know in reality what you have not experienced. Many today have been raised in Church and know all about Jesus being the Saviour of the world, but they have never experienced His life-giving power to change their lives.

I said for years that "Jesus lives in me", yet I had very little experience of that knowledge. I was taught in

Pentecost that because I spoke in tongues, I was filled with the Holy Spirit. I used to ask God, "If I am filled with the Holy Spirit, why am I so ungodly and doing so many things that are contrary to a Holy Spirit?" The Christian religious system is so full of confusion. That is why Revelation calls her *"Mystery, Babylon the great, the mother of harlots"* (Rev. 17:5). Babylon means confusion. There is *no hope* for that religious system. The only thing we can do is scrap it. That is why Revelation says, *"Come out of her, my people"* (Revelation 18:4). It cannot be fixed.

Paul says we are *"alienated from the life of God through ignorance"* (Eph. 4:18). Ignorance does not mean stupidity. Ignorance simply means that you do not know. I was a Christian many years in ignorance. I did not know that I could experience the quickening, life-giving Spirit of God in me to bring me into the reality of what I knew. You can have a lot of Bible knowledge and still be ignorant. We have also been *taught* a great deal of ignorance in Christianity. We are taught defeat and failure. We are taught how powerful the devil is and how he can defeat us. We are not taught that it is possible *in this life* to walk as Jesus walked. The Word clearly reveals that not only is it possible, but God expects us to mix faith with His Word and make it real in our lives. The Word says, *"He that abides in Him ought to walk even as He walked"* (1 John 2:6). If we are not walking as Jesus walked, then we need to seek Him until His Spirit arises in us. ***"Being alienated from the life of God through the ignorance that is in them, because of the blindness of their heart"*** (Eph. 4:18). These verses are talking to *us*, the present day people of God! We have had our understanding darkened to the abundant life that God has made available to us through Jesus. Jesus did not go to the cross only so you could die and go to heaven. He died that you ***"might have life and that more abundantly"*** (John 10:10). The Life of God lies dormant within us. When that Life begins to function, we begin to change. We don't *try* to change; it is a natural process of His Life coming alive within us. The Apostle Paul said that we should be ***constantly transformed from one degree of glory to another*** (2 Cor. 3:18).

The Transforming River

The book of Genesis, chapter two, talks about a river flowing in three directions and becoming four heads. The name of the first is *Pison,* which means "freely flowing". The second is *Gihon,* which means "bursting forth". The third is *Hiddekel,* which means "rapid". The fourth is *Euphrates,* which means "that which makes fruitful". In that land of flowing rivers there are also precious stones. Precious stones are transformed stones. In the book of Revelation, we again see a flowing river and precious stones. Stones are made precious by the flowing of the river. This picture shows us that God's will in Genesis is to produce precious stones for His building, which is seen complete in Revelation. Between Genesis and Revelation there is a long process to produce the City of God.

The key to spiritual understanding of the Bible is to discover that it is a Book describing and unfolding to you your own inner being. When you first receive God, you begin to experience from the depths of your being something that is moving and flowing. This moving and flowing is the Spirit of God, represented by the flowing river in the Word. Deep within your being there is something "freely flowing", something "bursting forth", something that is "rapid", and something that will "make you fruitful". Jesus said it this way: *"He that believes in Me, out of his innermost being shall flow rivers of living water!"* (John 7:38).

We need to be challenged in our walk with God -- not for condemnation, but to gain proper light and understanding. We need to experience what we say we believe. *Where is the flowing of the living water that we say is within us?* I used to go to God and ask Him, "Where is the abundant life and the living water that You said we were to have?" I knew it was there, because I did experience it from time to time. I knew the problem had to be with me, not with God. There were times when I would be greatly filled with the Spirit of God, but it would not last. God does this so that we will continue to seek Him for His fullness. I wanted to stay in that river, but I didn't know how. The more time we give to God to seek Him, the more we come into His flowing. Whenever you begin to sense even a little of His flowing within you, there is a transforming that takes place. The more the river flows over the stone of the natural man, the more you are transformed into a precious stone. A great many Christians have tried to die to the flesh and to be obedient to the Spirit, but it is impossible for the natural, carnal self-life to be like God. If you will learn instead to turn to the Spirit of God within, and begin to experience the presence of God within you, the river of His Spirit will begin to flow, and the river will transform you. It is impossible to enter into the presence of God and not have something of His essence flow into your soul.

The book of Revelation reveals to us that the New Jerusalem, the City of God, is made of gold, silver and precious stones. Gold represents God's divine nature, silver represents redemption. Precious stones are made precious only by transformation.

Religion has taught us that the New Jerusalem is a golden city, and that it is up in a place called heaven. It has golden streets, gates of pearl, and a river flowing out of the throne with a Tree of Life on both sides and in the middle. Someday this city is supposed to fall out of the sky, and we will all go into it and live happily ever after. I wish it were that simple.

We must begin to pray for God's people to have a spiritual understanding of His word. The entire book of Revelation is revealing to us our own inner life. You must realize that *you can begin to experience this City of God now.* You do not have to wait until you die to enter the New Jerusalem. Today! -- right now -- you can experience the flowing of the Spirit of God within you. This flowing will transform you into a precious stone, to be built up with the saints in your locality, until together you become a local expression of the City of God. This is God's plan for His Church. We are to be *a visible expression of the invisible God*

Ye also, as lively stones, are built up a spiritual house, an holy priesthood, to offer up spiritual sacrifices, acceptable to God by Jesus Christ" (1 Peter 2:5).

"But we all, with open face beholding as in a glass the glory of the Lord, are changed into the same image from glory to glory, even as by the Spirit of the Lord" (2 Cor. 3:18).

"But if the Spirit of him that raised up Jesus from

the dead dwell in you, he that raised up Christ from the dead shall also quicken your mortal bodies by his Spirit that dwelleth in you. Therefore, brethren, we are debtors, not to the flesh, to live after the flesh. For if ye live after the flesh, ye shall die: but if ye through the Spirit do mortify the deeds of the body, ye shall live" (Rom. 8:11-13).

I will never forget the time when the Spirit of God began to speak the above verses to me. That is when I began to change. I knew them and believed them and hoped for them. When the Spirit began to speak them to me, I began to seek God for the flowing of the river to transform me. The entrance of the Word brings light. In our natural state we are in darkness, in fact we *are* the darkness. God says, *"I form light, and create darkness"* (Isaiah 45:7) and *"the people that sat in darkness saw great light"* (Mat. 4:16). If you are in darkness, how can you see? You don't bind the darkness, you just turn on the light.

The book of Revelation says that the New Jerusalem has streets of gold. Gold typifies divinity, streets represent the walk. Those who are experiencing the New Jerusalem are walking in the divine nature and character of God. In the New Jerusalem there is a river flowing from the throne. Where is the throne of God today? It is within you. Paul told the Ephesians that *"He hath raised us up together, and made us sit together in heavenly places in Christ Jesus."* (Eph. 2:6). There is a realm, a consciousness in God, where we can experience these things. Many talk today about the believer's authority, but that authority comes only from the throne. If the Spirit of God does not have authority in your life, then you cannot exercise God's authority. If you are under the Spirit's authority, then you will have authority.

The Crossing of the Jordan

In the Old Testament, when Israel was about to cross the Jordan, it was told them in Joshua 3:3, *"And they commanded the people, saying, When ye see the ark of the covenant of the LORD your God, and the priests the Levites bearing it, then ye shall remove from your place, and go after it."*

When you see the ark begin to move, that's when you cross the Jordan. When you experience within your consciousness the Spirit of God beginning to rise, and when you begin to experience the tables of stone (the ten commandments) to be the regulating life-law within you, then you begin to cross the Jordan. The Ten Commandments were never meant to be a set of rules and regulations that you try to keep in an outward way with your fallen humanity. When you experience the resurrection power and Spirit of God coming alive within you, you will naturally express what was written on those tables of stone. It is effortless. No more trying to be that good Christian, but from your innermost being flows the Spirit of God to fulfill all the righteous requirements of the Law. Don't try so hard to be holy. All you need is one glimpse of the Ark, just a little taste of Jesus Christ in you, and all of a sudden you begin to live the life that you thought you had to die to receive. We used to think that death solved our problems, but not so. The hope of the Gospel is not merely to get saved and then someday to die and go to heaven. The hope of the gospel is *"Jesus Christ in you, the hope of glory"* (Col. 1:27).

Don't Be Devil Conscious

Another part of the darkness in these days is to be devil-conscious. One of the biggest-selling categories in Christian books today is writings on the Cults. Christians today are reading hundreds of books on Satanism and witchcraft. They read biographies of the experiences of people who have been in Satanism, with all the gory details about what Satan can do to you. The reading of all these books is causing such a consciousness of Satan and demonic activity that it is actually helping that activity. (Incidentally, one of the lowest-selling categories in Christian books is prayer.) Christians are spending millions of dollars to learn about witchcraft and demons, and how to deal with them. They think they need to learn about these things so they won't be trapped by Satan, but that in itself can be an entrapment. When Christians are so consumed with learning about demons and Satanic activity, it makes a statement that Christians are living in fear. They think they have to learn about Satan to fight him. Do you really think that learning about all the details of what Satan can do to you will help empower you to fight the hosts of darkness? *It will not!* However, if you learn to live in the presence of God, where you can say, ***"It is no longer I that live but Christ that lives within me"*** (Gal. 2:20), Satan has no power over you. If Satan comes to me and the Spirit of God rises up within me, what can he do to me? I can study all about demons and how to deal with them. I can study deliverance, but is it really going to help me fight the darkness? There is only one area of true deliverance that will have lasting effect. It is this: ***"Let God arise and His enemies be scattered!"*** (Psalm 68:1). If the Life of God never arises within your being, your enemies will never be scattered, no matter how much you study and learn.

The Word says that we have been delivered from the power of darkness and transferred into the Kingdom of God. Listen. If we have truly been taken out of the power of darkness and placed into the Kingdom of God as the Word says, then we need to experience it. The Word of God is not a theory, but a fact. If you have been taken out of the power of darkness and transferred into the Kingdom of God, then Satan has no power over you. You may say, "But look at the multitude of Christians who pray every day, yet the enemy is destroying their finances, and they are eaten up with sickness and disease. How can you say the devil has no power over them?" It is because of the darkness. Again I must repeat: ***"This I say therefore, and testify in the Lord, that ye henceforth walk not as other Gentiles walk, in the vanity of their mind, having the understanding darkened, being alienated from the life of God through the ignorance that is in them, because of the blindness of their heart"*** (Eph. 4:17-18).

Most Christians believe more in the power of the devil than in the power of God. By confessing and believing in the power of evil to prevail over you, you give it the power to do so. Whatever you believe in will work for you. You believe in your heart that the devil has power over you, you then confess it with your mouth, and it becomes yours by experience. It can be very difficult to believe God when your experience is totally different. However, if you will look away from your wrong experiences and begin to believe God, your experience will then line up with the Word. You can spend your whole life fighting the devil (as I did for many years), sometimes winning and sometimes losing, but never realizing that in actuality he has no power over you.

Not I, but Christ In Me

The Apostle Paul knew the power of the human mind, and the power of human beliefs and suggestions. That is why he said for us not to walk as the gentiles walk, in the vanity of their mind. The carnal mind is what keeps us in bondage to the flesh. We think, "How can I possibly walk free of Satan and in the power of God?" We know that the Word says we have been delivered from sin, sickness and death, but that is not our experience. I have sickness in my body and I know that for a fact. Some say that sin and sickness are not real, but that does not make them go away. Our problem is the darkness, the blindness, and the ignorance. The problem is in not knowing what we have inherited in Christ. It is the blindness of not seeing who He is in me. It is no longer I: *"I have been crucified with Christ, nevertheless I live, yet not I, but Christ lives in me"* (Gal. 2:20). If I, through the Spirit, put to death the carnal self-life, and I am no longer living, and the Life of Christ is coming forth in my body, I will begin to realize the resurrection power of Jesus giving Life to my mortal body.

We do have the Life of God in us. If you have experienced that Life, no one can take it away from you. Just as you have experienced His Life in you, you can experience everything that He is by that Life growing in you. We are alienated from that Life due to the darkened understanding and the ignorance. Paul told the Corinthians, *"In whom the god of this world hath blinded the minds of them which believe not, lest the light of the glorious gospel of Christ, who is the image of God, should shine unto them"* (2 Cor. 4:4). We must realize that this also applies to Christians. The god of this world is the spirit of the age that we live in. It is all the human beliefs that are contrary to the Word of God. Paul said in 2 Corinthians 10:4-5, *"For the weapons of our warfare are not carnal, but mighty through God to the pulling down of strongholds; casting down imaginations, and every high thing that exalteth itself against the knowledge of God, and bringing into captivity every thought to the obedience of Christ."* We must renew our minds to conform to the Word of God. If our experience does not line up with the Word, then our experience is wrong, not the Word. We must spend time seeking God so that His light may enlighten our darkness.

Coming out of darkness is a gradual experience. After the night has ended, the day gradually dawns. The Church has been in darkness for 2,000 years, but the day is beginning to dawn. You will soon see a people on the earth who walk in the reality of Christ in themselves. If you open to the truth of these words of

His indwelling presence, you will begin to come out of the darkness. If you are not consciously aware of God living His Life in you, then for you He is not real. You have only a story-book God. You cannot walk in the Spirit as a theory, or only as a good teaching. If you begin to walk in the Spirit, you will begin to see your enemies fall at your feet.

Paul also said that you need to be renewed in the spirit of your mind. The spirit of your mind is a renewed consciousness. Human intellect alone will never know the power of God. He must come alive in your consciousness.

The Glorious Church

"He has put all things under His feet and has appointed Him the universal and supreme head of the church which is His body, the fullness of Him Who fills all in all -- for in that body lives the full measure of Him Who makes everything complete, and Who fills everything everywhere [with Himself]" (Eph. 1:22-23, Amplified). There is enough revelation and power in these words alone that, if you believe them, they will bring you out of the darkness. I began a few years ago to learn the power in the spoken word. I learned that what I believed in the new heart God had given me was far past the reasoning capabilities of my natural mind. I had to learn to follow and listen to the

Spirit of God within me, instead of listening to my natural mind. I began to have an experiential encounter with God in my being. This is still a limited experience, but it is growing. There is a realm in God where there is no sin, no disease, no sickness and no death. The Church is not yet fully there, but we are beginning to enter into it.

The Apostle Paul said, ***"Put on the new man"*** (Eph. 4:24). *What does that mean?* ***We are seated with Christ in heavenly places*** (Eph. 2:6). *What does that mean?* ***We have been blessed with all spiritual blessings in heavenly places*** (Eph. 1:3). *What does that mean?* These statements are given to us as facts, as present realities, not as something to hope for someday. There is a realm in God where we can experience these things. It is a conscious awareness of being that which the Word declares. We begin to experience these things when we have a spiritual birth and begin to grow in the Spirit. The Word says, ***"Howbeit that was not first which is spiritual, but that which is natural; and afterward that which is spiritual. The first man is of the earth, earthy: the second man is the Lord from heaven. As is the earthy, such are they also that are earthy: and as is the heavenly, such are they also that are heavenly. And as we have borne the image of the earthy, we shall also bear the image of the heavenly"*** (1 Cor. 15:46-49). This is what the Church is coming into. We are to bear the image of the heavenly. *Just think of it!* A group of people on the earth who are manifesting the heavenly character of Jesus. Paul told the Corinthians, ***"He that is joined unto the Lord is one spirit"*** (1 Corinthians 6:17). In your spirit is the Holy Spirit. These spirits are not two spirits, but **ONE SPIRIT.** Paul told the Ephesians, ***"The two shall become one, and I speak a great mystery of Christ and the Church"*** (Eph. 5:31-32). *You are bone of His bone and flesh of His flesh.* As we are transformed and begin to live in our spirit, where the Spirit of God dwells, we become the visible expression of the invisible God. *What a divine mystery!*

Coming Out of Darkness

Chapter 5

Coming Out of the Wilderness

We have all been in the wilderness, and there is an awareness today that something is about to break upon the scene, that the Church truly is going to come out of the wilderness. What I carry within my heart more than anything else in these days is the desire that God's people would have the love of the Father revealed to them.

The Unveiling of the Father's Heart

We have all experienced the Father's love to a degree. But *for the Church to come out of the wilderness, we must have an unveiling of the Father's **heart**.* Though I experienced a revelation of the love of God when I was first saved, at times this takes place in a more special way. There have been times in my life over the last 40 years, and there are still times even now, when the presence and the essence of God is so lovely and so wonderful that I sit and weep and weep in the love of God. Even though you have experienced the love of God, there continues to be an unveiling of how great that love is.

Jesus said to His disciples in Matthew 13:11, ***"Because it is given unto you to know the mysteries of*** *the kingdom of heaven, but to them* [the multitudes] *it is not given."* To *you* it has been given. How can we understand that? Many times I have asked God, "Why is it that I have this burning desire, and this love in my heart—why is it that everything within my being cries to be conformed to the image of God?" And the only answer I have ever been given is, "Because to you it has been given. You haven't worked for it. You haven't been good. In fact you *can't* be good enough for it, but *to you it has been given to know the mysteries of the Kingdom of God."*

The Mystery of the Gospel

When you read Paul's writings, he speaks a lot about the mystery of the Gospel.

"Now to him that is of power to stablish you according to my gospel, and the preaching of Jesus Christ, according to the revelation of the mystery, which was kept secret since the world began" (Rom. 16:25).

"But we speak the wisdom of God in a mystery, even the hidden wisdom, which God ordained before the world unto our glory" (1 Cor. 2:7).

"Having made known unto us the mystery of his will, according to his good pleasure which he hath purposed in himself: That in the dispensation of the fullness of times he might gather together in one all things in Christ" (Eph. 1:9-10).

Can you be a part of this? If we take these verses

literally, then *there is hope for every one of us.* In the fullness of times, God will do this, because He is sovereign, because He is El Elyon, the Most High God, the supreme Ruler of the universe, and He has purposed in himself to bring all things into one in Christ. If you can receive this you have great hope, because there will come a day in your experience when *you will fully reveal and manifest to the world the glory of your Father God.*

When is this going to happen? Well, in one sense of the word, we could say that it has already happened. When were you put into Christ? I might say that it happened for me in 1969, when I heard the Gospel for the first time. I was raised in a church, one of our mainline denominations, but when I was 29 years old I was still going to church seeking for God, when someone told me the simple Gospel—that this God who I thought I served, the God I had been searching for all my life, all He wanted was for me to simply open my being to Him and receive Him as Lord, and then I could experience Him. And when I did that, I experienced being in Christ.

I could spend hours telling you of my experiences during the first few days. I knew that I had been placed into Christ, and everyone around me also knew it, not because I immediately went out and preached the Gospel, but because my life changed. Without my saying a word, the people I worked with began to say to me, "Gary, what's wrong with you?" I was not the same. To them, it seemed like there was something wrong with me!

In 1969, I entered into the awareness of being in Christ, but you know what? That's not when it happened! The Gospel plainly declares to us that *we were placed in Christ at the cross of Calvary*. Can you believe that? First of all, can you believe it for yourself? And then, can you believe it for those around you?

"How that by revelation he made known unto me the mystery; (as I wrote afore in few words, whereby, when ye read, ye may understand my knowledge in the mystery of Christ)" (Eph. 3:3-4).

"And to make all men see what is the fellowship of the mystery, which from the beginning of the world hath been hid in God, who created all things by Jesus Christ: To the intent that now unto the principalities and powers in heavenly places might be known by the church the manifold wisdom of God, according to the eternal purpose which he purposed in Christ Jesus our Lord" (Eph. 3:9-11).

"This is a great mystery: but I speak concerning Christ and the church" (Eph. 5:32).

"Pray for me, that utterance may be given unto me, that I may open my mouth boldly, to make known the mystery of the gospel" (Eph. 6:19).

"Even the mystery which hath been hid from ages and from generations, but now is made manifest to his saints" (Col. 1:26).

The mystery of the Gospel was made known and

revealed unto the early Church, especially by the Apostle Paul. After His resurrection, Jesus spent 40 days with His disciples, teaching them things pertaining to the Kingdom of God. That's why, on the day of Pentecost, a mere handful of people could turn the world upside-down. Some of them had spent 3½ years with Jesus Himself, and by the words that He spoke, He had put into them the revelation of the Kingdom of God.

The Essence of the Gospel

And you know, we as the Church are still waiting for the Kingdom of God, aren't we? Not realizing that the Kingdom of God is here! Although you might say it this way: "The Kingdom is here, but not yet." The Kingdom of God is here in the sense that God will, by the power of His Spirit, enable you to bring your whole being into subjection unto Him. That's the Kingdom. *The Kingdom of God is simply the rule and the reign of His Spirit.* But since that first period of revelation, first by Jesus and then by the disciples, so many things have come into the Church.

The Apostle Paul taught this revelation of the Kingdom, and he had not been with Jesus physically before His death and resurrection. Yet Paul had the most marvelous revelation I believe, of any man in the New Testament. However, *the Church at large has lost almost the entire essence of the Gospel that Paul preached.* If it had not been lost, you would not see the conditions that we have on the earth today.

In this country especially, *we have made the Gospel an intellectual Gospel.* "If you believe it, you can be a Christian. If you don't believe it, you can't be a Christian." Is it simply a matter of intellectually knowing all the right things? Jesus' substitutionary death on the cross accomplished my salvation, but do I have to intellectually know it to receive it? Or can I be in a foreign land somewhere, never having the heard the name of Jesus, and could there not be something that stirs within my being? Could I not look up at the stars and realize that through the creation of God there is a revelation of God? And even though I do not know His name, something within the very essence of my being cries out for more of life. Could it not be that even though I do not have an understanding of the Gospel, I might cry, "There must be someone out there greater than I am, and I want to know You!" *"For whosoever shall call upon the name of the Lord shall be saved!"* (Rom 10:13). Could that not happen? Could you not be in a foreign land, having never heard the name of Jesus, and be saved? Well, if you say no, you don't know the heart of God. If a man in a foreign land cries out to God, the same thing happens to him that happened to you when you received Jesus!

It is by the Spirit of the Lord, not by intellectual knowledge, that you are saved. You can know everything there is to know about the Gospel, you can quote chapters and verses out of the Bible, and still not know God. You know that is true. And here is this poor, humble man who has said, "There must be someone out there greater than I am, and I want to know You." There is something in us. We just know. That man is regenerated just like you and me. He may never hear the name of Jesus in his lifetime, and he may meet a Buddhist monk, who will instruct him in the Buddhist religion, and he will be a very, very confused man. Because in his heart he has met, and been regenerated by, and has within him the essence of, the Spirit of God—but in his mind, he has the Buddhist religion. And there are men and women all across America today who would say that because that man is a Buddhist, serving a false god, he cannot possibly be saved.

Please hear and understand! *It's not what you believe intellectually that counts with God.* When you go before God, your excuse will be no good if you say, "I received you intellectually. I cast out devils in Your name. I healed the sick, and I raised the dead!" What will Jesus say? ***"I never knew you"*** (Mt. 7:23). And that poor little, humble man, all he wanted was God, and he got screwed up in his head with Buddhist religion, but in his heart he had the God of the universe—you may see *him* ushered in to the presence of Abraham, Isaac and Jacob, and *you* will be on the outside. And you had it all intellectually right!

Don't ever judge a man by what he believes in his head. Get to know his heart. No, I wouldn't go worship in a Buddhist temple, but I would never condemn someone who has the genuine love of God in him—and you can tell the difference between religion and love. And you know what? That Buddhist is no different than a Christian. *Whether you are in church or out of it, you have been influenced by 2,000 years of religious tradition, and you can be just as screwed up in your head, intellectually, as a Buddhist is.* But if you have God, that is what matters. You might be a Lutheran. You might be a Catholic. You might be a Pentecostal, you might be anything. But if you have met the God of Abraham, Isaac and Jacob, you'll know it. And would I look at you, because you go to a Lutheran church, and say, "You don't know God"? I wouldn't dare! Yet that happens all the time. Let's get to know one another by the spirit. Spend some time in my presence, and get to know my heart. You'll hear me say things that you can't agree with, and that's okay, but if you get to know me, and you get to know my heart, you will love me and I will love you. The differences in our intellectual beliefs don't matter.

Oh, I want so badly for the Church to hear this! *On the day of judgment, what is going to matter—whether you had all the right doctrine, or whether you had a heart hungry for God?* If you sought after God, if you relieved the suffering of your neighbor, if you opened your home to the needy—what is going to really count? "Oh God, I believed everything just right." "Sorry about that. I didn't know you. I was in prison, and you didn't come to Me. I was thirsty, and you didn't give Me to drink. You had a church of 10,000 people, and you didn't give them to drink. You gave them all of your knowledge. You taught them the seven steps to this and the eleven steps to that, but you didn't give them anything to drink. You didn't really feed My sheep. I don't know you." It's going to happen. It's going to happen if we don't understand, and have revealed to us, the heart of the Father.

How Will Oneness Happen?

God's plan, His eternal purpose, is that He would gather all things in Christ, so that, as it says in Ephesians 5, He may present to Himself a glorious Church without spot or wrinkle. How is that ever going to happen? We must have a revelation of the Father's heart.

There was a time when, if you asked me what I thought it would take to bring everyone into oneness, I would have said to you that for that to happen, everyone would have to be Lutheran. Really! That is what I would have said. Everyone must know that they are not justified by what they do, but as Martin Luther taught, they must be justified by faith. So I would have told you that for everyone to be in oneness, we would all be Lutheran, we would all be justified by faith.

If you would have asked me a few years later what I thought the Church needed to understand in order to come into oneness, I would have told you right away that everyone would have to get filled with the Holy Ghost and speak in tongues. That would bring in the oneness. But I think now that we've had a few years' experience in that, we can look back and see *there was no oneness brought in by people being filled with the Spirit and speaking in tongues.* (I shouldn't say "no oneness," of course; there was some oneness, but not generally.)

The only thing that will truly bring us into oneness is the revelation of the heart of Father God, realizing that He's not just the God of the Jews, He's not just the God of the Lutherans, or of the Pentecostals, but He is the God and Father of all humanity! The Church has to have a revelation of the Father-heart of God! We must have revealed to us that God had a perfect plan, as Ephesians says, and that His eternal purpose, all of this, was already worked out by God. Jesus was the Lamb of God even before the foundation of the world (John 17:24, Rev. 13:8).

What It Means To Be Holy

Now I'm going to touch on some things that may cause you some problems, but just bear with me. One of the biggest problems that we have in the Church is bigotry. The Church has come a long way in bigotry—or I should say, has come a long way *into* bigotry, and now it is coming *out* of bigotry somewhat. There was a time when, if you were within a certain denomination and you were black, you had to be segregated out and you could not be a part of that major denomination. Well, we've come a long way from that. Recently, that major denomination has repented for that concept.

We have so many concepts that we pick up which cause us to be, in our mind, separated, and maybe just a little bit better than the other guy. For instance, I mentioned a little earlier about being filled with the Holy Ghost and speaking in tongues. There was a time, and there still is among some Pentecostals, when you were told that if you do not speak in tongues you cannot possibly be filled with the Holy Ghost, because that is the evidence of being filled with the Spirit. And there has been so much division and so much strife brought in just from that one concept. *To tell someone that they are not filled with the Holy Ghost because they do not speak in tongues is almost the height of ignorance in the Church!*

Those of you that are familiar with me know the concept that I teach of being filled with the Holy Ghost. It's not that you may *not* speak in tongues, but if you are filled with the Holy Ghost, if you truly are one who has opened to God and have invited Him to take Lordship and dominion of your life, you will be a holy person. And you won't have to *try* to be holy; you won't have to get up every day and try to live according to a standard. You won't have to memorize ten chapters of Scripture a day. You won't have to try to pray for four hours a day.

The Lord sat me down for about four years and would not allow me to minister, because although, even as a young Christian, I had been given a revelation of some things that the Church is just about to come into, I wasn't able to share it because the time wasn't right. But God sat me down, to the point where I told my wife at one time, "You know what? I don't think that I even have it anymore. I can't teach." God totally stripped me of everything. There was a period in my life of 3½ years when I prayed and sought God for a minimum of eight hours every day. And my wife can tell you she was almost a widow, because of the times that I would go 12 or 13 or 14 hours. I was so desperate to know God! And out of those 3½ years, the Lord gave me much revelation and in-depth knowledge of His heart and how He feels toward all of humanity—not just toward the Church.

In the eternal past, God had a plan and a purpose. He is El Elyon, the Most High God, and He uses people, He reveals Himself to people, according to His plan and His purpose. It's not according to our plan and our purpose. God sat me down for four years and wouldn't allow me to minister, with the exception that I wrote a couple of books. And I really thought that I had lost my anointing. I told Carol, "I can't even stand up before people anymore. I don't know what I'm going to do!"

I went down to visit Love Link Ministries one day about a year and a half ago, and Pastor Ada said to me, "Do you have a message for us today?" and I said, "No. God hasn't released me yet to preach." And as far as I knew, He hadn't. The next day, we were in church, and she didn't ask me again, she just said, "Gary is going to minister today." That was one of the greatest moments in my life in recent years, because when she called I knew it was God, yet on the way up I felt so empty. For four years, I had been empty. But when I took the microphone, God filled me up! And everything came back.

The only reason I share that story with you is so that you might know me, and understand that what I teach I didn't read out of a book, and I didn't pull it out of a hat, and I'm not copying someone else's ministry. One of the things God revealed to me is that in these coming days, *there is a wonderful, glorious, magnificent revelation of the heart of God coming to the Church!* God truly does love humanity. But we take the things of God, and we create wedges. We become bigots. "If you don't speak in tongues, you're not filled with the Holy Ghost." Jesus told His disciples to tarry in Jerusalem until they were— not *filled* with the Holy Spirit, but *clothed* with the Spirit. In Luke 24:49, He said, ***"Tarry ye in the city of Jerusalem until you be endued,"*** which simply means to be clothed with the Spirit. And then we read in John 20:22 that on the very first day of the Resurrection of Jesus, He appeared among His disciples and He said to them, ***"Receive ye the Holy Spirit,"*** and it says He just breathed on them! What does that remind you of?

In the very beginning, God breathed upon a man of clay. And in the very breath of God is the very essence of

God. Everything that God is, is contained in His breath, His Spirit. And when Jesus breathed on those disciples and said, *"Receive ye the Holy Spirit,"* they were absolutely filled with the Spirit of God! That is the only way, my friend, that you will ever be filled with the Holy Spirit—by receiving the breath of God. You can't live physically without breath; neither can you live spiritually. That's why God told Ezekiel at the valley of dry bones to speak to the wind to breathe—breathe life, breathe the Spirit—into the dry bones (Ezek. 37:4-10). In the words are the very breath of God. Just speak to those bones and watch them stand up and live!

If you are filled with the Holy Ghost, you are just simply holy. Now what does that mean? We don't even really know what it means. We think that to be holy we would probably stop all secular activity and would pray a lot and read the Bible a lot. In other words, our concept of holiness is way out of whack. The simplest way to explain it is that *holiness is wherever God is.* The first time holiness was revealed in the Bible was at the burning bush, where Moses was told, *"Take off your shoes, for you are standing on holy ground"* (Ex. 3:5). That ground was only holy because the presence of God was there. I have heard holiness taught until it becomes a bondage. "You have to wear your hair long, your shorts long. You can't cut your hair this way or that way. You can't go to movies. You can't dance. You can't take a drink!" The way holiness has been taught has brought people into bondage, rather than liberty!

Transformation By the Presence of God

God loves for His people to be set free to live according to the awareness of His presence. Yet generally speaking, the people of God as a whole don't really carry the presence of God within them. We all know that He is there, but I am speaking from conscious experience, because a lot of times I have no awareness of the presence of God. Sometimes I'll begin to speak to someone on the street, and immediately I am just aware that God is on the scene. At that moment, I don't think about my condition, I don't think about where I have missed God for the last three or four days, I don't think about what I need to do, but when the essence of God appears, at that moment I become a holy person.

There is no way that you can learn to be godly, a better word for it is transformation. You cannot learn it with the natural mentality. I have often shared that I tried for 13½ years to be a good Christian, and I never made it. I couldn't even quit some of the simple habits that I had—either couldn't quit or didn't want to. But God is my Father, and one day He spoke to me, "Gary, I have a plan and I have a purpose for you. You can fight back. You can rebel, and it is going to cause you a lot of grief, a lot of heartache. You are going to go through a lot of trials, a lot of tribulation. But I am El Elyon, and I can guarantee that there will come a day when you will fully reveal and manifest My glory to My creation. Not because you are good enough. Not because you are always obedient when I speak. Not because of anything you have done, but because I have a design, an intent and a purpose for you. Because of that, you will be what I say you will be. Fight it if you want to."

The biggest obstacle I hit with this is, what about the human will? He is El Elyon. It is said in religious circles that God will not violate your will. Well, tell me about the story of Jonah. Didn't Jonah try to say no? And what did God do? Have you ever said no to God? And when you have said no to God, has He turned His back on you? Well you might have thought that He did, because you might lose the awareness and the sweetness of His presence, but He comes back, does He not? Oh, there is nothing in all the world that I desire more than to be a carrier of His presence on the earth! And my desires have become so strong in this area that the other things that kept me down for 13 years don't bother me anymore. But it's not the overcoming of those things that got me to a place in God where now I am worthy to receive His presence and carry it throughout the earth.

Any man who feels that he has *earned* a place in God where he is now acceptable by the Father to be a teacher, or a carrier, or anything that has to do with God, is a man most deceived. If you stand before people and you see that you are where you are today because you have been obedient, you do not understand the Father-heart of God. Now in a sense, you do learn obedience. But your obedience does not come out of anything that is in the natural, soulish makeup of man. There is nothing in that old creation that is willing and obedient—*nothing*! And if you think there is, you will find out otherwise.

There is only one hope that we have. Paul said it this way: *Christ in you is your hope* (Col. 1:27). There is absolutely nothing in your natural personality (the natural human makeup, the carnal mind) that God can use. Nothing. We haven't learned that yet, because as long as you look at another human being and say, "If they would only do certain things; if they would only stop this, and do that," you are a person who would bring other people into utter bondage.

There is nothing in Adam that will serve Christ, although he may want to. I teach a lot on the Tree of the Knowledge of Good and Evil, that there is a good desire in a lot of us. We do, some of us, want to become like God, but we can't. How could we? The desire is there, but even that desire can be a carnal desire of a good man who just wants God. That doesn't work either. The only hope is to have a revelation of the Father-heart of God. And when you do, you will realize that God truly is no respecter of persons. Sometimes that's hard for the Church to accept, because we want to feel like we're special. There is something about us that wants to feel like "I have a heart for God, and because I have a heart for God, He really blesses me. And if only you had a heart for God like I do, you would be blessed as I am."

Oh, that is so wrong. Where did I get that heart?

When I was 11 years old, I told my mom, "Please buy me a Bible that I can read and understand, if there is such a thing." All we had at that time was a King James Bible. I asked my mom to buy me a Bible because I said, "When I grow up I want to be a preacher." Why? I hated church! I told my mom that when I grew up, I would never go to church again. It wasn't Church. I was born with a desire, a hunger, for God. I used to think it was just for me, that it was kind of exclusive. None of the other friends I had seemed to have a strong desire for God as I did. Now, I realize it was grace.

God's Plan

God is El Elyon, and He has a plan and a purpose. He placed His Seed not just in you and me. God has placed His Seed in all of humanity. The Gospel of John says that Jesus was the true light that lights every man that comes into the world (John 1:9). Is this true or false? Proverbs tells us that the spirit of man is the candle, or lamp, of the Lord (Prov. 20:27). *Every person has within their being the Seed of God,* and that Seed needs the Divine Sperm to quicken it and regenerate it. God calls out the Church, reveals Himself to the Church, and then begins to impart unto the Church His essence, His nature and His character, so that they in turn can go to the world and bring reconciliation to the creation that fell.

God has been with us in the wilderness. When we

suffer, God suffers. Why? Because, more than you ever realize, God and man truly are one. In the very core, in the very center of your being, lies the Seed of God. And when you are regenerated, that Seed of God is what brings to you the feeling, the emotion, the regeneration of God. Every person that was ever born is special, but you are not any more special because you know God than the man who doesn't. Didn't Jesus say, *"No man can come unto Me except the Father draw him"* (John 6:44)? Then how can you take credit? How can you say that the reason you know God is that you have done certain things, or you haven't done certain things? *When God chooses you for His own plan and purpose and generates His Divine Seed within you, all of a sudden you become aware, you become conscious of God.* Why? It is His plan and His purpose to restore the creation back to Himself.

Romans 8:21 says that there will come a day when all of creation shall be loosed from the bondage of corruption into the glorious liberty of the children of God. Is that true or not? If you are typical in your Christian thinking, it is not yet true for you. But who does "all of creation" include? Those who have run to an altar? Those who have said some words? Sometimes we think it's a magical phrase: "Jesus, I receive You." Will there really come a day in the history of the world when all of creation shall be loosed from the bondage of corruption into the glorious liberty of the children of

God? Oh, I can't wait for the revelation to come to the Church! Oh, we have such a message! We have the hidden mysteries of the Gospel yet to be revealed.

Our country is in such a mess, yet even as Christians, we say, "Well, if we could just get rid of the whole political system and start over." But let me tell you that we, you and I, are responsible for what is happening in Washington today It's not the Democratic Party's fault. It's not the Republicans' fault. The people of God have lost the reality of the Father-heart of God, and *we have not become the salt of the earth.* What is the salt of the earth? If I am the salt of the earth, I am the flavor, and if I am truly salted with His essence, I am absolutely free to do *anything!* But in the doing of whatever I do, I am salt, and from the very essence of my being, something will permeate, and people will be affected. If you have the essence of God, you don't have to preach the Gospel, in the sense of the "religious" Gospel.

I worked at NASA for six years, and for at least half of that time, I didn't try to preach the Gospel at all. But I tried to be the best worker, the best friend. That is a gift that God has given me, I just love people. But after three years, I mentioned to a man who worked with me, "John, have you ever been aware of God in your life?" and this big bruiser of a guy almost hit me. He said, "Don't you ever mention that name in my presence again." Because, he said, "I'll tell you one thing, Gary. If there is such a thing as a God, I can't wait to see Him, and I'll tell Him,

'You SOB,' for the mess that He made this creation to be." But I want you to know that when I left NASA, this man had tears in his eyes, and he said, "Gary, all of my life I've heard about the love of God, about, you know, preaching and this and that," and he said, "You're the first person I've ever met whom I could say actually *has* the love of God and walks in what they say they believe."

You don't have to preach the Gospel. And if you are around me, you find out that I'm just a joker. I have a lot of fun. Yet I know that deposited within my being, there is such a precious, precious anointing of His love for humanity. Again, does that make me special? Please! NO! No, it doesn't. As I said, for 13½ years I did everything; I never prayed less than an hour a day. I never read less than ten or twenty chapters of Scripture a day. Yet for 13½ years I was a failure. Not totally, for I did make some progression, but I wasn't free. But when I realized that holiness is wherever God is, then God began to speak in small ways and reveal to me, "You've been *saying* for years that Jesus lives in you—don't you think it's about time that you became *aware* of it?" And today, I'm still not. I'm aware of it, but not nearly enough, because *when we have the heart of the Father unveiled to us, we will be world-changers.*

God is not a bigot. I was taught as a young Christian, "If a Jehovah's Witness comes to your door, slam it in his face, because those people really believe what they say, and you will become so deceived." That's the kind of love that I was taught. And the Mormons? "Oh my God, don't even get close to those guys! Some of the things they teach are demonic!" We have no concept of the Father-heart of God. We don't really have an experience of what we say we believe, or we would not be in fear of a Jehovah's Witness, we would not be in fear of a Mormon, we wouldn't teach our kids not to play with the "JW's".

If we had the essence of God and we were the salt of the earth, what would we fear? Because we would salt the earth. You really are the salt of the earth. But the Lord said, *"If the salt has lost its flavor . . ."* (Mt. 5:13), and for the most part that is what happened. In 2,000 years, we lost the flavor. The Church isn't really able to salt that much anymore. What did the Lord say? ***"It's good for nothing. It needs to be cast out."*** Some people will tell you that means that if you lose your salt, you lose your flavor; you've lost your salvation and you will go to hell and burn forever. Let me tell you what it really means. *When you lose your saltiness, the fire of God begins to bring purification.* It's not a negative experience! El Elyon knows just exactly what you need to cause you to bow the knee, just as He knew what it would take to turn Jonah, who was running away from Him.

You are free to do anything you want to do, you are free to turn your back on God. But I have news for you. Try it! Sure, you can make the choice. You are free. But *you really don't have a free will.* Your will is either captivated by the enemy through the fall, or you have given yourself to God. I used to drive out into the desert every morning in California, and I would say, "God, I give you permission to do whatever it takes. I say to the principalities and powers in heavenly places, I give God permission to do anything He wants to do in my life." I lost my free will. If I ever had it, I lost it then. God became El Elyon to me, whether I liked it, or whether I didn't. And there have been many times when I didn't like it. The fire gets hot.

But although we look at these experiences as negative, we have to understand the Father-heart of God. *He will burn you to a crisp.* You will be judged, but it won't be a religious judgment. God is not that big, ugly being up there full of vengeful wrath. I know that the Bible talks about the wrath of God, and I know that the day of His wrath is coming, but the concept of "sinners in the hands of an angry God" is really not the right concept of your Father God. God as your Father will put you through the fire. What happens to gold if you throw it in the fire? It is purified. Gold, silver and precious stones. What is in you? The gold. Do you have the Divine Life and Nature of God, or do you not? If we can say, as the Apostle Peter taught us, that we have the Divine Life of God in us, then we have the gold, but we will have to be purified by the fire.

I hope you can hear what I am saying and go a little

bit further with it. God has no pleasure in the death of the wicked (Ezek. 33:11). John said that Jesus would baptize with the Holy Ghost and with fire (Mt. 3:11). Well, we have taken the Holy Ghost and Pentecost, but we left off the fire, because the fire isn't the fun part. But we need the fire, because when we have the heart of the Father unveiled to us, we will be world-changers.

I was born with a nature that loved all of the wrong things. On the inside of me, I had a desire for God, but my natural character and makeup was much stronger than my desire for God. So, everywhere I went, ministers would say, "I can't help you. You have to make a choice. You have to decide, are you going to obey God or obey your flesh?" Well, what am I going to do if my flesh is stronger? I tried obeying God, but it didn't work. So God put me in the fire.

All of us will go through the fire. Your natural, human character and personality—all of those human traits that you have inherited from your father Adam, all of the disobedience, all of the erring of your ways, everything in your being that is antichrist (and the Church is full of antichrist today) must be burned. El Elyon will put you in the fire until you come up out of it a pillar of smoke, and this is not just for you alone. You are only fortunate in this sense of the word: that God is calling you now. *God has called us out now to begin to purify us so that we can take the message of reconciliation to the world.*

I had a prophecy given to me a few years ago, and

when this prophecy was given to me, God spoke right behind it and said, "This word was not for you, this word was for the Church." It *was* for me, but not *just* for me. You know what I mean. And the word was this: *"There is going to be a day when people will look into your eyes and immediately be ushered into the presence of God, be regenerated, and be filled with the Spirit of God."* When that happens, you'll know for a surety that we have come up out of the wilderness.

We need to be the offering that is consumed upon the altar by the fire of God, and it hurts. But you know what was said of Jesus (and you would have this same attitude if you understood the heart of God), it said that for the joy that was set before Him, He endured the cross. And *if you have the plan of God for your life revealed to you, then for the joy that is set before you, you also will endure the fire!* And you will endure the pain, you will endure the suffering.

There is not much talk in the Church today about suffering, but *if you will be godly, you will suffer!* And it won't be by people persecuting you (although that could be a part of it); you are going to suffer in the very essence of your being, because *everything in you that you thought was godly is going to be stripped away.* And if you haven't had this experience yet, there will come a day when God will rip that flesh away from you and let you look at it and see it as it is, and you will realize that, if not for the grace of God, you could be a murderer, you could be a rapist, you have all of the tendencies that any man ever has had embodied in your flesh and you are capable of the most vile acts, were it not for the grace of God. It's worth the suffering to be rid of the flesh. *"And He will baptize you with the Holy Ghost and with fire"* (Mt. 3:11).

Prayer: Burn Within Us

Father, by the power of Your Holy Spirit, by the very essence of your being, I ask You to burn upon the altars of our hearts. I ask you to send forth that holy fire that would consume every area, every avenue of my thought and my being. O God, I ask that you would burn, and burn, and burn within my being, and that You would cause the essence of Your being, the Seed of Your Life, that is within me to rise and to stand. O Father, may that Seed of Your Life come forth within Your people! Lord, we, as the collective Body of Christ, stand undivided. We say, "Come, O Holy One, come, fire of God, come and burn within our being." Father, only You can burn out the rebellion. Only You can burn out the disobedience. It is only by the purifying fire of Your Holy Ghost that we can live and not die. Oh God, bring the fire. El Elyon, reveal to us your Father-heart.

Coming Out of Darkness

Chapter 6

The Appearing of Christ

God still speaks to His people today through prophetic words. I love to hear the word of a true prophet, and I especially like to hear the word of a prophet without conditions. There are times when God will say to you, "If you do this, then I will do that—and if you don't do this, I'm not going to do that!" So I always listen for conditions when I hear a prophet prophesy. When there are no conditions, that means that God has given a promise which He alone will fulfill.

This reminds me of what He said to Abraham. When God called Abraham, He said, ***"I am going to make you a father of many nations"*** (Gen. 17:4), and God promised him a son (Gen. 17:19). Then we read the story of Abraham and see that Abraham failed miserably many times. He lied, and he did all kinds of things, but I want to tell you something. *When God makes you a promise, you can take it to the bank!* And, like Abraham, when God gives us a promise, we tend to do everything we can possibly do in the natural to make it happen, and all we produce are Ishmaels. That is all we can produce in the natural.

But God has a Son of promise. And God made His

covenant with the Seed of Abraham, which Paul tells us is Christ (Gal. 3:16). Therefore, that covenant between God and Abraham was really not with Abraham, although Abraham participated in it. The promise was to the Seed, which is Christ. I want you to get that! The promise that God gives to me is not a promise to Gary Sigler. He doesn't have anything for me. He says, "You know what, Gary? You're good for only one thing, and that is to give yourself up unto death. But I have a promise, and I have a covenant with the Seed, and I placed that Seed in you."

Has God made a covenant with you? No! He has made it with the Seed. Therefore, even though we talk a lot about obedience, we had better be careful what we are thinking. The reason we want to become an obedient people is so that the Seed of God can swallow us up. But the natural person is not to be the one obedient unto Christ. In other words, Gary Sigler has nothing in himself of obedience to offer unto God. I may want to try. I'll try with all my heart to fulfill what God has promised me, but I can't, and I need to find that out. That is the experience of Romans chapter 7. We all need to go through that experience. You need to find out that you can't maintain that perfect obedience which will cause the Seed of promise to come forth and appear in you. But because you can't, that doesn't mean that God throws you on an ash heap. All it means is that He will throw you into the fire of His presence, and you'll burn! *The promise is not to you, but to the Seed within you.*

The Appearing of Christ

I want to speak here about the appearing of Christ. What I say will probably be a little different from what it has been tied in with before, but nevertheless we all know the goal is the appearing of Christ. Paul said something very interesting. He said, ***"Henceforth know we no man after the flesh"*** (2 Cor. 5:16). He says that today we don't even *want* to know Jesus Christ after the flesh, but that we should learn to know every person by the spirit. So let me give you a few verses on the appearing of Christ.

2 Thessalonians 1:10 says, ***"He shall come to be glorified in His saints, and to be admired in all them that believe."*** Can you imagine that? The God of Heaven is to be admired in you! Can you look at your sisters and brothers, and see Christ? Well, it may be pretty easy in an environment where we all are in worship and fellowship together, but if you get around them on their job, or in their homes among their family, you have to be able to look beyond what you see in the natural. You have to look *into* them and see Jesus. You have to admire in them that which He is.

Psalm 102:16 declares, ***"When the Lord shall build up Zion, He shall appear in His glory."*** We know that Zion is the City of God, and is He not beginning to appear in Zion? *No one who has been in fellowship with*

His people for any period of time could deny that God is beginning to appear. I'm sure all of you are like me in this—we have desired for so long to see the beauty of Zion, the City of God.

Colossians 3:4 states, *"When Christ who is our life shall appear, then shall you also appear with Him in glory."* These are some verses that I have clung to, sometimes without any hope, sometimes in despair, sometimes in utter depression. I've held on, knowing that there will come a day when I shall appear with Him in glory—not because I've done anything in myself, but because God has covenanted with the Seed. I have within me, and you have within you, the most precious essence of His being. That is where that covenant stands.

1 John 3:2 reads, *"Beloved, now are we the sons of God, and it doth not yet appear what we shall be, but we know that when He shall appear, we shall be like Him, for we shall see Him as He is."* When you really see Him as He is, you will be like Him. Why? Because you will see Him in yourself and in others! And I want to take this one step further. You won't see Him only in Christians. You won't see Him only in the glorious Church which is going to be manifested. You won't see Him only in His special saints, but *you will see Him in all of humanity.*

Mother Theresa took a lot of flak from the Christian world, which is saying that she is tried to bring in a New Age Gospel. But I saw a video of her once, and it wrought some real change in my life. It showed how she would go into the hospitals. One scene I remember very plainly was when she walked into a certain hospital where there were the sick and the dying, and there was a man in bed. Those in attendance said they didn't know how long he could last. He just shook and shook, and you could tell he was in great agony. And this poor, tiny little lady walked over to him. She laid her hand on his head, and she just patted his head, and immediately the shaking stopped and the peace of God came to him.

Oh, people, don't talk to me about New Age! If that is New Age, then I will be a part of the New Age to bring God to people. Don't misunderstand me when I say that, but we just cannot ignore the principles of God. We cannot see someone who is so full of the love of God that they would go among lepers, they would go among the filth of the world and hug them and love them, and call that New Age. We have churches all across America today who are saying that is a New Age Gospel, and I feel sorry for them. She was asked, "Sister Theresa, how can you do this? How can you go to the scum of the earth? How can you reach down into the pits of India, and pick up the filth and hug them, and cry, and love them, and pray for them?" Her answer was this: "Because I see God in every person."

"We know that when He shall appear, we shall be like Him, for we shall see Him as He is." When you see Him as He is, you will be like Him! But I was taught,

when I first went into Pentecost many years ago, that there is going to be a day when we'll all be raptured into the heavens, and we'll look at Him, and when we look at Him, we'll be changed into His likeness. That is a fallacy! I wish it were true. But there are other verses we need to remember. As John said, *"Beloved, you had better abide in His anointing, so that when He does appear you won't fall on your face in shame before Him at His coming"* (1 John 2:28). The "fly-away" Christians better wake up!

The truth is seen in Zechariah 14:5, *"And ye shall flee to the valley of the mountains, for the valley of the mountains shall reach unto Azal: and ye shall flee like as ye fled from before the earthquake in the days of Uzziah the king of Judah: and the Lord my God shall come and all the saints with thee."* When Jesus comes in His physical form in the heavens, you will probably be right along by His side! 1 Thessalonians 3:13 says, *"To the end that He may establish your hearts unblameable in holiness before God, even our Father, at the coming of our Lord Jesus Christ with all His saints."* God's goal is to call out a people unto Himself, that He may, by the power of His Spirit, the drawing of His Spirit, the workings of His Spirit, work into that corporate group of people His Life, His nature, and His character—that they may stand upon the earth not as Baptists, Lutherans, Pentecostals, but that they may stand upon the earth as one new man, to bring forth judgment unto righteousness.

God's True Business

I literally weep in intercession when I see some of the things that are on so-called "Christian" television. For instance, not long ago there was an example of the concept that every believer will be suspended in the air for seven years, and then God will pour out great anger and wrath and horrible tortures and judgments upon humanity. Now I know that concept, but I just can't imagine it. I have experienced the depths of the love of God, and I have been into some of the heights of the love of God, but I cannot find a God who is so angry that He would want to pour out a vengeful wrath upon His people. Yes, the wrath of God is coming. Yes, judgment is being poured out. But you know, Jesus Himself tried to destroy that concept of an angry, vengeful God. He said, "It has been written in your very own law . . ." (He did not deny the law of the Old Testament). He said, "It has been written in your very own law, 'an eye for an eye and a tooth for a tooth.' I know what is there. But I say to you, love your enemies! Do good to those who despitefully use you! I know what is written in your law. You would like me to take this prostitute and stone her" (Mt. 5:38-44, John 8:3-11).

Christians all over the world today would like to stone prostitutes and homosexuals. We would like to get rid of sin in the manner of some of the other religions of the world. We'd like to see a cleansing take place. That's our concept of God, so that's easy for us to accept. But Jesus revealed a different concept to us! "It is written in your very own law—but you had better listen to Me. You know, you run to the Scriptures, because in them you think you have eternal life, but you won't come to Me, because when you do, I'm going to tell you some things, and I'm going to reveal to you an understanding of God and the Father-heart of God that you've never had. And because it doesn't fit with what you have been taught in the past, because it doesn't fit with the law that you have received, you will reject the love of God. That is why you cannot have the Logos in itself" (John 5:39-40).

You can take the scriptures and justify the most heinous, horrible crimes with it, and people have done so, thinking they have done God a service. But *God is in the business of restoring humanity back to Himself.* He has no thought of destroying, but of uplifting. Yes, there is judgment. Yes the fiery indignation and wrath of God is on the earth and is coming to the earth. But it is a righteous judgment! There is passage in the Old Testament where God says that when He brings judgment, He will take into account where a man was born (Ps. 87:4-6). What does that mean? It means He will take account of where you were born. Were you born in India where you had no knowledge of God? Or were you born in America where you've had nothing but religion, and you've rejected not God but that which religion has said He is? (I rejected Christianity years ago, but I didn't reject God, and I never would.)

Yes, there is judgment. And yes, you need to fear God, because when He appears, who can stand in His presence? When He appears, if you are full of greed, if you are full of back-biting, if you are full of envy, if you are full of jealousy, if you are full of competition, I feel sorry for you! Yes, you will be judged, and I guarantee that you will pay to the very last farthing. But I can also guarantee to you that the covenant is with the Seed of God within you, *not* with your human, natural personality! That thing is going to fall into the ground and die. It's going to be consumed and burned up. And out of the rubble, out of the ash heap, out of the pain and the suffering that you may experience, will come the gold and the silver and the precious stones.

You must realize that God is God. We speak about the sovereignty of God, but even that is not understood. I'll tell you what the sovereignty of God is. It means that He is El El Elyon, He is the Most High God. And if He has decided to place His Seed within you, if He has decided to make yyou a son of His glory, if He has decided that there will come a day when you will manifest to the world His glory—guess what? It's going to happen. Say no to God all you want. Cause yourself such suffering and agony that words cannot describe it. I am an example of this, and I know what hell is. I've been through hell. I know what it is to get into disobedience to the uttermost. But I also know El Elyon, the Most High God! I know a

Father who loves me so greatly that I could turn my back upon Him, I could swear at Him in the heavens, I could even walk away and say, "Never again do I want anything to do with that God," but He is El Elyon! And He would say to me, "Gary, I have a covenant, and you have nothing to do with the covenant of My Seed that I have placed within you. And I say unto you that judgment will come. I'll throw you into a fiery furnace. I'll cause whatever it takes, but I guarantee you that I am your Father, and I love you with an everlasting love. And because I have the heart of a Father, and because I love you so dearly, I know how to make you submit."

We have to let God be God! It's not just a theory. God *is* God! You can't get away. I've tried. You know, if you really want to get away from God, and if it's really in your heart to go back into the world and to give up on God, you should do that, and then you'll find out that what I'm telling you is the truth. He is El Elyon. He has called you. What do we do with this verse: ***"He is the author and He is the finisher of our faith"*** (Heb. 12:2)? It took me years to find that out. I had nobody who would tell me, "Gary, be at ease. God will work it out." We don't even like to hear that. But if the responsibility for the Christian life is on Gary Sigler, I'm in a whole lot of trouble, and so are you.

The reason we have so many problems in the Church is that we have not understood the Father's heart. We have thought, and we have been taught, "He loves us unconditionally," but yet there has been that undermining concept that if you get into disobedience, if you don't do exactly what He says, then even though He still loves you, He can't help you anymore, because your will will nullify His ability to help you. If that is the truth, I wouldn't be here today. You have to realize that Jesus is your Redeemer! Do you want to know what the penalty for sin is? Read it in the Bible. Do you know who paid the penalty for sin? He bore the iniquity of us all, and with His stripes, we were healed. Behold the Lamb of God that takes away the sin of the world! He took it, He took your judgment!

Eternal Is Not Forever

There is a word in the New Testament, and I'm not going to elaborate on it here, I'm just going to throw the thought out to you (I have loads of material I can refer you to on it.) It is the word "eternal" in The Revelation, where it talks about "eternal torment" (Rev. 20:10). The word has been grossly misinterpreted. All Bible translations have their errors, and the word "eternal" has been one of the most mistranslated words. The words *aion* and *aonios,* are sometimes translated "eternal", but they literally mean age (eon), a finite period of time with a beginning and an end. There is no concept in the mind of God to throw somebody into an eternal torment, an endless anguish of fiery indignation and wrath. That's not our Father, but that is the God of some Christians, and that is the concept of God in the King James Bible and most other translations. (There are some translations which render those passages properly, and I can refer you to them.) Is there a hell? Absolutely! And you either have experienced it, or you will. There is a passage in The Revelation (21:8) that says all liars, murderers, and unbelievers will have their part, or a portion, in the Lake of Fire. You better believe, Christian, that you are going to be judged! But in that judgment, God will bring forth sons to His glory. You need to experience judgment now, and it will surely come (if it has not already done so), but it will not be eternal. It will not be done in vengeful wrath, it will be done in love.

Let's just remember to continuously seek God and go before Him with these concepts. Ask Him about His heart. Go to God and ask Him if He could toss someone into a fiery, unending torment. If a man has lived for seventy years and been the most vile sinner, would God be just, causing him to suffer eternal torment because of seventy years of sin and disobedience? I don't think so.

Why the Church Is In Darkness

I can't tell you how many years I sought after God with wrong concepts. Because I have always been very honest and open, I would go to pastor after pastor and I would confess, "I do this, and I do that." But all I was told was, "You know, you have a free will. It's your choice, Gary, so if you are going to continue to do this, then I can't help you and neither can God." And that's why this country is in such a mess. There are a lot of

Gary's out there in the world who have tried religion and found that it doesn't work. We don't all have strong characters and strong wills. We're not all able to whip our flesh into line and be righteous and good Christians, but that is the requirement you have out there. You have the survival of the fittest. The honest heart, the heart admitting its inability to transform itself, cannot make it in religion.

I'll never forget when I first experienced the Lord and wanted to join an Assembly of God church. The pastor gave me a card (I'm sure many of you have seen it) and on the back of the card it said, "I promise I won't dance, I don't smoke, I won't drink, I won't go to movies." But I often tell people, "Do you know what Jesus would do today, if He came on the scene? (I can see this so plainly, and all you religious devils can just go ahead and scream.) I can see Jesus going down to the corner pub. I can see Him pulling up a bar stool and ordering a cold beer. I can see Him taking a sip of that beer and turning to the fellow next to Him and saying, 'You know what? This is good, but I've got something that is so much better!'" You say He wouldn't do that? Well, I do that, and I never lose His presence—in fact His presence becomes sweeter. Now, if you want to misinterpret that and imagine that I am saying that drinking is okay (I know what the flesh does) that is all right. You see, *you cannot withhold the truth because of being afraid of what God's people will do with it.* That's why the Church is in darkness. I know pastors who know the truth that I preach, but they will not preach it, because they say, "If I taught that to my church, I'd have chaos on my hands." That is because these pastors don't know how to build their people up, and they don't know how to minister by the Spirit. They have to keep them in darkness in order to keep them.

Walking In the Love of God

I recently participated in a week of wonderful worship and fellowship in the Lord. We can easily get the concept that these are special times, and they are; that this was a special visitation, and it was. But then we have to go back to our jobs. In fact, somebody asked me the other day, "Can we keep this? This is wonderful, but what happens next week?" I used to ask that same question. I've been going to these kinds of things for about thirty years. I used to go to two or three weeks of meetings at a time and be in the glory, and then go back to work and immediately fall into depression. "My God! I've got to face the world again!" But *there comes a day in your life when there are no more highs and lows, when you just begin to walk in the love of God, come what may.* Where I used to work, when my wife and I walk into the dining room, people just love us. We don't preach to them (although I do hold meetings there on Sunday evenings, and any of them can come up and listen). I don't preach to them, but they just love us. But if I were typically religious, they wouldn't even like us. I can guarantee that, because I hear them talk about religious people.

It cannot be what you *say,* it has to be what you *are!* We have a message, but it is not a message of mere words. You know, God gives you a message, and then you go out, and it's just like the Abraham and Ishmael process—you go out to give the message, and all you do is create chaos. When God gives you a message, it can take years, because you have to *become* the message. And if you don't, the message that you give will not help anyone. People tell me all the time, "You speak with such boldness!" Why? It is because I know what I am saying; I've heard God speak these things to me. The things that I'm teaching today, God revealed to me over twenty years ago, but I never taught them. Then, about a year ago, the Lord released me to start teaching some of these things. I had pastored a church for 3½ years, and if you go back and listen to my messages, you'll hear in seed form that which I'm teaching today, but I didn't have the liberty to bring it out fully then.

I can remember that when I was saved, I wanted to be a pastor with all my heart. When I was eleven years old, I told my mom that I wanted to be a pastor. And in time, I applied to the Lutheran seminary, because that is what we were. I wanted so much to be a pastor, because I already had told my mom that when I grew up, I would not be going to church. You see, my concept was that if I became a pastor, then I could maybe bring some change to the Lutheran church. But my family had no money to support me in that field, and the seminary would not accept me without finances (bless God), so I couldn't go. But I wanted all my life to work for God. And when God finally called me into the ministry full time, it was to a church in Springfield, Oregon. After years and years of prayer and seeking God, and knowing that I had been called to go into the ministry, I knew that this was it. I'll never forget the first time that I walked on the church property and God spoke to me. I knew I was coming there! I had a vision burned within me of what God wanted to do in that place. But when I went there, you cannot believe the hell that my wife and I went through! I had thought pastoring was going to be just the greatest thing in the world, but we had folks tell us, "We don't like your music; we don't like what you teach." They went just a little bit short of saying, "We don't like you, either." But my wife can tell you, I never got angry. Honest to God, I never got angry; I didn't get upset in the presence of people. You know what I did? I went into my room, and I fell on my face, and I wept, and I said, "God! Help me! I know what You have placed within me, God. Help me. Give me the expression, because I know these people. If I have the expression, and if I can give them the understanding that you have given me, they're going to love the Word."

Rejecting False Concepts of God

People react against you because they don't understand. People rail against the Gospel because they are in darkness. It's not because they are mean and hateful (although some are) but because they are in darkness. But if the rest of the people of the world could have the vision and experience the love of God as I have experienced it, there is no way that they would reject Him! People today are rejecting the concept of God that America has given them. I don't want that God either. I don't want a God I have to be in fear of all the time, thinking that I might serve Him for twenty years, and then I might hit a weak point, I might backslide and get into sin, never come out, die, and then have to face an eternal torment. I don't want that kind of a God! I want a God I know is my Father. Yes, He may throw me into a fiery hell of His indignation, but no matter what it takes, it is going to be for correction, it is going to be for reproof, and it is going to be for my good. That's the only kind of God I know. I don't know the God of so-called "Christianity", I don't know who He is.

I know we all get our concepts from the Bible. But Jesus Himself said, "I know what your law says [Lev. 24:19-20]—if somebody kills your brother, you just take him out and kill him," but Jesus said, "Listen! Something is wrong with that concept" (Mt. 5:38-42). Am I saying that the scripture was wrong? I will tell you this: Some of the concepts that we saw in the scripture were not godly concepts. I know what your word says, and I know there are Christians who even delight to think that there are people who are going to suffer eternally in agony and torment—because "they deserve it". There are Christians like that, and there are people like that, because they think God is like that! And *whatever you think God is like, you will feel justified in being.*

You need a much bigger God than that. *You need a God who is able to save you to the uttermost.* You need a God who is able to reach down into the depths of your despair and your disobedience. You need a God whose arm is not shortened that He cannot save, who will reach down and lift you up—yes, a God who will correct you in His righteous indignation and wrath, but only because He loves you, not because He is angry. If we get an understanding of the heart and the love of our Father God, we will turn this world upside-down. And you who think that you are on the verge of being manifested as a son of God should know that you will never be a manifested son of God until you understand these concepts and get to know the heart of God—until you realize that He is not one who is vengefully angry, but who seeks only to do you good.

Don't you need that kind of a God? I do! As much as I have sought after God, there are still things in my life that pop up occasionally that I haven't been able to deal with fully. I need a Savior. I need to know that *what God desires more than anything else, what He desires even more than our obedience, is a heart that seeks Him!* That's why I used to go out in the desert, and say, "God . . . God! I don't have the will to serve You." (I both did, and I didn't. You know what I mean.) My flesh simply could not help me. I needed Him!

Today God is permitting this message to come forth. The Church is coming out of the wilderness, but *when we come out of the wilderness, we cannot come out with those old concepts that have kept us in there.* We have to have another Gospel than what we have had in the past. In fact, there is even a verse in The Revelation which speaks of an angel flying and having the everlasting Gospel to preach to the world (Rev. 14:6). Believe it or not, that is the Gospel that is beginning to be declared to you in these days. And not only by me—there is a whole group of men and women on the earth today whom you need to hear.

God's Loveliness Leads to Repentance

We are coming up out of the wilderness, and we are going to be a people, you and I. We're not going to have a critical eye for anyone; we're going to be able to see with eyes of the spirit. As I shared before, we're going to be able to look into the eyes of a prostitute and say, "There will come a day when you will shine forth in the glory of the Father, because He has decreed it to be so." And when you learn the heart of God, and you begin to speak words like that, you will find that the words you speak will create and generate life in the hearts of those to whom you speak. It's not a matter of their obedience. It's a matter of your understanding that you can speak to the Seed of God and cause it to come forth from within your innermost being. Do you realize that you have the Seed of God? Do you realize what that means? I can guarantee you, friend, there will come a day when you will be so filled with God and so richly blessed—not because you have been a good child, but because you understand and have had revealed to you the love of God. And you won't have to wait very long! That love will make you a good child, if you are not one. It will make you a good man or woman. Does not the Word say that it is the love of God that leads us to repentance?

The Revelation says that men will see the judgments of God and they will curse God rather than repent (Rev. 16:8-11). But when men see the loveliness of God, when they understand why the judgments are coming, they will repent in sackcloth and ashes, even those as wicked as the people of Sodom. You will remember that Jesus said to a certain group of people, *"It will be more tolerable on the day of judgment for Sodom and Gomorra than it will be for you."* He said that in two different instances (Mt. 10:15, 11:24)! Could that possibly mean that Sodom and Gomorra may have a chance? Is God going to throw them into an eternal, fiery hell simply because they did not have the knowledge that would have caused them to repent? I don't think so! You need to think about these things. Jesus said, *"If the mighty works, which were done in you, had been done in Sodom and Gomorra, they would have repented long ago in sackcloth and ashes"* (Mt. 11:21). So the reason they didn't repent was because of the darkness. They had not the knowledge of God that came through Jesus Christ. That's why John says, ***"The law was given by Moses,"*** (and Christians today still want to live by the law) ***"but grace and truth came by Jesus Christ"*** (John 1:17). If you understand the true concept of our Father God, you will become a most obedient person through the love and the drawing attraction of His Spirit. The Christian life is effortless— because it is His life!

Transformation

It is just natural for you to live the human life, is it not? You don't have to get up in the morning and figure out how you're going to be human today. And *when God begins to arise in you, you do not have to try to figure out how to live the godly life.* Out of your innermost being shall flow rivers of living water, and everywhere that river flows, it brings life and healing and restoration. Do you have sin in your life? You can either fall under condemnation, or you can seek God until the river begins to flow in you. If you are under condemnation because the sin is there, and you feel that you are cut off from God because of your sin and your disobedience, you will never experience the flowing of His river. You must realize that no matter how far into sin you may go, no matter how much disobedience you get into, no matter how far away from God you may fall, if you can but find within yourself the faintest cry, "Oh God!" He will run to you, and out of your innermost being shall flow rivers of living water.

The Spirit is represented, beginning in Genesis, by the flowing of a river, and there are precious stones in that river—which simply means that as the river flows, it causes the stones to be transformed into precious gems. And that doesn't happen today; it doesn't happen tomorrow; it doesn't happen next year. *Transformation takes a very long time.* What you need is not condemnation for the way you are. You are what you are, and you cannot change that. But if you get into the river, if you learn how to release from the very essence of your being the flowing of His Life, it will bring life not only to you, but to everyone who comes into your presence. You will bring life and healing and restoration.

In the river of life are the precious stones. So all the years that I've sought after God, year after year, sometimes being in hopeless despair of ever becoming what God wanted me to be—all the time that I was seeking after Him, unbeknownst to me, the river was flowing. There were times when I would experience the joy of God. We all experience it from time to time. But the river was flowing, and in the flowing of the river is the transformation process of the spirit. And if you realize that it is not your obedience, it is not your effort, but that through the spirit you put to death the deeds of the flesh, you will also realize that you can do that only in His presence. And again, if you have the concept that sin separates you and keeps you from His presence, you cannot be helped. But if you realize that there is nothing in all of creation that can separate you from the love of God, no matter how great your sin and failure, then all you need is to turn to God with an honest heart and say, "God, I need your help!" *We need a Savior every day.* And He is available to us every day. And my friends, *if the Life of God never arises in you, your enemies will never be scattered.* But oh, it will arise in you if the Sun of Righteousness appears with healing in His wings! Let God arise, and His enemies be scattered! In the presence of your enemies of anger, and bitterness, and resentment—in the very midst of those enemies that beset you and torment you, there is a table spread out before you.

Prayer: To Experience the Love of God

O Father, we ask for the fire of Your Spirit. O God, I am so glad that You have changed my concept of an angry, vengeful, wrathful God into One who is a Father, who loves beyond all comprehension. And Father, I ask that each of us may begin to more deeply experience Your love.

Prophecy: If You Turn Unto Me . . .

And I say unto you that if you turn unto Me in the midst of any situation and any trial, if you will but turn to Me in the very midst of sin and depression and anger and hatefulness and bitterness, and cry out from deep within, "O God! I need You!", out of your innermost being will flow My transforming power. So come unto Me, all ye that labor. Some of My people have labored so strenuously to enter into My rest, but I say to you today, that it is so easy to enter into My rest. All you have to do is to cease from your own works. And realize that I am El Elyon, the Most High God, and that I have a will, a plan, and a purpose for your life. And I say to you, because I have covenanted with that Seed that is within you, I look far beyond your mind, your emotion and your will. I look far beyond that natural person that you are, and I see deep within the center, the very core of your being, and I see that Seed of My Life that I placed there, and I say to you, that the Seed of My Life shall come forth. The Seed of my Kingdom shall reproduce within you, and you shall manifest My glory unto this earth.

Coming Out of Darkness
Chapter 7

Three Stages of Spiritual Growth

We have been thrilled with the response we have received from these messages. The reports are coming in from all over the country that people are so excited and appreciate the love of God much more since realizing His heart as a Father. I must admit that I was somewhat surprised. The system of Christianity has given us many wrong concepts of God, which makes it very confusing and hard for some to realize that our Father will perfect *His plan and purpose* in our lives.

Jesus said to His disciples, ***"It is given unto you to know the mysteries of the kingdom of heaven, but to them it is not given"*** (Matt. 13:11). God is revealing to His seekers in these days the reality of walking in the Kingdom of God. This revelation is not given to the masses of Christianity, but to those who have a heart-cry to know the reality of His indwelling life. God has been restoring many things to the Church since the days of Martin Luther. I believe that one of the last revelations to be given before the complete manifestation of the "Sons of God" is that *the hearts of the children must be turned toward God to see him as their Father, who is perfecting them according to His plan and purpose.*

God has certain times and seasons in your life when He will bring to you that which you need for your spiritual growth and understanding. I will never forget when I was introduced to a book by E.W. Kenyon. I was going over my bookshelf one day looking for something to read when I found a book called *In His Presence* by Kenyon. I have no idea how that book was placed on my bookshelf. I was amazed at the revelation, and yet the simplicity that was in that writing. When I read *In His Presence,* I was so excited that I wrote to Kenyon's publishing company and ordered every book he had written. I saturated myself in his writings for about three months and they literally changed my life. I had such a revelation of the living and abiding Word of God. After I read those books, I gave away hundreds of Kenyon's books, but not one person that I gave them to seemed to have their lives impacted the way I did.

I really believe that ***Jesus is the author and the finisher of our faith*** (Heb. 12:2). He brought me to a point where I could receive more light and understanding. My burden in ministry today is to bring people out of the darkness of religion, and human effort, into the glorious light of the gospel message proclaimed by the writers of the New Testament. I believe that God is beginning to remove the veil that has been cast over all nations (Isa. 25:7). He is beginning to reveal His heart toward His creation. No matter how much Bible knowledge we have, only God can open our understanding and our hearts to be able to receive that which He has. This is according to His timetable and not ours. As I have shared before, ***"For as in Adam all die, even so in Christ shall all be made alive. But every man in his own order: Christ the firstfruits; afterward they that are Christ's at his coming"*** (1 Cor. 15:22-23). God has a specific plan and purpose for every person. For some, it takes much more time and dealings by God before they will submit to His will.

There are basically three stages of spiritual growth in the Christian life, as revealed by the Apostle John, *"I write unto you, little children, because your sins are forgiven you for His name's sake. I write unto you, fathers, because ye have known Him that is from the beginning. I write unto you, young men, because ye have overcome the wicked one. I write unto you, little children, because ye have known the Father I have written unto you, fathers, because ye have known Him that is from the beginning. I have written unto you, young men, because ye are strong, and the word of God abideth in you, and ye have overcome the wicked one"* (1 John 2:12-14).

Little Children

When we are first born again, we are newborn babies, and it takes some time for spiritual growth. We need the liberty to be babies and little children until we grow up. John says in 1 John 2:1, *"My little children, these things write I unto you, that ye sin not. And if any man sin, we have an advocate with the Father, Jesus Christ the righteous."*

The ideal is that once you come to know Jesus, "I would that you sin not." But if you do sin, remember you have an advocate with the Father. John is saying here that right from the very beginning we need to realize that God is our Savior. If you are saved, you have a heart for God and you do not want to sin. When you have a heart for

God, deep inside you want to be conformed in His image. So John says, "Little children, I would that you sin not, but if you do, remember that you have an advocate, *Jesus Christ the righteous.*" Little children do not know a whole lot. They need, more than anything, to be properly fed. You do not teach a baby how to be a full-grown man. As parents, we do not expect a whole lot from our little children. One of the great problems in the system of Christianity that hinders spiritual growth is that after we are born again they will not allow us the time to be little children. They expect us to be born again and then start being a spiritual man. Religion condemns all the little children because they are not grown up. Little children are still worldly. They still do many things that a mature person wouldn't do. The one thing a little child has is confidence in their Father. They never feel like they cannot go to their Father, regardless of what they do. A child always knows that they can go to their Father and receive love and forgiveness. We Christians have a hard time believing that God is good enough to receive us just the way we are. He knows our habits and sins, yet He loves and forgives us anyway. When God called you, you may have been a prostitute or a king. When He called you, He knew exactly what you were and what it would take to transform you. He looks way beyond where you are today and He sees you in eternity fully transformed and walking in the realm of the Kingdom. Romans chapter 8 says that we have been called, predestinated, justified and glorified, all in the past tense. God looks at the finished work.

God's Unlimited Forgiveness

You cannot sin more than God's ability and willingness to forgive. In fact, He has already forgiven you. On the cross, every sin ever committed, past, present, and future, was forgiven. At the cross, sin, the world, the flesh and the devil were taken into death and did not come out of the grave. In God's eyes, sin is no more. He fully dealt with the sin problem. This cannot be just a doctrine. We need the revelation to see the full redemption that was purchased at Calvary. When we have the light and revelation of God concerning redemption, we will never be condemned again for the areas in our lives that need transformation. There will come a day when the veils will be fully removed from our eyes and we will see that sin is no more and we will be free from it. The fear of sin is what keeps many in bondage to it. I am no longer afraid of sin. I know I still experience it in certain areas, but I no longer fear it. I know sin is a product of the carnal realm. As long as I am not fully transformed, the carnal man will affect me at times. However I no longer fear this, I just continue to seek God and know that as I seek Him, as I touch Him, He will flow into those areas and bring transformation. When you no longer fear sin, it loses power in your life.

One of the greatest problems today is that we do not feel good enough to partake of the riches of Christ. We do not see the power of God operating in our lives because we feel that we are not worthy. We do not believe in the simplicity of the gospel. *Jesus bore the penalty for our sin* and we should not feel condemned, but rather forgiven. We are God's children, born from above. We have a new nature, but we are still for the most part little children. Because we are still more natural than spiritual, we condemn ourselves for what we do in the flesh. We feel we deserve condemnation rather than God's forgiveness. We feel, because of our sin and our carnal nature that from time to time rises up in us, that we are not worthy.

It would be wonderful if, when we come to God, we could be born a fully mature Son of God, but that just does not happen. God wants to transform us into what He is, and that is a long process. The religious ones look at the little babies and say, *"Look at them, they call themselves Christians and they do all kinds of things that they shouldn't. They must not be born again."* To them, being a Christian is a matter of conduct, of being right and doing right. They do not realize that they need to feed the babies, not condemn them. So precious few ever realize that to change the outward conduct only makes them a better person in the natural. No matter how good you are, it does not give you an entrance into the Kingdom of God. I have witnessed, time and time again, that it is much harder for a good person to enter into the realm of the Kingdom than a bad person. A good person has a hard time recognizing their need for God. If you have followed these messages on *Coming Out of Darkness* from the beginning, you know it doesn't matter how good or how bad you are, you still need God to be able to live the Kingdom life. God takes natural men both, good and bad, and transforms them into Sons of God. This is *the good news of the gospel.* Living in the Kingdom of God has absolutely nothing to do with the natural man.

We are not fully transformed yet. There are times when our flesh will get the best of us. There are still times when we say no to the prompting of the Spirit. If you are 95% transformed in the spirit and still have 5% carnality, that 5% will rise up and get the best of you at times. If you do not understand that, you will always be condemned. If you think that because you have been a Christian for 20 years you should not have any carnality, you will always condemn yourself, rather than recognizing it as the flesh and looking away to the sin offering and accepting forgiveness. Again, the penalty for our sin was paid at Calvary. That is why Jesus died and that *offering* **was for all** of humanity. He died so that you could find your way back to God. This is according to God's plan and purpose, which is **"every man in his own order"**. God **will** bring you into the fullness of His plan for your life.

Even though God will bring you fully into His purpose for your life, you still have a part to play in it. That is why it is **"every man in his own order"**. Our actions and responses to God affect our lives, whether for good or bad. The more that we hunger and seek after God, the quicker He can work His will in our lives. If we are not willing, we need to ask Him to make us willing. It is going to take ages for some to submit fully to God's working in their lives. The choices that we make do play a part in God's working in our lives. However, we must also understand that it is not a matter of the flesh. We know that the things we do in the flesh do not please God, but we cannot just lay back and do nothing, thinking that God will do it all. The key is that we must seek God. Don't try to perfect yourself in the flesh, but every day of your life, seek after God. Learn to worship Him and fall in love with Him.

There have been periods in my life when I would get so discouraged and downcast that I would lose hunger for God. I have gone for periods when I wouldn't read the Bible and I wouldn't pray much, but I never quit being honest with God. I used to drive to a place in my car or find a place in my home every day where I would just talk to God. I have said to God many times, "I do not have the hunger anymore, please help me." I believe that is how I found the strength to keep going on. Most Christians never get beyond the stage of a little child because of condemnation. It is OK to be a child, and you will always be a spiritual child until you realize that it is OK to be where you are today. It does not matter what your problems or hang-ups are. What matters is that you have your eyes unveiled to the fact that the price for your redemption was fully paid. You need to go to God and ask Him to reveal the depths of Calvary to you. You need your understanding opened to the fact that there will come a day when you will fully reveal and manifest His glory to the world, because that is why you were created. You do have a part to play in this. Your choices can deter His will but they will not stop it. Don't let anyone tell you that you are a puppet on a string. God does have it all worked out, but how long will you wait before going to Him and trusting Him to do in you what you cannot do in the flesh? I have been saying for years that Christians will do everything except take the time to sit quietly in His presence, because they are so busy. If you do not spend time with God, no matter how many good works you do, it does not matter. People may benefit from your good works, but you won't. You must begin to spend time with God. That is when the veils and the darkness begin to lift off of you. Only God can reveal to you the depths of His love. His love is not a doctrine; it must be experienced.

As Christians, we should not know one another according to the flesh, but according to the spirit. There are Christians who have been Christians for many years and are still babies because they have not known these truths. Let's not condemn the babies, let's feed them the riches of redemption to release them from condemnation so they can grow.

Young Men

"I write unto you, young men, because ye have overcome the wicked one. I have written unto you, young men, because ye are strong, and the word of God abideth in you, and ye have overcome the wicked one" (1 Jn. 2:13-14).

The Word of God abiding in you is much more than just memorizing the words of the Bible. Years ago, I had entire chapters of the Bible committed to memory without much experience of the Word operating in my life. When the Word of God abides in you, it becomes a part of your being. It becomes the Word again made flesh. It is the *living* and *abiding* Word working in you that enables you to live godly and overcome the wicked one. As the Word begins to operate in you, you begin, in small ways at first, to think and speak according to the principles of the Word and begin to see change take place in your life. Whenever we speak from our spirit the words of God that abide in us, those words have just as much value as the words spoken from the lips of Jesus. *This is not the name it and claim it doctrine.* Many people try to use positive confession and thinking, trying to manipulate God to do what they want. Most of them do not realize what they are doing, but this is the case. Whenever you take the written Word of God that He spoke to someone else long ago and use that as positive confession you are not abiding in the Word. However, if you are reading the Bible and God speaks it again to you and it becomes a living thing to you, then you can speak it in true faith and assurance that what you speak will come to pass. The key to speaking the Word is to *only speak what God has spoken to you.*

An Example of Acting on the Spoken Word

I will never forget a few years ago a former pastor of ours rose one Sunday morning and in his prayer time God spoke to Him and said, "Joe is going to walk today." Joe had been in a wheelchair for quite a while unable to walk. In church that morning, the pastor went up to Joe and said, "God spoke to me today and said you were going to walk, so **get up."** Joe just looked at him and said "I can't do it" but the pastor said, "God said you were going to walk, so get up." Still Joe just shook his head no and said he could not get up. Then the pastor spoke to two ushers and said, "Get Joe out of his chair." They pulled Joe out of his chair and the pastor said, "Make him walk." The ushers dragged him back and forth across the front of the church with the pastor saying, **"In the name of Jesus you will walk,"** over and over for about ten minutes. By this time everyone in the church was thinking the pastor had missed God, but he just kept on saying **"Walk."** All at once, as the ushers were dragging this man across the church, strength came into his legs and he began to stand on his feet and walk alone. Well, you can imagine the praises that ascended to God that morning. This is the only way true miracles happen in ministry. You cannot just read in the Bible that God heals people and then start speaking the Word to everyone you see that is sick. Don't misunderstand me, I am **not** saying you shouldn't pray for the sick, you should. If God doesn't give you a Word for a miracle, pray for them but don't make a fool of yourself and do disgrace to the Spirit of God by speaking a word of healing to someone and it not happening. You won't have to make excuses why the person did not get healed like, "You just didn't have enough faith. I spoke the Word but you did not believe." There is so much of that kind of trash in the church which just brings condemnation on people because *you* were not acting out of faith. Joe did not have faith to be healed, but God had spoken to the pastor, and what God speaks to you, **HE** will do.

An Example of Speaking a Word You Haven't Heard

A few years ago, I saw one of the leading "Word of Faith" teachers line up about 15 wheelchair patients and begin to speak the "Word of Faith" to them to rise up and walk. When nothing happened, he began to exhort them to try to move their legs and he began to pull them from their chairs. They began to fall on the floor, still being exhorted to put their faith to work and begin to walk.

They were squirming around on the floor desperately trying to believe and be healed. I will never forget that pitiful sight as long as I live. Not a one of them received the ability to walk. This took place on nationwide television. What a disgrace to the miracle-working power of God. People of God are doing the same thing across the world today, speaking a word that was given to someone else two thousand years ago, and nothing is happening. They are speaking for healing, cars, lands and prosperity, thinking they are rich in the Word and faith, not knowing they are miserable, blind, wretched, poor and naked. Jesus said, *"I do only those things I see my Father do,"* not those things I read in the Old Testament. Jesus told his disciples to heal the sick and cast out devils and they had a marvelous ministry. If He says to you to do the same, then when you speak a Word of healing, healing is what will take place. I know I can be misunderstood here, but you must hear the spirit in these words. If we will take the time to sit in God's presence, He will begin to speak to us, and then when we do speak the Word it will come to pass. I am not against the "Word of Faith" teaching. It is just that you must hear God yourself and then live, act, speak, and do that which He speaks. When I become full of the Word of God as a living reality, as I begin to hear God speak to me in my daily life, then I take that which He has spoken to me and I speak, and I live, and I center everything around that which God has spoken to me. I become that which I speak. Again, this is the experience of the Word becoming flesh.

"As a man thinks in his heart so is he" (Prov. 23:7). Jesus said, *"Out of the abundance of the heart the*

mouth speaks" (Luke 6:45). Whatever you think in your heart, you will speak out of your mouth, and the creative words that you speak bring to you your experience of tomorrow. The words that you speak can be very powerful. They can work for you either positively or negatively. We must, by the grace of God, have revealed to us the heart that we were given at the new birth.

You Have Overcome the Wicked One

When we hear a word like this, we can immediately interpret it with the natural mind and think of the devil *out there somewhere.* The devil outside of you is not the problem. Jesus took care of him at the cross. The Word says, *"And having disarmed the powers and authorities, he made a public spectacle of them, triumphing over them by the cross"* (Col. 2:15, NIV). One who has realized the power of the cross and has had their mind renewed to see that the devil is not the problem is on the way to a great spiritual awakening. The devil on the outside of us has been defeated. We have been taught so much the power of the devil that we believe in it and that is what gives it the power. The devil we need to overcome is that carnal mind that was received by the Fall. The wicked one is that rebellion, that consciousness we received at the Fall. It is that consciousness we have of being separate and alienated from God. The flesh, the carnal man, is the wicked one we need to overcome. If the Word abides in you, and you become the Word, then you have overcome the wicked one.

This, of course, is a matter of transformation. Your growth from a little child to a young man is a long process. I believe God is speeding up the process in these days, because we are very close to God bringing *"many sons into glory"* (Heb 2:10). We are very close to God removing the veil cast over all nations (Isa 25:7). The covering cast over America is most deceiving. We are in the darkness and covering of religion disguising itself as Christianity. The system of Christianity is included in that *"wicked one"* that we must overcome. How many people realize that this beautiful, full of good works, system is a part of **BABYLON** the mother of HARLOTS **spoken** of in The Revelation chapter 17? Larry & Betty Hodges, in their publication, *The Shofar Letters,* issue 2, 1997, say:

Some are loathe to leave the stain-glassed cathedrals, the pews and pulpits, the hirelings and hierarchies, the Sunday morning *meeting* at 10:00 A.M., three songs, an offering and 30 minutes of freeze-dried prepackaged pabulum, and have therefore, in many cases, chosen these very things over the Lord Himself. They do so because they have been made drunk with the wine of the fornication of harlotries. Although espoused to the Lord, their hearts have gone after other lovers. Men who would never be caught dead in a real brothel think nothing of frequenting spiritual houses of ill-repute for the same reasons, though spiritual.

Before I continue further, let me make it clear that I am not referring here to those who are still in need of keeping the feast of Pentecost; who still very much need to gather together with others of like precious faith, or of those who come together *in the Spirit.* I am referring to those who remain in *Babylon* and refuse to leave it, or its ways, customs, rituals, or ceremonies.

Lest you misunderstand who Babylon is, it is all the religious systems, groups, denominations and non-denominational denominations, including Charismatic, Pentecostal, *and some home-meetings.* It is that which bears the stamp and spirit of the Mother of Harlots and Abominations of the Earth! It is ***Things, men, movements, institutions, organizations, etc. which draw the multitudes after themselves and attach the crowds to themselves. It is the principle of Anti-christ; that which definitely supplants, or intends to supplant Christ. It is an alternative to the whole Christ in man-made Christianity; an imitation life borne and carried on by it's own momentum.*** *(The Shofar Letters,*

We Must Overcome Bigotry

Someone asked me a short time ago, "Why is it that most of God's people get angry when they are told about the possibility of God saving everyone?" In the Old Testament, the Jews thought that they were the only people of God on the earth. The Jews were very bigoted. When Jesus came they were so sure that the gospel He brought was only for them. They would never have gone to the Gentiles with the gospel. Peter had to have a vision from God to convince him to take the gospel to the Gentiles. Acts tells us, ***"On the morrow, as they went on their journey, and drew nigh unto the city, Peter went up upon the housetop to pray about the sixth hour. And he became very hungry, and would have eaten: but while they made ready, he fell into a trance, and saw*** *heaven opened, and a certain vessel descending unto him, as it had been a great sheet knit at the four corners, and let down to the earth: wherein were all manner of fourfooted beasts of the earth, and wild beasts, and creeping things, and fowls of the air. And there came a voice to him, Rise, Peter; kill, and eat. But Peter said, Not so, Lord; for I have never eaten any thing that is common or unclean. And the voice spake unto him again the second time, What God hath cleansed, that call not thou common"* (Acts 10:9-15).

We can see by these verses that God no longer calls any man unclean. In this vision, He was telling Peter that God has cleansed everyone and **He is not a bigot**. His love and His redemption are for the world, not just a select group of people. He *does call* a select group out of the world to dispense Himself into them so that they can go to the world and bring them the word of reconciliation. Christians are the most bigoted group of people on the earth today. Christians get upset with me when they hear me talk about God being the Father of all and redeeming all and being able to save someone who does not know about Jesus. Even those who claim to know Jesus fight among themselves. Even within their own denominations they argue over doctrinal differences. The Baptists are divided over baptism. The Lutherans are divided amongst themselves. The Pentecostals are divided. These religions are all divided because of man's carnal interpretation of the Bible. Anyone who sees the oneness of Christ and the Church could never be a part of that HARLOT system. Revelation 17:3 says that she is *"full of names of blasphemy"*. We should not call ourselves anything. Not Baptist, Catholic, Pentecostal or anything else. Paul told the Corinthians, *"And I, brethren, could not speak unto you as unto spiritual, but as unto carnal, even as unto babes in Christ. I have fed you with milk, and not with meat: for hitherto ye were not able to bear it, neither yet now are ye able. For ye are yet carnal: for whereas there is among you envying, and strife, and divisions, are ye not carnal, and walk as men? For while one saith, I am of Paul; and another, I am of Apollos; are ye not carnal?"* (1 Cor. 3:1-4). How could the Word be more plain? Jesus Himself said in Matthew 12:25, *"A house divided against itself cannot stand."* The Institutional Church could never be a testimony to God because of the division among her. We must drop all bigotry and division. God is our Father and we are one family. You may be a Catholic or Pentecostal, but regardless of your affiliation, you are my brother and I love you and will minister to you.

Our Oneness Is in His Life

Our oneness is in *His life,* not in our doctrines or carnal knowledge. A doctrine, no matter how good or correct it is, should never be used to divide the people of God. The Apostle Paul said, *"Till we all come in the unity of the faith, and of the knowledge of the Son of God, unto a perfect man, unto the measure of the stature of the fullness of Christ: That we henceforth be no more children, tossed to and fro, and carried about with every wind of doctrine, by the sleight of men, and cunning craftiness, whereby they lie in wait to deceive"* (Eph. 4:13-14). A doctrine held in esteem above fellowship with another person is a wind that will carry you away from Christ. There is a people on the earth today who are coming into the unity of the faith, and they see the futility of the organized church with its forms, programs and rituals. They are not, as some suppose, *"forsaking the assembling of themselves together"*. They are coming out of Babylon and becoming a chaste virgin unto Christ. These are not sectarian or exclusive. They realize there are precious saints of God in all denominations and groups, but they themselves cannot any longer partake of the HARLOT system that keeps people in bondage. God's people are beginning to realize that they have *one life and one nature.* Jesus prayed, in John, chapter 17, verses 11,20-23, ***"And now I am no more in the world, but these are in the world, and I come to thee. Holy Father, keep through Thine own name those whom Thou hast given me, that they may be one, as we are. Neither pray I for these alone, but for them also which shall believe on me through their word; that they all may be one; as Thou, Father, art in me, and I in thee, that they also may be one in us: that the world may believe that Thou hast sent me. And the glory which Thou gavest me I have given them; that they may be one, even as we are one: I in them, and Thou in me, that they may be made perfect in one; and that the world may know that Thou hast sent me, and hast loved them, as thou hast loved me."***

This, very simply stated by Jesus, is the basis of our oneness. It is not what we intellectually believe, it is not the church you go to or the physical ground you meet on. Our oneness is *His life in each of us.* The Christ in me is the same Christ that is in you and *Christ is not divided.* The Christ in me loves and ministers to the world regardless of their condition in life. If I will not fellowship with you because you have different beliefs than mine, then my doctrines are IDOLS that need to be torn down. The Protestants talk about the Catholics bowing down to idols and images of saints, but *they bow down and worship their own doctrines.* They are, as Paul said, *"Little children, tossed about with the winds of doctrine."* Jesus is calling out a people and teaching them by His Spirit and they will one day stand on the earth as *one new man.* The world will then know that Jesus was sent of God and that He loves them. The sons of God will minister to the world the love of the Father and all bigotry will be put down. **Hallelujah!**

Fathers

"I write unto you, Fathers, because ye have known Him that is from the beginning" (1 Jn. 2:13).

John repeats the above sentence twice. The Fathers know Him that is from the beginning. Their understanding of God goes way beyond the comprehension of Christianity. When you know God as Father, you realize that you came out of His substance. Adam is your Father according to the flesh, but God is your Father according to the spirit.

*"Furthermore we have had fathers of our flesh which corrected us, and we gave them reverence: shall we not much rather be in subjection unto the **Father of spirits, and live?"*** (Heb. 12:9).

*"And they fell upon their faces, and said, O God, the God of **the spirits of all flesh**, shall one man sin, and wilt thou be wroth with all the congregation?"* (Num. 16:22).

*"Let the LORD, **the God of the spirits of all flesh**, set a man over the congregation"* (Num. 27:16).

"The burden of the word of the LORD for Israel, saith the LORD, which stretcheth forth the heavens, and layeth the foundation of the earth, and formeth the spirit of man within him" (Zech. 12:1).

God is spirit and He is our Father. All mankind have a spirit. *"He that is joined to the Lord is one spirit"* (1 Cor. 6:17).

God is the God of your spirit, not your flesh. This is one reason that all men are included in redemption. Your spirit was brought forth from the very substance of God. In your spirit, you and God are one. If you learn how to live and function from your spirit, then God is once again manifested in humanity.

There will come a day in your spiritual growth when you will become a spiritual Father. A Father is one who is a mature believer who carries the presence of God within him. He will reproduce God's life, God's will, and His glory in others. *A Father in the natural is one who reproduces human life. A Father in the spirit reproduces spiritual life.* Jesus said, ***"It is the spirit that quickeneth; the flesh profiteth nothing: the words that I speak unto you, they are spirit, and they are life"*** (John 6:63). When we learn to speak from our spirit the words of God, then our words also become spirit and life. We can impart life to others by our speaking. True ministry imparts life and builds up the saints. ***"Ye are our epistle written in our hearts, known and read of all men: Forasmuch as ye*** *are manifestly declared to be the epistle of Christ ministered by us, written not with ink, but with the Spirit of the living God; not in tables of stone, but in fleshy tables of the heart"* (2 Cor. 3:2-3).

To become a Father means that God's life has swallowed up the carnal life and you are now a representative of Him on the earth. *It is no longer I who live but Christ who lives in me.*

Another way to share the three stages of spiritual growth is:

1. God to you

2. God in you

3. God as you

As God to you, you understand that God came to man. He came *to you* to redeem you and restore you back to fellowship with your Father. He came not just to the Jews, not just to the Christians, but he came to the world. God to you is the first revelation in the mystery of God. Every man has a spirit, the substance of God. And God came to you to quicken and regenerate your spirit, so that you could once again have fellowship and commune with Him. As we have seen, Adam sold the human race into sin and death and Christ came to us with redemption. *"For since by man came death, by man came also the resurrection of the dead. For as in Adam all die, even so in Christ shall all be made alive"* (1 Cor. 15:21-22).

God **to** you means that God is **for** you. No matter how much sin I am in, no matter how many times I fall and fail God, He comes to me every day with the offer of pardon and redemption. I must state again that it is not our fault that we are in Adam. Has anybody ever told you that when you sin it is not your fault? The nature of Adam is to sin, That is why *God is to you.* You need to understand that God paid the price for every act of disobedience and transgression so that He could reconcile you to Himself. ***"God was in Christ, reconciling the world unto himself, not imputing their trespasses unto them; and hath committed unto us the word of reconciliation"*** (2 Cor. 5:19). These verses tell us that God in Christ comes to you realizing that you are not responsible for the condition you are in, so it is not your fault. You are a product of Adam's fall. God, willing to show His love, sacrificed Himself on the cross so you would understand that He knows that you can't in your fallen condition help yourself, so He came to help you. He came to be the reconciler that would reconcile you back to God. When Adam and Eve fell, God wasn't mad at them; He had already made provision for their redemption. Their redemption was based on God's choice, not on their choice. There are people who have never heard the gospel, but that does not stop God's provision from working for their good. Eventually God's redemption will be realized fully **in** them. *That is God to you.*

God In You

When you realize that God is to you and you begin to seek Him and come into a deeper understanding, and begin to hunger and thirst after Him, you then begin to realize God is in you. Paul told us that our hope is "CHRIST IN YOU" (Col. 1:27). Our hope is not in a "rapture" that will automatically change us into Christ's likeness. *That is a fairy tale and a fallacy.* The only hope we have is Christ in us. Because He is in us, that is our hope of glory. If Christ is truly in you and you are not experiencing Him, even though He is in you, it is, at least in this present time, doing you no good. Knowing it intellectually is not enough. All Christians know God came to them to save them, but most never experience God in them to deliver them from a life of self. We have people in churches around the world who say they are born again but never experience God in them to deliver them. God wants not only to come to you with redemption, but He wants you to realize that *He can live in you, instead of you.* I was a Christian for years before I experienced Christ in me. I knew intellectually and was taught that Jesus was in me, but I had no experience of His living through me. I experienced God's love and forgiveness, but I didn't know He could live His life in me. God in me is a marvelous revelation. That's the "young man" that John talks about. God in us with His ability and creative Word to change us and the very atmosphere in which we live. That is God in us and that is wonderful. However, when you experience God in you, you still have the flesh to deal with. So yes, God is in me, but the self-life still raises up so there is a certain amount of warfare we must do, *not with the devil,* but with self. There are Christians who have spent years fighting the devil and trying to pull down strongholds, when they themselves are still little children in the spirit.

What we need to deal with is not the devil outside of us, but the spirit of antichrist that is in our flesh. Some get upset when I say that Christians have a spirit of antichrist, but nevertheless, that is the case. Has God ever asked you to do something and your flesh said NO? That is antichrist. Anything in you that is against the workings of God is antichrist. In the mass of humanity, both Christian and non-Christian, *the antichrist is at this present time ruling and reigning in a people.* Christianity is looking for this man to come in an outward way, when all the time he is working and growing in their flesh and they do not recognize it. Our carnal nature is permeated with the antichrist spirit. Most Christians are in the darkness and do not understand the very basic things of God because of the antichrist nature that is in their flesh.

The experience of God in you is the first step in learning how to deal with that antichrist nature that is in us. *You should never be condemned for this.* You have inherited the antichrist spirit. You did not do *anything* to cause you to be this way. Everyone is born with this nature.

There are only two men growing on the earth today: Adam and Christ. (We will deal with this more in another chapter of *Coming Out of Darkness.)* These two men are growing on the earth at the same time. There is a mass of humanity that is growing within them the antichrist spirit. I know this is hard for some to accept, but you can be a Christian, go to church, read your Bible, give a tithe to the church, be full of good works, and still be growing the antichrist within you. This antichrist is not always easy to identify. The Revelation calls this spirit *"MYSTERY, BABYLON THE GREAT, THE*

MOTHER OF HARLOTS AND ABOMINATIONS OF THE EARTH" (Rev. 17:5). A mystery is not always easy to figure out. Babylon means confusion. I do not know of a more confused group of people of the earth today than the people of Christianity. This is not the fault of the people. Our leaders have taught us confusion for years. We have some of the most popular ministries of our day winning people to Jesus, telling them after they are saved to "Go to the church of your choice. If you want to be a Catholic go to the Catholic Church. If you want to be a Lutheran go to the Lutheran Church." *This is confusion!* God is redeeming people and calling them **out** of confusion, not bringing them to Him and putting them in it. Christians need to realize that antichrist can and is growing in the Christian system.

I am not against the Catholics, Lutherans, or any other people. I will go to a Catholic or any other church to minister to the people, but I will not and cannot support that ungodly antichrist system. That system is absolutely robbing God's people of their heritage. There are two mysteries in the book of The Revelation and they are both growing at the same time. They are both growing within us, and one of them is going to overcome the other. This is why I say that the choices you make are very important. The choices that you make will either feed the antichrist carnal nature within you or will feed the spirit of the living God that is within you. People quote scriptures like *"I can do all things through Christ"* (Phi. 4:13). No you can't, if you are a carnal Christian. But if the Spirit of God begins to grow in you and begins to swallow up that carnal nature, then you can be like the Apostle Paul and say, "I can do all things through Christ." Please don't take a spiritual baby and put that burden on them when you yourself can't do it.

There are two men coming into maturity: Adam and Christ; the antichrist spirit and the Bride. We can be a part of the Bride. God is calling out a people in this present time for His end-time purpose. I understand the strong pull of the flesh. The flesh cannot perfect the flesh, but we can choose to seek the Lord for grace to help in overcoming the antichrist spirit. If you choose to do something, it doesn't mean that you necessarily have the ability to do it. You are just going to make the right choice. *Just start making the right choices*. If your flesh rises up and overcomes that choice, don't fall under condemnation. When a baby is learning how to walk and he falls, he doesn't just lay there and get discouraged and say, "I'm never going to try again." He just gets up and tries it again and again. This is what I call exercising your spirit. A natural baby keeps exercising his legs until he is able to stand and walk alone. If you will continue to make the right choices, looking away unto Jesus for your help, and keep exercising your spirit, eventually your spirit will become strong and you will grow into that "young man". *"I write unto you, young men, because ye have overcome the wicked one."*

We need Christians who understand these principles and can minister them to the Body and help them grow. It doesn't matter how many times we fall and miss the mark. Just keep making the right choices and keep seeking God until He grows in you. *"For he that cometh to God must believe that he is, and that he is a rewarder of them that diligently seek him"* (Heb. 11:6).

Anything in you that is saying no to God is antichrist. That could be anger, resentment, bitterness or anything else that is not godly. Some people think they have been good Christians all their lives, and then something happens that they don't understand, and they get mad at God. When you get angry with God, you have a serious problem and do not know the heart of your Father. You get angry with Him because of circumstances beyond your control. That is an antichrist spirit. We need Christians who will be honest with God and take responsibility for their actions. Just be honest and come to the light, don't run away from it.

God As You

As little children, we realize that God is **to** us. As young men, we realize God is **in** us. Then we begin to experience God **as** us. All three of these stages are progressive. The Spirit of the Lord changes us from glory to glory. As a little child, we can experience something of the Father's reproducing life. Unlike natural babies, spiritual babies can reproduce spiritual babies. In fact, you can and will reproduce what you are. However, when you begin to mature and become a Father, you will be able to impart life to the babies that will help them grow into children, and then young men, and eventually, Fathers.

I can't tell you a whole lot about being a Father because I haven't experienced a lot, but I can tell you what it is. It is no longer just God to you or God in you, but it is God as you. This does not mean that your human carnal nature is God. This does not mean that Gary Sigler is God. What it means is that God's Spirit in my spirit has totally swallowed my carnal nature. I am now as He is. I and my Father are one. The Apostle Paul experienced this, he said, *"I am crucified with Christ: nevertheless I live; yet not I, but Christ liveth in me: and the life which I now live in the flesh I live by the faith of the Son of God, who loved me, and gave himself for me"* (Gal. 2:20). This is what will produce the glorious Church. A group of people who no longer live in themselves. Their carnal life has been swallowed up in the victorious, transcendent, resurrected life of Jesus Christ. It is no longer just God **in** His people but God **as** His people. I have experienced at times being so caught up in the Spirit of God that I have known that it was God appearing **as** me. That is what tabernacles is all about. *"For ye are the temple of the living God; as God hath said, I will dwell in them, and walk in them; and I will be their God, and they shall be my people"* (2 Cor. 6:16). What a wonderful revelation, God **to** you, God **in** you and then God **as** you.

I feel I must clarify again that I am not speaking according to the natural. This natural person that I am, Gary Sigler, and the natural person that you are, is only good for one thing. He must decrease and go into death until he no longer rises up to take control. Whenever self rises up and says, "I am God," that is an abomination. You hear this in the New Age movement, people saying, "I am God." That is "THE ABOMINATION" spoken of by the prophet Daniel. Whenever self sits in the temple of God, declaring himself to be God, that is the abomination of desolation *and that is the antichrist*. However, whenever the self is totally consumed by the Spirit of

God, you can say it is no longer I who live, but Christ who lives in me. It is no longer just God *in* me but God *as* me, that is God's revelation and mystery revealed.

The antichrist spirit that controls your carnal nature has the ability to reproduce in your soul a counterfeit of what God wants to do through His Spirit in your spirit. Declaring yourself to be God is a counterfeit. We know there has to be a reality for that to be a counterfeit. The antichrist is not some man that is going to someday go sit in a temple in Jerusalem and declare himself as God. **We are the temples of God.** Listen again, whenever your self, your carnal nature, sits in the temple of God and is ruling your life, that is the abomination of desolation that is saying no to God. That is the antichrist spirit sitting in the temple of God.

About ten years ago I was the studying the antichrist and rapture doctrines. I was seeking God about how we were to know this man called antichrist. God very clearly spoke to me and said, "YOU ARE THE ANTICHRIST." There may come a man someday who claims to be Christ. That has happened many times already. There are multitudes of Christians sitting around waiting for a man to come, thinking that the antichrist is all outside of themselves. This is a great deception. Paul warned the believers that in the last days (and according to the Word, we have been in the last days ever since the crucifixion of Jesus), *"some shall depart from the faith, giving heed to seducing spirits, and doctrines of devils"* (1 Tim. 4:1). We have been seduced for years by Christianity. We have been taught that our problem is the devil, when all the time the devil was not our problem. We have been taught to fight spirits in the airwaves. We think the problem is with the government, or the coming antichrist, or any number of things. We were never taught that the problem *was not outside of us, but in us.* The real problem lies hidden within us. Our problem is not the environment, it's not who your parents are, the problem is *the heart of man.* The Word says, *"whenever the heart shall turn to the Lord the veils shall be taken away"* (2 Cor. 3:16). Why are the veils so dark and thick in America? Because most in Christianity are not seeking God and turning their hearts to Him. They are being religious and going to church and doing lots of activities, but very little seeking of His will for their lives. Don't deceive yourself into thinking you have a heart for God if you don't want to be conformed into His image, if you won't take some time out of your day to seek Him and to know Him. A lot of the condition of Christians is due to the confusion that is taught. If you have a heart for God and you don't understand that you need only to seek Him, that heart will get you into a lot of religious activity. You will be hungry for fellowship, so you may go to church and be taught ignorance. In the pulpits across America, you can go to church and learn ignorance.

An Example of Ignorance Being Taught

I was listening to Christian radio the other day, and there was a pastor teaching ignorance. If I mentioned his name, almost everyone would recognize him. He is one of the most listened to preachers on the radio today. He has a church of several thousand members in California. This man was saying that in the beginning the church was in so much darkness and sin was so prevailing that they needed Apostles and Prophets and the miracle-working power of God to get the church started. However, after John penned the last words in The Revelation, God's revelation was complete, the book was shut, and God no longer needed to perform miracles. He said, "Miracles passed away with the apostolic age." He said that the Apostles, Prophets and the gifts of the Spirit were no longer needed and they had passed away. This man is teaching his people ignorance and sowing darkness and blindness over their eyes so that they cannot experience the reality of God for themselves. There is no way those people, if they believe what their pastor is saying, could receive a message from God. He has cast a veil over them, so they cannot see the truth. This is why I say that Christianity is the deception, and the seducing spirits and doctrines of devils that keep people in darkness and bondage. You can go into Catholic churches, Pentecostal, Nazarene, Lutheran, Baptist or any other church and be taught ignorance that will keep you in darkness. WAKE UP, CHURCH OF THE LIVING GOD, AND SHAKE YOURSELF! *"Wherefore he saith, Awake thou that sleepest, and arise from the dead, and Christ shall give thee light"* (Eph. 5:14).

If you have a heart that only hungers after God, He said, *"Anyone who comes to me"* (not to the system of Christianity), *"I will in no wise cast out"* (John 6:37). All you have to do is say "God I want you and I want to know the truth." Ask Him to grant you a heart that seeks only Him. We need to drop all of religion and turn to Him for a fresh revelation that will give us hope and inspiration.

God to me—*little children,* God in me—*young men,* God as me—*a Father.* When we have these realities revealed in us we will be able to bring reconciliation and restoration to all of God's creation. When God fills us and saturates us and we become a Father, we won't have to wonder what His will is, because we will become His perfect will on the earth.

Coming Out of Darkness
Chapter 8

Understanding Judgment

In coming into an understanding of the heart of God, I found that judgment is a *wonderful* thing. The judgment that we have been taught in traditional Christianity has given us a false concept of God. One of these false concepts is this: "There is going to come a day when God is going to pour out His vengeance, wrath and anger upon humanity because of their rejection of Him, and disobedience to Him. God is so angry at mankind that He is going to pour out horrible tortures upon them and then send them to a fiery torment where they will be tortured in unending agony throughout all of eternity." ?

We are taught this concept mainly due to two things:

1. Mistranslation of God's Word.

2. Natural understanding, rather than spiritual interpretation.

A natural, carnal understanding of the Word has caused almost all the conflicts between believers. You can have a natural understanding of the Bible and still miss God. Spiritual understanding of the Word only comes through seeking God intimately and spending much time in His presence. The Bible was never meant to be taken strictly intellectually with the natural understanding and interpretation. The Apostle Paul said that the Word of God is a mystery. The plan of God is hidden from the natural, carnal mind of man. The natural mind cannot understand deep spiritual truths. Natural man can only understand with his natural mind. To be able to understand the mysteries of the Kingdom of God, you must have a heart that is seeking only God and His truth. It is very easy to get this heart just by going to God in a very simple way and asking Him to capture your heart for His purpose and to open to you the mysteries of the Word. Ask Him for the spiritual interpretation of His Word.

We will see in this message the way in which God judges. We will see that His judgment is just and righteous, not vengeful and hateful. *"With my soul have I desired thee in the night; yea, with my spirit within me will I seek thee early: **for when thy judgments are in the earth, the inhabitants of the world will learn righteousness"** (Isa. 26:9). **"Arise, O God, judge the earth: for thou shalt inherit all nations"** (Ps. 82:8).

You can see from the above verses that judgment is a thing to be desired. When God judges the earth, the people will learn righteousness and then God shall inherit all nations. God sends His judgments for correction, to teach you His righteous ways.

Judgment Is to Be Taken Seriously

Judgment is not to be taken lightly. If you sow to the flesh, you will most certainly reap the flesh. *"For if the word spoken by angels was stedfast, and every transgression and disobedience received a just recompense of reward; how shall we escape, if we neglect so great salvation; which at the first began to be spoken by the Lord, and was confirmed unto us by them that heard him?"* (Heb. 2:2-3).

In these days, we are hearing the wonderful message of reconciliation and sonship. We can all feel the nearness of the day of Jubilee for us. There is soon coming a day in which the firstfruits of God will be loosed from the bondage of corruption and shall fully reveal and manifest to the world the fullness of God. If we neglect the prophetic voices in the land today proclaiming the gospel of the Kingdom, we will be among the most sorrowful. We shall not escape the judgment and the reward of our disobedience. We must all seek the Lord as never before, asking Him to enlighten our darkness and enable us to rise in the power of His Spirit to conquer the flesh.

The writer of Hebrews tells us that the gospel of the New Testament far transcends the Covenant given in the Old Testament. The Gospel of grace far surpasses the message of the law in that in the Gospel of grace is the power to deliver you and to cause you to walk in the character and nature of God. That is why God judges us. His judgment is for correction to cause us to turn back to Him as our source of life.

Three Ways God Judges

There are basically three ways that God judges us:

1. For past sins.

2. As sons.

3. As servants.

The First Judgment Was for the Sins of the Past

"For Christ also hath once suffered for sins, the just for the unjust, that he might bring us to God, being put to death in the flesh, but quickened by the Spirit" (1 Pet. 3:18).

"To wit, that God was in Christ, reconciling the world unto himself, not imputing their trespasses unto them; and hath committed unto us the word of reconciliation. Now then we are ambassadors for Christ, as though God did beseech you by us: we pray you in Christ's stead, be ye reconciled to God. For he hath made him to be sin for us, who knew no sin; that we might be made the righteousness of God in him" (2 Cor. 5:19-21). It is very clear by these verses that God is not imputing sin to us, which means He is not holding us accountable. In Christ, we are made the righteousness of God.

"Who his own self bare our sins in his own body on the tree, that we, being dead to sins, should live unto righteousness: by whose stripes ye were healed" (1 Pet. 2:24).

"The next day John seeth Jesus coming unto him, and saith, Behold the Lamb of God, which taketh away the sin of the world" (John 1:29).

I often ask this question: Did Jesus really take away the sins of the world? Most Christians don't really believe that He did.

"And he is the propitiation for our sins: and not for ours only, but also for the sins of the whole world" (1 John 2:2).

"For all have sinned, and come short of the glory of God; being justified freely by his grace through the redemption that is in Christ Jesus: Whom God hath set forth to be a propitiation through faith in his blood, to declare his righteousness for the remission of sins that are past, through the forbearance of God" (Rom. 3:23-25). Romans 3:23 is used repeatedly in gospel messages and normally is read as a standalone verse, but verse 23 should never be read without verse 24. Verse 23 is not the end of the sentence, but goes on to say that all who sinned have been freely justified by His grace. This is the good news.

"All we like sheep have gone astray; we have turned every one to his own way; and the LORD hath laid on him the iniquity of us all" (Isa. 53:6). For every wrong that I have ever done, Jesus took the iniquity on Himself, and not only for my sins but also for the sins of the whole world.

"When Jesus therefore had received the vinegar, he said, It is finished: and he bowed his head, and gave up the ghost" (John 19:30). When Jesus said, "It is finished," the word "finished" meant the debt had been paid.

Strongs #5055: teleo (tel-eh'-o); from 5056; to end, i.e. complete, execute, conclude, **discharge (a debt):**

accomplish, make an end, expire, fill up, finish, go over, pay, perform. (Strongs Concordance)

As Jesus was dying, with His last breath, He said, *"The debt has been paid."*

Oh, how we need to know the depth of those words "It is finished!" Your debt has been paid. Do you have things in your life that aggravate you from time to time? Do you have problems with your temper? Do you have things in your life that just pop up once in a while that you would rather not be there? I'm telling you according to the Word of God that the debt has been paid. The judgment for your sin nature has been paid. As I have said so many times before, you need not be condemned for the nature that Adam gave to you. You need to be transformed by the Spirit of God growing in you. God has already judged the sin of the world at the cross. The sin is that carnal nature that the Apostle Paul talks about in Romans, chapter 7, that you were born with. That is the debt which has been paid in full. Everything that your carnal nature does was paid for at the cross. Although God is not condemning us for our carnality, He is judging us. A better word for judgment is "correction", because the word judgment today has a bad connotation to it. Most people relate God's judgment with a terrible wrath and anger. Correction doesn't sound so harsh; *it is,* but it doesn't make us think of anger and wrath. Because God loves us and wants us to be transformed into His likeness and image, He brings chastisement upon us.

The Penalty for Sin

If what we have been taught in the past is true about judgment, if the penalty for sin and unrepentance is eternal torment, then Jesus could not have possibly paid that price for sin, or He would have to be eternally tormented. There is something drastically wrong with the concepts we have received from the Word due to translation errors. When Jesus said, "The debt has been paid," it was like a divine eraser that erased the sin of the world. Oh, how the world needs to hear the good news of the gospel! They are not going to be judged because of the nature they received from Adam. We have been taught that God is a vengeful God and that because some have lived many years in disobedience and rejected God, He is going to pour out His vengeful wrath upon His creation. God *is* going to pour out His wrath, but His wrath is for correction and reproof and is not vindictive. We are taught that because man has inherited this antichrist nature, and because he does what his nature dictates, that God will torture him forever in unending torment. This ungodly message, more than anything else, has so distorted the image of our Father God. *It makes the cross of none effect for those who have not the will power to change and accept the religious traditions of modern day Pharisees.* God does not condemn you for acting out of your human life. It is natural for you to live from the life that Adam gave to you. God is judging you and will continue to judge you, not because of you living by the life that you inherited from Adam, but because He loves you and His judgment and correction is to get you to turn to Him.

We Are Judged As Sons

"Beloved, now are we the sons (children) *of God, and it doth not yet appear what we shall be: but we know that, when he shall appear, we shall be like him; for we shall see him as he is"* (1 John 3:2).

When you look at me, I still reflect so much of my carnal nature. I am not even close to being perfected, but *it does not yet appear what I will be.* God is doing a work in me (and in you), and one day we shall be like Him. Because of His judgments and corrections and because of His great and mighty love for us, there will come a day when He shall appear, and when He appears, we shall be like Him. That's because when He appears, He is going to appear in us. He is not only coming physically as the man Jesus our redeemer, but He will also appear in us.

We are children of God right now by position. We are children because God paid the price to redeem us. Whether a person realizes it or not, the blood of the Lamb has redeemed them. In position, we are the children of God, but we must not just settle for the knowledge of our position, we must grow up to become sons in character and in nature. That is one reason why we are judged.

"For if we would judge ourselves, we should not be judged. But when we are judged, we are chastened of the Lord, that we should not be condemned with the world" (1 Cor. 11:31-32).

To judge yourself means simply to be transparent. Don't try to hide and cover yourself up. I go to God every day with things in my life that are still carnal and not fully dealt with. We must be honest and transparent before God.

"And ye have forgotten the exhortation which speaketh unto you as unto children, My son, despise not thou the chastening of the Lord, nor faint when thou art rebuked of him: for whom the Lord loveth he chasteneth, and scourgeth every son whom he receiveth. If ye endure chastening, God dealeth with you as with sons; for what son is he whom the father chasteneth not? But if ye be without chastisement, whereof all are partakers, then are ye bastards, and not sons. Furthermore we have had fathers of our flesh which corrected us, and we gave them reverence: shall we not much rather be in subjection unto the Father of spirits, and live? For they verily for a few days chastened us after their own pleasure; but he for our profit, that we might be partakers of his holiness. Now no chastening for the present seemeth to be joyous, but grievous: nevertheless afterward it yieldeth the peaceable fruit of righteousness unto them which are exercised thereby" (Heb. 12:5-11).

You can see by these verses that God judges us as sons. If we really understood what judgment was for we would go to God daily for His correction. I want God to judge me now. I do not want to pass from this life and then realize how far I have missed God. It is much better to go to God every day and ask Him to deal with us now in whatever way it takes to correct us.

Most Christians, because they do not understand

judgment, think that the devil is their problem. Nothing could be further from the truth. I can boldly tell you that *the devil is not your problem*. We have been so blinded by some of the religious teaching we have had. We have a *tremendous* problem and it is right between our ears. It is called the mind. **Carnal nature and carnal thinking is our problem**. The devil does exactly what he was created to do. The devil is a tool in the hand of the Lord that He will use to perfect His saints. I realize this is not a traditional concept of the devil, but *he is not your problem*. The only power that the devil has over you is in your unrenewed mind. Once your mind begins to be renewed in the things of God, and you go to God daily and seek Him for His correction and reproof, seek Him to have a nature transformation on the inside of you, you will find that the devil is not the problem. Christians for years have blamed their problems on the devil outside of them, instead of taking responsibility for their actions.

I have been through some horrible chastisements in the past, thinking it was the devil trying to destroy me. There is the law of sowing and reaping that has nothing to do with the devil fighting you. *"If you sow to the flesh, you will of the flesh reap corruption"* (Gal. 6:8).

Jesus said, *"Narrow is the way that leads to life"* (Matt. 7:14). I used to think that meant that narrow is the way to go to heaven and few there be that find it. That is the traditional concept. I thought if I did good all my life that when I died I would go to heaven. However the narrow way that leads to life is referring to God's life. Jesus said, *"I am come that you might have life"* (John 10:10). The life that He refers to here is the life of the Spirit, the abundant life of the Spirit of God flowing in us. The reason that Jesus died was so that He could take away your stony heart and replace it with a heart of flesh and cause you to walk in His statutes. *"And I will put my spirit within you, and cause you to walk in my statutes, and ye shall keep my judgments, and do them"* (Ezek. 36:27). *This is why we are judged.*

"Can the Ethiopian change his skin, or the leopard his spots? Then may ye also do good, that are accustomed to do evil" (Jer. 13:23). God doesn't correct you, thinking that you're going to whip yourself into line with your carnal nature. The judgment is to get you to turn to Him, and then from His Spirit within you, you will find the strength to live for Him. When you learn to turn to Him instead of trying to get your natural carnal life to live godly, His Spirit begins to operate in you and enables the Spirit to infiltrate all the areas of your life that need transformation. This judgment has nothing to do with the natural man learning obedience. Yes, you must learn obedience, but your obedience must come from the new creation man created in Christ Jesus. *"If you through the spirit put to death the deeds of the body you shall live"* (Rom. 8:13).

Turning Your Heart to Him

If you will just spend time with God every day to get to know him, you will find yourself being transformed into **His** desire for your life. Whenever the heart turns to the Lord, the veil begins to be removed (2 Cor. 3:16). *We must learn to turn our hearts moment by moment to the Lord.* There is none of us who are so carnal that we cannot turn our hearts to Him at least a little every day.

This is why we are judged as sons. We are judged so that we will turn to God for the supply of the Spirit, not to get us to try and make new resolutions to do better. I used to say "Lord, today *I will do this and I won't do that."* That does not work. If you have been a Christian very long, you know it doesn't work. However, if you turn your heart to Him, in your seeking of Him, you will realize that the debt has been paid. I may have some things in my life that shouldn't be there, that haven't been overcome yet, but that is why He died. I cannot save myself from the works of my flesh. WE need a saviour. Just because we are Christians doesn't mean that all of a sudden we are super spiritual persons that will always be obedient to God. There are times when our flesh gets the best of us. If, on the other hand, you don't want to be obedient to God, then you are probably not born again. The Spirit probably has not yet regenerated you. However, wanting to do something does not necessarily give you the power to do it. Only God can give you the strength and power to overcome the dictates of the flesh and live according to the Spirit. That is why we must seek God. Remember that every time you seek God and contact Him in your spirit, something of His divine essence is added to your being and a killing aspect is released to your flesh. *"God is a Spirit: and they that worship him must worship him in spirit and in truth"* (John 4:24).

There is no other way to be an overcomer. We cannot be good enough in ourselves to please God and overcome the flesh. *We must contact God in spirit.* We must be transformed by the power of the indwelling Spirit of God. Even if we do have a strong natural will and can be obedient, it is to no avail. Of course, it is better to be obedient than disobedient, but in God's eyes, our obedience must be by His Spirit in our spirit, flowing into and transforming our natural life for God to be pleased. *"But we are all as an unclean thing, and all our righteousnesses are as filthy rags; and we all do fade as a leaf; and our iniquities, like the wind, have taken us away"* (Isa. 64:6). Our righteousness is anything we do from the natural man, or good man. The best we can produce for God from our natural goodness is as filthy rags.

We Are Judged As Servants

"For the Son of man shall come in the glory of his Father with his angels; and then he shall reward every man according to his works" (Matt. 16:27).

We are judged according to what we do and how we do it. Do you go to church every Sunday? Do you read your Bible every day? Are you a "Good Christian"? You may discover when God judges you that some of those things were to no avail. How could that be, you say? When God comes in judgment, He is not looking for good people, He is looking for Christ. *He is looking for His Son in you.* How much of Christ has been worked into you? If you stand in God's presence and hear Him say, "Well done thou good and faithful servant," it will be because Christ has been formed in you. You would have to fall at His feet and give Him the glory for working His life into you. In all the things that I have accomplished for God, I can never see where *I* have done anything, but I can always see the miraculous power of God that has been working in my life. I cannot personally take credit for anything. This is why if we are given a crown in the natural sense of the word, we will throw it at His feet. It is He who deserves the crown. It is God who has worked in us both the willing and the doing of His good pleasure.

We Shall Be Tried by Fire

"For other foundation can no man lay than that is laid, which is Jesus Christ. Now if any man build upon this foundation gold, silver, precious stones, wood, hay, stubble; every man's work shall be made manifest: for the day shall declare it, because it shall be revealed by fire; and the fire shall try every man's work of what sort it is. If any man's work abide which he hath built thereupon, he shall receive a reward. If any man's work shall be burned, he shall suffer loss: but he himself shall be saved; yet so as by fire" (1 Cor. 3:11-15).

The judgment here is what you used to build on the foundation and how you did it. The foundation is *"Christ in you".* When we are regenerated by the Spirit, the foundation is laid. How you build on that foundation in yourself and in others is what you will be judged for. You can build with gold, silver and precious stones, or wood, hay and stubble.

Building with wood, hay and stubble represents building with our human nature. Anyone who has studied typology will tell you that wood represents human nature. For instance, the Ark of the Covenant in the Old

Testament was a type of Christ. The Ark was made of wood overlaid with gold, signifying that Jesus was human and divine. Gold represents the divine nature.

To build on the foundation with wood simply means that we work by and with our human nature. This can be very good. We can teach Sunday school, be a missionary in Africa, give a tenth of all we receive, and write Christian books. These are all very good things, but if they are done out of our natural human effort, our works will be burned up when the fires of judgment come. Wood is consumed in the fire. An example of this is Cain's offering. He brought the best his hands could produce and offered it to God, but God rejected it. Able didn't bring anything of himself; he just brought an offering according to God's direction.

We can build with wood or gold. Gold represents divinity, the divine life. So these two items, wood and gold, represent two ways to build on the foundation of Christ. I can build by, through, and in the Spirit, or I can build with the natural human religious concept and work for God all of my life, and when judgment comes, everything will be burned up. I won't be lost, but I will go through the fire. This judgment is not just a future event; this takes place at various times in the Christian life. Many work for God for years, and then realize they did it with human effort and not by the Spirit.

Building With Gold

We must learn that everything that has lasting value and can withstand the fires of judgment is only that which we do *out of the Spirit of God within us.* ***"Except the LORD build the house, they labor in vain that build it: except the LORD keep the city, the watchman waketh but in vain"*** (Ps. 127:1). Unless it is Jesus Christ in me, by His divine life and nature flowing through my humanity, my work is in vain. It is what we do by the power of the Spirit, not by natural human resources, that will gain the Lord's favor. In the book of the Revelation, we are told that the New Jerusalem has streets of gold. Streets represent the walk and gold represents the divine nature. This simply means that those who are living in the reality of the Kingdom of God, which is the city of God, are walking in the divine nature. The New Jerusalem is to be entered into now. John said, ***"And I John saw the holy city, New Jerusalem, coming down from God out of heaven, prepared as a bride adorned for her husband. And I heard a great voice out of heaven saying, Behold, the tabernacle of God is with men, and he will dwell with them, and they shall be his people, and God himself shall be with them, and be their God"*** (Rev. 21:2-3). Christianity always puts things off in the future. There is a day coming when the New Jerusalem will be realized fully in a people, but we must begin to enter into the experience now or we will miss it in the future. If we are progressively walking in the Spirit, we are being transformed into His image and are walking at least in a degree today in the New Jerusalem.

Building With Silver

We must not only build with gold, but with silver. Silver in typology means redemption. There should not be anyone on this earth who does not know that they have been redeemed. Jesus paid the price of their redemption on the cross. There will come a day, because of our Father's heart and His love for humanity, that He will cause all to bow before Him in worship. No one should feel as though they are not redeemable in His sight, no matter how bad or corrupt they are. We should be building on the foundation with the redemption of Jesus. No matter how many times we sin and miss the mark, we must realize the silver. We have been redeemed back to God, purchased by His blood, and we belong to Him. And because we belong to Him, He will continually judge us and work in us, until one day we will stand complete in Him, giving Him all the glory and honor. His fire will one day purify everyone who comes to this earth.

We are not transformed by lighting candles, by saying long and repetitive prayers, by reading the Bible or by anything else we may do. Our redemption is based on **His work.** If we could have possibly made it into the Kingdom by our good works and human effort, then the Cross would not have been necessary. Oh, how the world needs to know that they are redeemed! The price was paid. *God was in Christ, reconciling the world unto Himself, not holding men's trespasses against them.* To build with silver means to build with redemption in mind. We are not trying to get people saved. We realize that the Blood of Jesus redeemed every person. We just need to let people know of their redemption. We are not saved by our performance. The system of Christianity is a performance-based religion. Christians are not built with redemption, but with performance. If you are good, God will bless you, if you are bad, you go to hell. How sad that the gospel of salvation for all has been reduced to a performance. If you understand redemption, you can minister to a prostitute without condemning her. You get her to understand that God loves her just the way she is and that he paid the price for her sin at Calvary. Because of that, she can turn to Him and fellowship with Him and find that her life will be transformed, not by her performance, but by His Spirit arising within her. Once God begins to grow in her, she will forsake her old way of life and begin to flow in the new. Oh, how I wish the world could have the realization of His redemption! One day all the peoples of the earth will know of this marvelous plan.

Building With Precious Stones

We build on the foundation with **gold** (the flowing of divine life), with **silver** (redemption, what he has done for you, not what you can do for Him), and with **precious stones** (the transformation of the inner man). Precious stones are precious by transformation. A natural stone has gone through a process and become precious. In the books of Genesis and the Revelation, we see a river with precious stones. The river represents the Spirit. In our spirit is the flowing of the Holy Spirit and as we continually turn our hearts toward the Spirit in our spirit, the river in us begins to flow. As the river flows from our spirit into our soul, our soul is transformed into precious stones. The natural man becomes transformed by the flowing of God's Spirit within. If you minister as a precious stone, then your ministry changes people. A true minister dispenses the life of God. We become ministers of the New Covenant, not of the letter, but of the Spirit.

As we speak or write, people are fed with the Spirit of life, and life always brings change. If you are living, you are always changing. *Dead things never change.* That says volumes about the system of Christianity. If you never advance beyond the fundamentals of Christianity, then *you are dead and not alive.* If you have been a Christian for a few years and you are the same today as when you were saved, you are not alive, but dead. To be alive means that Christ has quickened you by His Spirit and He is constantly bringing change and transformation to your life. You can only be effectual in ministry by ministering what you have experienced. *What you have experienced of God, you can minister to another.* You can go to Bible school and learn how to prepare sermons, how to market your ministry, and learn homiletics and hermeneutics, but that will not qualify you to minister life. When people feel a call of God on their life, most of them immediately fall into the trap of religion. When the Apostle Paul was called, he was taught of the Lord. Larry Hodges, in his article on the "Oxcarts" from **The Shofar Letters, issue 6, 1997, says:**

When God had summarily arrested this man, Saul of Tarshish, He did not send him to the *Bible School* at Jerusalem with its noted teachers and preachers. They undoubtedly had the credentials. They had been eyewitnesses to things others would never know unless they told them. They had personally been with Jesus for more than three years. They heard more fall from His very lips than most men of that day ever hoped to hear in their lives. They had been designated by the Lord Himself to help lay the foundations of the Church! What a wonderful opportunity for this young man, Saul of

Tarshish! A year or two under this sort of ministry and he could be trusted to be sent (of Man) any place with the gospel of the kingdom.

But God did not send His man, who was to become the apostle of apostles, to Jerusalem for instruction and training for ministry. ***"For my thoughts are not your thoughts, neither are your ways my ways, saith the LORD. For as the heavens are higher than the earth, so are my ways higher than your ways, and my thoughts than your thoughts"*** (Isaiah 55:8-9). God turns this young man toward the *desert's school of obscurity and isolation* and a crash course in intimacy with God. *There is something infinitely better than merely knowing the Bible. It is* knowing *the Bible's Author.*

"But when it pleased God, who separated me from my mother's womb, and called me by his grace, to reveal his Son in me, that I might preach him among the heathen; immediately I conferred not with flesh and blood: neither went I up to Jerusalem to them which were apostles before me; but I went into Arabia, and returned again unto Damascus. Then after three years I went up to Jerusalem to see Peter, and abode with him fifteen days. But other of the apostles saw I none, save James the Lord's brother."

This is why the apostle Paul could say he was a minister, not of the letter, but of the Spirit. He ministered by the Spirit, not from a book of prewritten sermons or learned Bible knowledge. He was ministering as a precious stone in God's Kingdom. He had the transforming power of the

Spirit of God in his life. To minister by intellectually learned knowledge is to build with wood, hay and stubble. When God comes to bring judgment, **wood, hay and stubble will be burned up.** The fire does not consume the gold, silver and precious stones.

The Ten Virgins

"Then shall the kingdom of heaven be likened unto ten virgins, which took their lamps, and went forth to meet the bridegroom. And five of them were wise, and five were foolish. They that were foolish took their lamps, and took no oil with them: but the wise took oil in their vessels with their lamps. While the bridegroom tarried, they all slumbered and slept. And at midnight there was a cry made, Behold, the bridegroom cometh; go ye out to meet him. Then all those virgins arose, and trimmed their lamps. And the foolish said unto the wise, Give us of your oil; for our lamps are gone out. But the wise answered, saying, Not so; lest there be not enough for us and you: but go ye rather to them that sell, and buy for yourselves. And while they went to buy, the bridegroom came; and they that were ready went in with him to the marriage: and the door was shut. Afterward came also the other virgins, saying, Lord, Lord, open to us. But he answered and said, Verily I say unto you, I know you not. Watch therefore, for ye know neither the day nor the hour wherein the Son of man cometh" (Matt. 25:1-13).

Here there are ten virgins. The wise had oil in their vessels. The vessel represents our soul. The lamp represents the spirit. Jesus said, *"That which is born of*

Spirit is spirit" (John 3:6). That part of you that is regenerated, quickened and made alive begins in your spirit. Proverbs 20:27 says, *"The spirit of man is the candle* (light) *of the Lord, searching all the inward parts of the belly."* The spirit of man is the lamp. When God comes to you in judgment, it is not enough just to have your spirit regenerated. God wants your whole being—spirit, soul and body—to be transformed into His likeness. First our spirit is regenerated, then our soul is to be transformed and then even our body will be made like unto His glorious body. God is processing a group of people today who will be the manifested sons of God. This is why judgment comes. And it is not just a future judgment but we are judged continually. If it was only a future judgment, then when we pass from this life, we will have it all to face then. We need to pray for God's judgment and correction in our lives now, so that when we do pass on, we will be judged as faithful and true servants. Judgment is a wonderful thing when you understand that it is for your correction and your lessons in righteousness. God's judgment comes out of His love for us.

The Wise Had Oil in Their Vessels

The wise virgins had paid the price during their daily lives to have the oil in their vessels. *"I counsel thee to buy of me gold tried in the fire, that thou mayest be rich; and white raiment, that thou mayest be clothed, and that the shame of thy nakedness do not appear; and anoint thine eyes with eyesalve, that thou mayest see. As many as I love, I rebuke and chasten: be zealous therefore, and repent"* (Rev. 3:18-19).

Our vessel (soul) represents our unrenewed mind, emotion, and will. Our mind desperately needs to be renewed. The natural (carnal) and especially the religious mind need to be renewed. In our spirit dwells the mind of Christ. This mind that is in Christ Jesus can also flow into your natural mind so that you begin to think like God thinks. As the mind of Christ begins to infiltrate your natural mind, you begin to realize first of all that you and God are one. *"He that is joined unto the Lord is one Spirit"* (1 Cor. 6:17). Everything that God is, is in our spirit waiting to flow into and saturate every fiber of our being. You begin to have true discernment between your flesh and spirit. You are never condemned, because you know the flesh will never be able to please God. Our only hope is Jesus Christ in us as the transforming power to change us into what He is. When you come out of religion you begin to see and experience true spirituality, and it is nothing like you thought it was while you remained in Babylon. In Babylon (the religious systems), you will always be condemned for not measuring up to a standard. The only standard there is for the Christian life is Jesus, and the natural man can never meet that standard. However, the Spirit of God in you will transform you totally into what He is. *We are one with God,* not in our soul (mind, emotion & will), but *in our spirit.* When we learn to contact God in our spirit is when the oil begins to flow into our vessel. We then become one with Him in our vessels. This is a life-long process, so be patient with yourself. You must learn unlimited forgiveness for yourself; *you're going to need it.*

Our natural will and emotions need to be renewed. When you begin to seek God for who He is, and He begins to grow in you, then from your spirit where the light, life, character and nature of God is, God begins to infiltrate every area of your being, transforming your soul into His image. That is having oil in your vessel. It is not that you take your natural will and try to be obedient to God. That doesn't work. We need the will of the Spirit that has been birthed within our spirit to grow up and flow into our natural will so that we become soft and pliable to do His will.

Our untamed emotions must be brought under the control of our spirit. A Christian functioning from natural emotions is what we used to call an "elevator Christian"; one day they're up; the next day they're down. One day you're full of love for someone and the next day, when they do something you don't like, your love turns sour. When someone hurts you, you feel rejection, bitterness and resentment. When the spiritual emotions begin to flow into your natural emotions, they too become transformed. You then experience what Jesus taught in Matthew 5. You can bless those that curse you and do good to those that despitefully use you.

The wise virgins had paid the price, they had judged themselves in their daily life and the spirit flowed into their vessels.

The Foolish Virgins

The foolish virgins had not enough oil in their vessels. They had not taken the time to spend in His presence to have His spirit overtake their natural man. They had been regenerated. They had oil in their lamps (spirits) but they were not transformed into His image. The foolish were told to go and buy for themselves. They still had to go and pay the price to have the oil in their vessels. Christians think that when they die they are going to go to a place called heaven and everything is going to be wonderful. There are many verses in the Bible that prove this is a false gospel. I have said many times, death has no power to change you into His likeness. You enter the Kingdom of God through much suffering and tribulation. That is because everything we are must decrease so that He increases. The majority of God's people are lazy, indifferent, and never seek God with all their hearts and then they are taught that when they die they will be changed into His likeness and everything will be wonderful. This is a devilish doctrine.

Many foolish virgins today are waiting for a rapture that is going to lift them from the earth and then they will party while the rest of mankind suffers the wrath of God. This is a grievous doctrine to the Father-heart of God. If you were raptured into His presence and you stood there in your carnality and your foolishness, His presence would be a fire that would consume you. You cannot look upon God until you are transformed into His likeness.

Some of us, when we pass from this life, may hear these very words: "You cannot come in to the wedding, you have no oil in your vessels, so now you must go and buy. Even though you have passed from the earthly plane to the spiritual plane, you still have to pay the price." You may think today that you are getting away with a lot, but when judgment comes, you will still pay the price of transformation. Praise the Lord that the foolish will still have the opportunity to buy, but they will miss the wedding feast.

Being Cast Into Outer Darkness

"His lord answered and said unto him, Thou wicked and slothful servant, thou knewest that I reap where I sowed not, and gather where I have not strawed: thou oughtest therefore to have put my money to the exchangers, and then at my coming I should have received mine own with usury. Take therefore the talent from him, and give it unto him which hath ten talents. For unto every one that hath shall be given, and he shall have abundance: but from him that hath not shall be taken away even that which he hath. And cast ye the unprofitable servant into outer darkness: there shall be weeping and gnashing of teeth" (Matt. 25:26-30).

Can you imagine hearing these words when you thought all your life you were a pretty good Christian? You have gone to church, tithed your money, maybe taught Sunday school, you have done all these things and you're looking to go to heaven and be happy ever after. Instead you hear, "Cast that unprofitable servant into outer darkness." You said no to the Lord too many times. He didn't ask you for a lot. Do you know what He asks of you? He simply asks, "Will you come unto Me?" He doesn't say come and work, come and teach Sunday school, or go to Africa. He just says, *"Come unto Me and I will not put you to work but I will rest you. Religion will work you, but I give my servants rest. When you come to Me you can learn to just rest and sit in My presence and get to know me. And I will reveal to you the inner depths of your being, your spirit, where you will find that I dwell. Then from our communion and fellowship you will begin to be like I am."* That is all He asks for. Your time given to sit in His presence and learn of Him will cause the oil of His spirit to flow from your spirit into your vessel.

"And I say unto you, That many shall come from the east and west, and shall sit down with Abraham, and Isaac, and Jacob, in the kingdom of heaven. But the children of the kingdom shall be cast out into outer darkness: there shall be weeping and gnashing of teeth" (Matt. 8:11-12).

He said this to the Jews, but the Christians of today are not much different. They think they are God's chosen people, and everyone else is going to hell. Jesus said, "Many will come from the east and west and sit in the kingdom, but the children of the kingdom will be cast out." Do you know what that meant to the Jews? To their way of thinking, they were the only people of God and everyone else was a gentile. What He said to the Jews of His day he would say to the Christians of today. "Many of the people you consider *'unsaved'* will be ushered into the Kingdom and you will be cast into outer darkness." There are people sitting in our churches today who will be cast into outer darkness, while many of the people they consider unsaved will be ushered into the Kingdom. I know that is hard to believe but it is the truth. How could a prostitute be ushered into the Kingdom and a Christian be cast into outer darkness? It is a matter of the heart. God does not require perfection; he requires honesty of heart. This is not just a future happening, but is also happening now.

Coming to the Light

Jesus said, *"He that does truth comes to the light."* God wants us to be transparent. It doesn't matter how bad we are, if we have a heart that seeks after God. No matter how many faults and hang-ups you have, if you are seeking God in your daily life, you will be ushered into His presence before someone who is self-righteous, and always goes to church, and always reads their Bible. What you only know intellectually will do you no good when judgment comes. Everything of the natural man is of no use to God. This is why the way that leads to life is so narrow (Matt. 7:14). The way to life is so narrow that nothing of our self-life can get through the gate. You cannot carry anything with you of the old carnal nature. *"He must increase, I must decrease."* Everything that we are in the natural must be transformed into the spiritual. This is a hard and fearful thing on the flesh. However, we will continue to be judged until we are fully submitted and conformed to His will.

To come to the light simply means that we need to always be transparent. Do not try to hide, as Adam did in the garden. Not only do we need to be transparent as individuals, but we also need to be transparent as a Church.

I have often shared about Alcoholics Anonymous meetings. If our churches would only be like their meetings, we could win multitudes for Christ. The alcoholics that attend those meetings are very transparent. They are not performing when they come to meetings. They do not try to be something they are not when they meet together. You can go to their meetings and no one expects you to be or do anything. You are perfectly welcome to be just who you are with no pretense. No matter how bad you are, no one tries to change you in an outward way, but they all try to help you. You can go into an Alcoholics Anonymous meeting and say, "I really blew it last night and got drunk again," and they will just forgive you and help you no matter how many times you fall back into it. If our churches would allow people to be transparent and still love them, they would find themselves ministering to many more than they are now. You wouldn't dare to come to church and say, "I fell into fornication last night." We judge each other so wrongly sometimes. Do you know that a man who falls under temptation and commits fornication is not necessarily a fornicator? A fornicator is a fornicator by lifestyle. We all have things in our life that occasionally get the best of us. What did Jesus say? *"He who is without sin let him cast the first stone"* (John 8:7). A lot of God's people are hurting because they have fallen into fornication, or their flesh has gotten the best of them in other areas and the church won't have anything to do with them. It takes the Spirit of the Living God to rise up in you before you can totally overcome in any area of the flesh.

There were some things in my life that I thought I would never overcome, but eventually, one by one, the Lord infiltrated those areas and I was set free. We cannot be transparent in our churches, because we all have to pretend to be "Holy" and righteous. We have to act religious because we don't dare let people really know some of the things that are inside of us. We don't dare let them know some of the things we suffer in the flesh. We are all in the same place, but *nobody wants to admit it.* We have to hide under the guise of a Christian code of conduct. This hiding under the religious cloak is why the children of the Kingdom will be cast into outer darkness. This is not just a future judgment. Many of God's people today have been cast into outer darkness because of hiding from the light. To be in outer darkness simply means you cannot see spiritual things. You can understand some religious things with the natural mind, but you cannot take and understand the meat of the Word. If Christ is not being formed in you, if the living water is not flowing in you, if you are just going to church and being religious, then you are in darkness.

Let God Expose Your Darkness

You must come to the light and let God expose your darkness. *"This then is the message which we have heard of him, and declare unto you, that God is light, and in him is no darkness at all. If we say that we have fellowship with him, and walk in darkness, we lie, and do not the truth: but if we walk in the light, as he is in the light, we have fellowship one with another, and the blood of Jesus Christ his Son cleanseth us from all sin"* (1 John 1:5-7).

I have, in the past, sought God in ignorance, asking Him to cause me to walk in the light, because I used to think that to walk in the light would mean that I would have no habitual sin in my life and I would be totally obedient to

God. Then one day, God revealed to me what walking in the light really means. If you are in darkness, you can't see. In a dark room, nothing is visible. However, if you turn on the light, you immediately see all things. You can see the beautiful furniture as well as the dirt in the corner.

When you are walking in the light of God, you can see all the good changes He has wrought in your life, but you can also see all the imperfections and habits that still need to be overcome. You are always humbled in the light, because no matter how much transformation has taken place in you, there are still so many unholy things about you that need the Spirit's transforming power. This is truly wonderful, because if we walk in the light, always exposed and transparent to God, the Blood of Jesus continually cleanses us from all sin, and because we are transparent, we have fellowship with one another, knowing that none of us are yet perfected, but we are cleansed by the Blood of Jesus. **Hallelujah for such a gospel!** This takes all the performing out of the gospel. We are free to be who we are and still love God and one another, knowing that He is working in us, and will continue to bring judgment to us until we are fully transformed in spirit, soul and body. Transformation is a lifelong process.

We must begin to understand that everything that comes in our life, *without exception,* is there for a reason. I know that's a hard thing to hear, but nevertheless true.

My brother, Dal Quackenbush, often comments about how I can laugh in any situation. Carol and I have gone through some terrible things, but nothing can take our joy. We know Who is in control and "know that all things work together for good". We must receive in simple faith, that God has a perfect plan and purpose for our lives and He is in control of even our adverse circumstances. The more we fight against what we think are adverse circumstances, and the more we don't realize the hand of God in it, the longer it will last.

The Wedding Garment

"Then saith he to his servants, The wedding is ready, but they which were bidden were not worthy. Go ye therefore into the highways, and as many as ye shall find, bid to the marriage. So those servants went out into the highways, and gathered together all as many as they found, both bad and good: and the wedding was furnished with guests. And when the king came in to see the guests, he saw there a man which had not on a wedding garment: And he saith unto him, Friend, how camest thou in hither not having a wedding garment? And he was speechless. Then said the king to the servants, Bind him hand and foot, and take him away, and cast him into outer darkness; there shall be weeping and gnashing of teeth" (Matt. 22:8-13).

This is an amazing parable. Those who were bidden to the wedding feast were not worthy. He is not talking here just about the Jews, but also New Testament Christianity. This is the wedding feast of the Lamb. Those who were bidden (the Christians?) were not worthy. I can hear many saying on that day, "But Lord, we received Jesus as Savior. I remember walking up an aisle and confessing it. I was told that if I confessed you, I would go to heaven and everything would be OK. I even cast out devils and healed the sick in Your name. I went to church and read my Bible." He may say, ***"Depart from me"*** (Matt. 7:23).

Those who were bidden were not worthy, so He said to go out and gather both **bad** and **good**. To the Christian mindset, this verse does not make sense. According to our concepts, the ones who were not worthy should have been the bad people, but not so. The requirement for being in the wedding feast was to have on a wedding garment. I have repeatedly said that it doesn't matter how good or how bad you are, what matters is your heart condition. There are a lot of people in the world whom Christians would call bad, who have a heart for God but have not been able to overcome the flesh. And it is mainly due to the religious traditions that have kept them in darkness and bondage. It isn't really their fault.

What Is the Wedding Garment?

"Kings' daughters were among thy honorable women: upon thy right hand did stand the queen in gold of Ophir" (Ps. 45:9).

"The king's daughter is all glorious within: her clothing is of wrought gold. She shall be brought unto the king in raiment of needlework" (Ps. 45:13-14).

In relationship to the Father, we are the daughters. In relationship to the Son, we are the Queen.

The requirement for being in the Lord's wedding feast is that you must have on a wedding garment. This wedding garment is much more than just a regeneration

225

experience. To have on a wedding garment, you are one who walks in the Kingdom of God as a living reality.

The Queen standing in gold means that she stood in the divine life of God. The daughter is all glorious within. She shall be brought to the king in raiment of needlework. Her clothing is of wrought gold

The wedding garment is both raiment (outer clothing) and needlework (inward transformation). This simply means that God is working *(stitching)* His Spirit into us. This gold *(divine life)* is being wrought into us. Wrought gold means that the gold has been beaten and formed. The Spirit is inworking His life into our inner man until we are transformed from the inside out. This is why we never need to be condemned. As we continue to seek and fellowship with the Lord in our daily life, He is continually working *(stitching)* His life into us. Again, I must stress that this is a life-long process. The Spirit of the Lord changes you day by day from glory to glory. In the eyes of religious self-righteous Christians, you may be a bad person. But they are in the dark and cannot see the working that God is doing in your life. It is a hidden work and someday it will be revealed.

To not have on a wedding garment simply means that you have not given of yourself enough in your daily life to sit in His presence and be taught of Him. You may have studied the Bible, graduated from a Bible school and may have been a pastor, but you did not sit quietly in His presence to learn and be taught by Him. It is in the stillness and quietness that we find God in reality. As long as you are continually busy, you may learn much about God, but you will not know **Him**. Most Christians only know the God of Christianity and that is a false concept of God. Their God is a God fashioned after the carnal mind of man. Most of them believe that a loving God who created them will one day allow billions of His creatures to suffer in an endless torture of a fiery hell. They believe that He would like to save all men, but He can't. They don't believe that *"All who die in Adam will be made alive in Christ"* (1 Cor. 15:22). They believe that man's will is stronger than God's will. Poor God, He wants to do so much, but His rebellious creatures won't let Him. They do not believe that *"God works all things after the counsel of His own will"* (Eph. 1:11). They do not believe that *"God was in Christ, reconciling the world unto himself, not imputing their trespasses unto them"* (2 Cor. 5:19). They do not believe that *"this is good and acceptable in the sight of God our Saviour; Who will have all men to be saved, and to come unto the knowledge of the truth"* (1 Tim. 2:3-4).

I could go on and on with the false concepts we have been taught. Those who are only taught by the letter of the Word and their religious teachers will be *"ever learning and never able to come the knowledge of the truth"* (2 Tim. 3:7). These are those who will be cast into outer darkness until they pay the price to have the oil in their vessels. I beg of you to seek God on these matters until you hear Him speak to you.

The greatest thing you can do for God is to spend time in His presence. That will afford Him the opportunity to work Himself into you.

God's Judgment Will Be Just

Most religious leaders teach us that God's judgment is not just. They would never say that, but that is what they teach. According to their concept, you can be a sinner for seventy or so years, and when you die you will suffer all eternity without any hope of escape. That would be an unjust judgment. This is taught because of Bible translators mistranslating the Word. The teaching of eternal torment **is just not true**. It was never in the original Word that was given by the Apostles.

"And whosoever shall not receive you, nor hear your words, when ye depart out of that house or city, shake off the dust of your feet. Verily I say unto you, It shall be more tolerable for the land of Sodom and Gomorrah in the day of judgment, than for that city" (Matt. 10:14-15).

"Woe unto thee, Chorazin! Woe unto thee, Bethsaida! For if the mighty works, which were done in you, had been done in Tyre and Sidon, they would have repented long ago in sackcloth and ashes. But I say unto you, It shall be more tolerable for Tyre and Sidon at the day of judgment, than for you. And thou, Capernaum, which art exalted unto heaven, shalt be brought down to hell: for if the mighty works, which have been done in thee, had been done in Sodom, it would have remained until this day. But I say unto you, That it shall be more tolerable for the land of Sodom in the day of judgment, than for thee" (Matt. 11:21-24).

Why is it that these verses on judgment are never taught

by most Bible teachers? It is because if you believe them it does away with the concept of eternal torment.

We know that Sodom was the wickedest city on the earth at that time. Yet Jesus said, if the mighty works had been in Sodom that had been done in His day, they would have long ago repented. Now God, being just, is not going to punish Sodom for their iniquity more than anyone else, when they never saw the mighty works of Jesus. Jesus said that if they had, they would have long ago repented.

"The LORD shall count, when he writeth up the people, that this man was born there. Selah" (Ps. 87:6).

This means that on the day of judgment, God is going to take into account where you were born. Were you born in India and had no teaching of Jesus the Savior? Or were you born in America, where all you heard was the religious gospel based on man's performance, not on God's love and grace? Did you reject the God of Christianity because of their religiosity and tradition? Did you reject the God of the Christian system, yet in your heart you were hungry and sought after God? Then when judgment comes, it may be more tolerable for you than for them.

"And the Lord said, Who then is that faithful and wise steward, whom his lord shall make ruler over his household, to give them their portion of meat in due season? Blessed is that servant, whom his lord when he cometh shall find so doing. Of a truth I say unto you, that he will make him ruler over all that he hath. But and if that servant say in his heart, My lord delayeth his

coming; and shall begin to beat the menservants and maidens, and to eat and drink, and to be drunken; the lord of that servant will come in a day when he looketh not for him, and at an hour when he is not aware, and will cut him in sunder, and will appoint him his portion with the unbelievers. And that servant, which knew his lord's will, and prepared not himself, neither did according to his will, shall be beaten with many stripes. But he that knew not, and did commit things worthy of stripes, shall be beaten with few stripes. For unto whomsoever much is given, of him shall be much required: and to whom men have committed much, of him they will ask the more" (Luke 12:42-48).

God is fair and just in His judgment. Did you know to do the Lord's will? Has the Lord spoken to you and you did not do what you knew He wanted you to? You will be beaten with many stripes. Again, I must say that this is not just a future judgment. If God is speaking to you right now to do certain things and you are refusing, then you are under judgment now. He will correct you, as a natural father would correct his children when they will not do what the father knows is best for them.

For the so-called sinner who doesn't know the Lord's will for their life, even though they do many things worthy of stripes, their judgment (correction) will not be as severe.

No one is condemned to an eternal torment or extinction. We all will be judged, but the judgment both now and future will be just. We will not suffer because God is vengeful and wanting to pour out His anger and wrath on us. That is a horrible concept perpetrated on us by our religious ancestors.

God's Judgment Is to Teach Righteousness

"With my soul have I desired thee in the night; yea, with my spirit within me will I seek thee early: for when thy judgments are in the earth, the inhabitants of the world will learn righteousness" (Isa. 26:9).

God's judgments will teach us righteousness. This is why I say that judgment is a wonderful thing when you understand what it produces. There will come a day, through the judgments of God, that all the inhabitants of the earth will learn righteousness. The only reason God judges us is so that we will learn to live righteously. As people begin to have revealed to them the truths of judgment, they will not be angry with God when judgment comes. They will run to Him and not away from Him. Of course, the unregenerate will not respond to God's judgment at first, but eventually they will learn of the Savior's love, and they too will submit.

Judgment by Fire

One of the ways God judges is by fire. The word "fire" in the original is "pur". We get our English words pure, purify, and purity from this word. This is also the meaning of the original word.

Almost all the teaching of the past has reserved the fires of judgment to be just for the unsaved. There is at least one passage in the King James Bible which shows that hell is not an eternal judgment and that many Christians are going to have a portion of the fiery judgment. That passage is Revelation 21:7-8: *"He that overcometh shall inherit all things; and I will be his God, and he shall be my son. But the **fearful**, and **unbelieving**, and the **abominable**, and **murderers**, and **whoremongers**, and **sorcerers**, and **idolaters**, and all **liars**, shall have their **part** in the lake which burneth with fire and brimstone: which is the second death."*

The word "part" is the Greek word "meros" (Strongs #3313). Thayer's definition is:

1) a part

a) a part due or assigned to one

b) lot, destiny

2) one of the constituent parts of a whole

a) in part, partly, in a measure, to some degree,

as respects a part, severally, individually

b) any particular, in regard to this, in this respect

These verses indicate that if you are a Christian and do not overcome all things, you will have a **part** in the lake of fire. Do you have a trace of any of the above negative things in your life? If so, you will experience the fire of God for purification.

"And now also the axe is laid unto the root of the trees:

therefore every tree which bringeth not forth good fruit is hewn down, and cast into the fire. I indeed baptize you with water unto repentance: but he that cometh after me is mightier than I, whose shoes I am not worthy to bear: he shall baptize you with the Holy Ghost, and with fire: whose fan is in his hand, and he will thoroughly purge his floor, and gather his wheat into the garner; but he will burn up the chaff with unquenchable fire" (Matt. 3:10-12).

What is the chaff? It is simply those things in our carnal nature that God needs to deal with. He will burn up the chaff with unquenchable fire.

"And of the angels he saith, Who maketh his angels spirits, and his ministers a flame of fire" (Heb. 1:7).

"For our God is a consuming fire" (Heb. 12:29).

"Behold, I will send my messenger, and he shall prepare the way before me: and the Lord, whom ye seek, shall suddenly come to his temple, even the messenger of the covenant, whom ye delight in: behold, he shall come, saith the LORD of hosts. But who may abide the day of his coming? and who shall stand when he appeareth? for he is like a refiner's fire, and like fullers' soap: and he shall sit as a refiner and purifier of silver: and he shall purify the sons of Levi, and purge them as gold and silver, that they may offer unto the LORD an offering in righteousness" (Mal. 3:1-3).

"For every one shall be salted with fire, and every sacrifice shall be salted with salt" (Mark 9:49)

"If a man abide not in me, he is cast forth as a branch, and is withered; and men gather them, and cast them into the fire, and they are burned" (John 15:6).

What God is saying here is that if you do not learn how to abide in His presence in your daily life, *you will dry up*. It does not matter how much you read the Bible or go to church, or how often you offer up your religious prayers. You must find the entrance into His presence and learn how to abide in Him. If you don't, then you will dry up, regardless of all your religious activity. He states here that if men dry up and become withered, then they are gathered and thrown into the fire. It simply means that if you don't abide in His presence, and your natural life is in control, then Jesus will not only baptize you with the Holy Spirit, but with fire. God will throw you into the fire of tribulation. God **will** burn up the chaff in your life.

"That the trial of your faith, being much more precious than of gold that perisheth, though it be tried with fire, might be found unto praise and honour and glory at the appearing of Jesus Christ" (1 Pet. 1:7).

All of us are going through the fire, but most of God's people do not recognize what it is. We keep thinking that the devil is causing all our problems. We continually focus on the devil's ability to harass us, thinking that the devil is in control, not God. With these concepts, we become devil conscious instead of God conscious. We must stop giving the devil so much attention. I know that many are going through some very hard times right now. However, the devil does not have the power to destroy that which God is doing in me. We are going through the fires of purification, but it is not caused by the devil. God will use the devil to bring judgment upon you, but it is not for your destruction, but for your salvation from rebellion and disobedience.

We need a vision that will cause us to submit to the correction of God. It was said of Jesus that He learned obedience through that which He suffered. Are we any better? The Word also says that we should be *"Looking unto Jesus the author and finisher of our faith; who for the joy that was set before him endured the cross, despising the shame, and is set down at the right hand of the throne of God"* (Heb. 12:2).

"That the trial of your faith, being much more precious than of gold that perisheth, though it be tried with fire, might be found unto praise and honour and glory at the appearing of Jesus Christ" (1 Pet. 1:7).

"I counsel thee to buy of me gold tried in the fire, that thou mayest be rich; and white raiment, that thou mayest be clothed, and that the shame of thy nakedness do not appear; and anoint thine eyes with eyesalve, that thou mayest see" (Rev. 3:18).

If we appear before Him with nothing but the natural, we will be naked and exposed and ashamed. The Apostle John tells us, *"But the anointing which ye have received of him abideth in you, and ye need not that any man teach you: but as the same anointing teacheth you of all things, and is truth, and is no lie, and even as it hath taught you, ye shall abide in him. And now, little children, abide in him; that, when he shall appear, we may have confidence, and not be ashamed before him at his coming"* (1 John 2:27-28).

Oh, how we need to seek God for a heart that hungers only after Him! As a Father, God knows what is best for us. We need to be able to say to God, *"I don't care what I have to go through, or how hot the fire of tribulations gets, God I don't care what I have to do, but on the day of judgment I want to shine forth with the glory of my Father. I want to be one who can bring the multitudes to the throne of His grace. I want to be able to touch the dead and sick and bring life and healing to a lost and dying world."*

God is raising up a people today and transforming them. He is not just gifting them, but He is bringing forth His fullness within them. When you are in their presence, you will be touched and healed, and you will know that God did it. Man will not get the glory. The fire of His presence burning in His people will cause the earth to learn righteousness.

"And out of the throne proceeded lightnings and thunderings and voices: and there were seven lamps of fire burning before the throne, which are the seven Spirits of God" (Rev. 4:5).

Once we have the revelation that *our God is a consuming fire* that burns the chaff in our life, and purifies us, we are well on the road to transformation. I know how the fire hurts, but our flesh is so strong. We need a Savior. He not only saved us from the sins of the past but He is continually saving us from the workings of our flesh. I am so glad that I experience a Savior who can reach down in my despair and disobedience and bring anything into my life that He needs to for my correction and reproof.

Father, I ask that you unveil our minds to the Father-heart of God. May Your love and Your fire burn upon the embers of our hearts. Oh God, release the fire of Your presence, baptize us in the fire that would purify us. Lord, burn out everything in our beings that is not according to Your will and purpose for our lives. Father, I thank you that, no matter what it takes, You will bring us through that narrow gate that leads to life. Father, put up the barriers that would hinder us from taking the broad way, and restrict us to the way of life. Amen.

I pray that this has helped the reader to understand somewhat the judgments of God. This by no means is a complete work on the subject, but with prayerful consideration, God will reveal to each of His seekers the truth of His correction, reproof and judgment. May we never again look at Him as an angry God just waiting to pour out His horrible tortures upon His lost and dying creation. He is judging them in righteousness to bring them fully into His plan and purposes for their lives.

Coming Out of Darkness

Chapter 9

God's Promise To The Seed

"The burden of the word of the LORD for Israel, saith the LORD, which stretcheth forth the heavens, and layeth the foundation of the earth, and formeth the spirit of man within him" (Zech. 12:1).

"But the hour cometh, and now is, when the true worshipers shall worship the Father in spirit and in truth: for the Father seeketh such to worship him. God is a Spirit: and they that worship him must worship him in spirit and in truth" (John 4:23-24).

Jesus said that to worship God you must worship Him in spirit and in truth. Another meaning for the word truth is *reality.*

We are beginning to enter in these days the Feast of Tabernacles. To experience Tabernacles in reality is to have the Spirit of the living God filling His temple, *which temple you are.*

What I was taught in the Pentecostal circles was that the Feast of Tabernacles represented the land of Canaan, a place we enter into when we die. We were taught that we experienced Passover when we were saved and Pentecost when we were baptized with the Spirit. However, to experience the Feast of Tabernacles, we were taught that we must die and go to heaven.

This is why in many Pentecostal circles today they sing songs like "When we all get to heaven, what a day of rejoicing that will be." We sing these songs because of our mindset. We have been taught that the crossing over of the Jordan river is physical death, and that we won't really be free and understand the reality of God and walk in the "Good Land" of Canaan until we die. They say that our hope is to live the best we can and then we die and go to heaven. I have met a lot of people who say they want to go to heaven but I never met anyone who wanted to die to self to go there.

Jesus taught some very simple things, such as, *"The kingdom of God cometh not with observation: Neither shall they say, Lo here! or, lo there! for, behold, the kingdom of God is within you"* (Luke 17:20-21).

The Kingdom of Heaven does not come with observation. You cannot see it just with your physical eyes. People are saying today that you need to go here or go there, God is really moving over there, and that may be true, but Jesus said, *"The kingdom of God is within you."*

To worship God in spirit, we must enter into the reality of walking *today* in the Kingdom of God. The Apostle Paul said, *"Now this I say, brethren, that flesh and blood cannot inherit the kingdom of God; neither doth corruption inherit incorruption"* (1 Cor. 15:50).

The Adamic nature cannot inherit the Kingdom of God. Those who teach that we enter heaven at death do not understand this Scripture. There is no power in death to change you and make you acceptable for heaven. Death has no power to change you into His likeness. If you pass from this earth realm today, you will still be what you are right now. Death has absolutely no power to make you into His likeness. This is why the Apostle John warned us to abide in Him so that when He appears we won't fall in shame before him at His coming. *"And now, little children, abide in him; that, when he shall appear, we may have confidence, and not be ashamed before him at his coming"* (1 John 2:28). God is *Spirit,* and He formed the *spirit* in man. The Apostle Paul tells us, *"He that is joined unto the Lord is one spirit"* (1 Cor. 6:17).

If you are joined to the Lord, if His Spirit has quickened and regenerated your spirit, you are one with God. Not in your mentality, not in your natural understanding, not in your thinking, but you are one with God in spirit. We *must* worship God in spirit and in reality.

To worship Him in reality means that you are walking in the Kingdom of God. To walk in the Spirit means that the flesh is no longer in control. To walk in the Kingdom of God today means that God is once again walking in humanity. The reality of the Kingdom is to see the life of the King come alive on the inside of your being. If Jesus isn't at least in a small measure coming forth in you, if you are not being changed into His likeness, if you are not seeing your natural, carnal human nature falling into the ground and dying, you *are not* in the Kingdom of God and neither will you go there when you pass from this earthly plane.

The Scriptures never have promises for Adam, the carnal man. The promises are made are to the *Seed*. The only promise to your carnal Adamic nature is that it will be put to death. Do not ever think that God expects you with your human intellect and understanding to become godly. He does not plan to take your carnal nature and make it into something better. The only thing your carnal nature is good for is to fall into the ground and die so that the Seed of the living Christ can come forth within you. You must understand this if you are to ever walk in the wonderful promises of the Scriptures.

The Divine Nature

"According as his divine power hath given unto us all things that pertain unto life and godliness, through the knowledge of him that hath called us to glory and virtue: whereby are given unto us exceeding great and precious promises: that by these ye might be partakers of the divine nature, having escaped the corruption that is in the world through lust" (2 Peter 1:3-4).

This is a promise to the one who has been regenerated by the Spirit of God. The promises are to the Seed. If you don't understand this, you will always be trying with your natural goodness to make your carnal nature better. God wants to expose, reveal and unveil to you that your carnal nature needs to fall into the ground and die, no matter how good it is.

Today you are living from either Adam or Christ. You are receiving your life source from one of these two natures. You may be a Christian, born again and regenerated, and still be living in Adam and not Christ. Adam can be very good. Adam can go to church and sing songs and dance, he can do all kinds of religious activity, he can have good emotional feelings, but Adam is still Adam and he cannot enter into the Kingdom of God. That is why Jesus said, "If you are going to worship me, you must worship me in spirit and truth." We cannot come into His presence with our natural goodness, or works of righteousness. We must enter into His presence *in spirit.* This simply means that we enter His presence from the Christ nature within us and not from the Adamic realm.

Blessed Are the Poor in Spirit

Jesus said, *"Blessed are the poor in spirit"* (Matt. 5:3). To be poor in spirit means that you understand your carnal nature, the goodness as well as the evil. You realize that you are so poor in being able to please God with your human living. When you look at the life that Jesus lived as an example to His followers, you hear Him teach the principles of the Kingdom in Matthew 5, 6, & 7, and sense a stirring and a longing to walk as He walked, but you know it is impossible with your human nature. Within you is a desire, a deep longing hunger to be as He taught, but you realize the hopelessness and the utter inability for you as a human to walk as God on the earth. You have that desire to be conformed in every way to His nature within you, but you feel so empty and unable to fulfill all the righteous requirements of the law. That is when you begin to discover that to worship God is not a matter of your intellect, not a matter of your good performance.

Some of us can be very good, but our goodness cannot enter into the presence of God. One of the best examples of that is Cain and Able. Cain from his natural abilities and talents tilled the ground, and I am sure that he produced some of the best crops that could be yielded. I'm sure that he brought the very best that his human hands could produce to offer to God, but God rejected his offering. For years I wondered why Cain's offering was not acceptable. It was because he tried to come to God based on his capability to please God through his natural ability and goodness.

Able just brought an offering to God and his offering was accepted. He did not do any work with his hands. Able realized he could offer nothing to God from himself. He knew he could not come to God with his natural ability and character. He understood that the offering was based on the coming Messiah, one who would come to be an offering for his sin. We cannot with our natural life be obedient and walk in all the precepts of the Law. It is wonderful that you have that desire. Anyone who has been regenerated has the Spirit of God within them and will have the heart-cry to be like He is. But unless you understand that it is *impossible* for a human to be godly, until you really understand that, you will always be a failure, because you will always be trying to make your carnal nature better, rather than letting it die.

The Religious Concept of Holiness

The past moves of holiness have, for the most part, always tried to make Adam (our natural life) better. Holiness has been taught in such a way that it has brought much bondage to God's people. We were taught that women must wear long dresses and long sleeves and not cut their hair and not chew or go to movies. The list of don'ts goes on and on. We have thought that to be holy we *must not do* certain things and we *must do* other things. We must read the Bible every day, pray, give 10% of our money, and this list also never seems to end. This concept makes us think that holiness is an outward condition.

If we clean up Adam, then like Cain, we feel worthy to enter into God's presence, not realizing that this attitude *keeps us from* entering in. This is why multitudes of God's people never experience His loving presence in their daily lives, because they are trying to enter His presence with the works of Adam (the flesh). We are always trying to make Adam better. When you understand who Adam is, you realize that he is under the Curse, he is and always will be separated from God.

Adam is the Adamic race of flesh and blood, with a carnal mentality, and separated from God. Adam will never be acceptable to God. Jesus did not go to the Cross to make Adam a better person. Jesus took Adam (the carnal nature) into death through the Cross and left him there, and even when we were dead in trespasses and sins, Jesus made us alive in our spirit with Christ. Now Christ is our new nature, and Adam is dead. We don't realize this, so we still keep trying to make Adam better, when God says he is dead. We teach our children holiness in an outward way, which brings them into bondage and causes them to rebel against the religious teachings of their parents. Holiness is not performance. Holiness has nothing to do with your natural character becoming better.

God's Concept of Holiness

Holiness is simply God Himself. If God by His Spirit is not living in you, if He is not being formed in you, if the Spirit of the living God is not flowing from you, you can never be holy. Holiness is the person of Christ living His life in you *instead* of you. Holiness is not a performance. You are either holy or you are not. Holiness is not something you can become. Holiness is wherever God is. When I first had my eyes opened to this truth, I understood that everything I had been trying to do for many years was missing the mark of holiness. I was trying to make myself obedient. I was trying to conform to the Law in an outward way.

One day, the Lord revealed to me a truth in the burning bush where God spoke to Moses. God spoke from the bush and told Moses to take off his shoes because he was on holy ground. The only reason that ground was holy was because God was there. That ground was not holy until the presence of God came upon it. Holiness is wherever God is. When you have the revelation of the Spirit of God living in you, you will then be a Holy person. You won't ever be holy in Adam, but when you see Christ in you and realize that is your true nature, you will then begin to live from that nature and you will be holy. You don't become holy in spirit, *you are holy already!* This is why Paul prayed in Ephesians 1:17-19,

"That the God of our Lord Jesus Christ, the Father of glory, may give unto you the spirit of wisdom and revelation in the knowledge of him: The eyes of your understanding being enlightened; that ye may know what is the hope of his calling, and what the riches of the glory of his inheritance in the saints, and what is the exceeding greatness of his power to us-ward who believe, according to the working of his mighty power."

Once your eyes of understanding are opened, you will never have to try to be holy. Christ in you will grow and swallow up everything of Adam until Christ is *all in all.*

If you have been regenerated, you have a desire for God. If you don't have a hunger to be like Jesus, if you do not have this desire, it doesn't matter how many times you go to church, read your Bible, or say some words. If you do not have a desire in your heart to be conformed into His image, if you have no desire to walk as He walked, if you have no desire to see your ugliness, your resentment, your bitterness, your hatred fall into the ground and die, then you might be religious, but you are not regenerated.

However, you must realize that Adam (the flesh man) cannot ever be holy. This is why the Apostle Paul said in Romans 7:14-24,

"For we know that the law is spiritual: but I am carnal, sold under sin. For that which I do I allow not: for what I would, that do I not; but what I hate, that do I. If then I do that which I would not, I consent unto the law that it is good. Now then it is no more I that do it, but sin that dwelleth in me. For I know that in me (that is, in my flesh), dwelleth no good thing: for to will is present with me; but how to perform that which is good I find not. For the good that I would I do not: but the evil which I would not, that I do. Now if I do that I would not, it is no more I that do it, but sin that dwelleth in me. I find then a law, that, when I would do

good, evil is present with me. For I delight in the law of God after the inward man: but I see another law in my members, warring against the law of my mind, and bringing me into captivity to the law of sin which is in my members. O wretched man that I am! Who shall deliver me from the body of this death?"

Saved at the Cross

Paul says the Law is spiritual but we are carnal. This is why we must learn how to touch God in our spirit. *In our flesh dwells no good thing.* We must worship God in our spirit. We delight in God, but there is a principle working in our flesh called the law of sin and death, and it brings us into bondage and captivity.

If this is your experience, then you know that you have been regenerated, or you wouldn't care about your sinful condition. I use the word regenerated instead of saved, because you were saved at the Cross of Calvary. The Apostle Paul clearly taught that we were crucified with Jesus at the Cross. At the Cross, the world, sin, the flesh and the devil were terminated. However, in our perception it is all very much alive. I have used before the illustration of a rose. If you cut a rose from a rose bush, the moment you cut it, it loses its life supply and is dead. However, in your perception the rose is still very much alive. Nevertheless, in a few days the rose will totally die. At the Cross of Calvary, Adam lost his life supply and was crucified with Jesus. When you really see that by revelation, your carnal nature will begin lose its hold on you.

You Are Made Alive in Your Spirit

When you are regenerated in your spirit, you are made alive, and then begin to experience God as your life. If you have been quickened or touched by God, you will never forget it. Everyone can remember the experience of being regenerated. When God touches and regenerates your spirit, it is the best experience of your life up to that time. His Seed within you is made alive.

From the Cross to the Throne is a long process in your experience. Time is for processing. From the time of regeneration until we are transformed into His likeness and image is a long transformation process.

The key to becoming godly is to understand that it is impossible for you to accomplish it, but like Abraham, we are able to believe God who justifies the ungodly. *"But to him that worketh not, but believeth on him that justifieth the ungodly, his faith is counted for righteousness"* Rom. 4:5).

As a Christian, for many years I had a lot of ungodly habits and traits. I had developed a lot of deep-rooted habits by the time I experienced the Lord at 29 years old. These habits did not all just fall away from me when I was regenerated. To become transformed can take a long time. However, if you get into the workings of the flesh to try to perfect the flesh, you cause yourself a lot of grief. The flesh cannot perfect the flesh. We must understand that it is God's responsibility to perfect us.

"For it is God which worketh in you both to will and to do of his good pleasure" (Phil. 2:13).

"Looking unto Jesus the author and finisher of our faith" (Heb. 12:2).

"Being confident of this very thing, that he which hath begun a good work in you will perform it until the day of Jesus Christ" (Phil. 1:6).

We must develop confidence in God's ability to perfect us according to His plan and purpose. One who has true faith in God's ability can look at all the areas in his life that need to be transformed, and realize that because of the sacrifice of Calvary, God says that I am justified. Justified means *just as if I had never sinned*. I don't have to look or feel justified, but nevertheless, because of the Cross of Calvary, God says we are justified.

"To wit, that God was in Christ, reconciling the world unto himself, not imputing their trespasses unto them; and hath committed unto us the word of reconciliation" (2 Cor. 5:19).

Almost all of Christendom knows these verses but has not really had a revelation of them. Many of the denominations today will teach you that Jesus lives in you. We have had this teaching for two thousand years, without much experience of it. In these days, we are being brought into a much greater revelation and understanding of God and His purposes than ever before. This is because the age is changing and the new age is going to usher in a people who are in the full likeness and manifestation of God. God is literally going to fill His temple, *which temple you are,* with His presence. Today, God is filling me with Himself. For 13 years, I tried desperately to be a good Christian and couldn't, but today I don't even have to try to be one.

We have had a lot of truth for years with little understanding and reality. One of my favorite verses today is, ***"Then the eyes of the blind shall be opened, and the ears of the deaf shall be unstopped. Then shall the lame man leap as an hart, and the tongue of the dumb sing: for in the wilderness shall waters break out, and streams in the desert"*** (Is. 35:5-6).

Today our eyes are being opened. It is not enough to just intellectually know the gospel. We think that because we know these things we have them. We think that because we have the knowledge that Jesus lives in us that He does, yet look at our condition. There is something drastically wrong with the church system. The condition of the system of Christianity is an indictment against the leaders of the system. This is because carnally minded men have taken the Scriptures with the natural understanding and have taught people with natural

251

concepts and reasoning. Every religion in the world, Christianity, Buddhism, Hinduism, Taoism, or any other religion, was birthed because men had a hunger and a desire for God. These religions were all started by good men hungering after God, but became polluted through the carnal mentality and understanding of men.

If Christian leaders really had a heart for God, with no selfish motives, not looking for gain, not trying to maintain their finances or promoting themselves, if they were totally unselfish, there is no way that they could do what they are doing today. There is no way according to Scripture that you can say, "I am of Paul, I am of Apollos, I am Baptist, I am Catholic, I am Pentecostal." Some today are even saying "I am of the third day." Jesus said, *"Every kingdom divided against itself is brought to desolation; and every city or house divided against itself shall not stand"* (Matt. 12:25). The religious systems of today, the Baptist, Lutheran, Pentecostal, *all of them* are falling, because they are not built on a proper foundation. They all started as a work of God, but soon unspiritual men took over the leadership and created another division in the church system.

One of the things that God says he hates is the doctrine of the Nicolaitans (Rev. 2:6). That is the doctrine of the separation between clergy and laity. God does not want a church hierarchy. His plan and purpose is not to establish a church hierarchy; that is a perversion.

There is no place in Scripture where we can find such a thing as a "senior pastor". The Apostle Paul, wherever he went, established churches and ordained elders (plural) in each city. There is no such thing in Scripture as the systematized churches we see today. That is why there is no reality in the church life. That is why they are not worshiping God in Spirit and in reality, because there is no reality in that form. The ministry gifts that Ephesians talks about is not a hierarchy. An apostle goes into an area and establishes and lays the foundation of the church life. He raises up elders and then the apostle moves on.

We have not understood in these days that the Aaronic priesthood has ended. You do not need a man today to counsel you and tell you what to do. The Melchizedek priesthood is God coming to you bringing the bread of His Word and the wine of His enjoyment.

There is a big difference between you having a desire for God and a call on your life, and you going out to perform that with the carnal understanding and mentality. That is why we have this big, ungodly, horrible whore of Christendom passing herself off as the bride of Christ. She is divisive and backbiting. You get some of the Christians of the same church group together and they will bite and devour one another, they will expose one another, all thinking they are doing God a service. They have no concept of the Father-heart of God.

What God is doing today is bigger than any

denomination. God has so many hungry people today that we can travel the length and breath of this country and have a meeting every night in a different home. Some say that because we don't meet regularly in a church building we are forsaking the assembling of ourselves together. Preachers use that Scripture to keep people in their churches. You don't have to meet in a building with a preacher and a choir. The Word simply says to not forsake the assembling of yourselves together. You need me and I need you, and we need to gather together and fellowship.

Giving and Receiving

Another item I love to discuss is giving and receiving. I have never in all my years of ministry worried about finances. I never take an offering in any of my meetings and I never sell anything. What we have is always distributed at no charge. The principle of the Kingdom is giving and receiving, not buying and selling. A servant is one who gives and receives.

The system of Christianity has not learned some of the basic principles of the Kingdom. Jesus said, *"Therefore take no thought, saying, What shall we eat? or, What shall we drink? or, Wherewithal shall we be clothed? (For after all these things do the Gentiles seek:) for your heavenly Father knoweth that ye have need of all these things"* (Matt. 6:31-32). Do not be concerned about tomorrow. God can control what we do through our finances. If God wants me to do something, I just say, "OK God." I don't have to worry about the finances if He wants me to do something. If He wants me to go to another country to preach the gospel, I don't have to do fund-raising to raise the money. If I have to raise the money by self-effort, then God is not really telling me to go. He finances what He wants me to do. Most of the money raised in Christianity is done by carnal means and methods.

We have not been taught the principles of the Kingdom, because most people think that in our day and age they won't work. When Jesus sent his disciples out, he told them to not even take a money bag with them. ***"And he called unto him the twelve, and began to send them forth by two and two; and gave them power over unclean spirits; and commanded them that they should take nothing for their journey, save a staff only; no scrip, no bread, no money in their purse"*** (Mark 6:7-8). If God sends you, He will provide. I used to say that I wanted to be like the men of faith in Hebrews. If you want to be like those men then you have to be like they were. God spoke to Abraham and he just started walking, not knowing where he was going. Will we do that today? It is very difficult.

(Note: God does not always send out His disciples with no provisions (see Luke 22:35-36). God is not limited; He does not always have to do things the same way with everyone every time. The key is to hear His voice, and to do whatever He leads you to do. You may have a genuine calling on your life, and have to wait for years before God enables you to act on it. It would be presumption to claim a verse and try to force God to do the same with you as He did for someone else. Just relax and let God lead in His own way, and don't be afraid to obey even if there is no precedent for what He tells you to do.)

Jesus also said, *"Lay not up for yourselves treasures upon earth, where moth and rust doth corrupt, and where thieves break through and steal"* (Matt. 6:19). This is another Kingdom principle. The Word of the Kingdom is not for the masses of people. When Jesus taught the principles of the Kingdom, he went up on a mountain and His disciples followed Him. There were only a few who heard the marvelous teaching of the principles of the Kingdom. Matthew 8:1 says that when he came down from the mountain, the multitudes followed Him again. The multitudes will not listen to the gospel of the Kingdom.

We quote the verse all the time, *"Seek ye first the Kingdom of God and His righteousness, and all things shall be added unto you"* (Matt. 6:33). We say that and we accept that with our natural understanding, but we live like we do not believe it. We really do not believe it or we would live like it. We just mentally assent to Scripture.

The natural mind goes absolutely crazy with Kingdom

principles. We preach a different gospel than what Jesus and His disciples taught. Jesus said, *"Love your enemies."* He said, *"Do good to those who despitefully use you."* Do you think that Jesus would tell you to love your enemies and to bless them and do good to them and then He would do something different? If you listen to the gospel that is being preached today, that is what is said. We hear a lot in Christian circles about what horrible tortures God is going to subject His creation to. They teach that God is not going to bless His enemies, but submit them to endless torment and agony. This comes from a carnal understanding of Scripture. God would never teach us to do good to our enemies and then do the opposite Himself.

God has many wonderful, precious people in the system of Christianity, however they are divided and blinded today by the system. It is not their fault that they are sitting in darkness. Every seed produces after its own kind. If you have been indoctrinated into a denominational theology, and that is all you ever know, then the denominational seed will reproduce in you. Only a revelation from God would ever cause you to seek more than you can find in the system of religion. God has placed His Seed within us, and will produce His life within us as we seek His presence above all else.

The problem with most of us is that we have mingled seed sown within us. We have the Seed of God regenerated within us, but we also have the seed of religion sown in us. We must turn away from all the religious things and seek to hear God for ourselves. The principles of the Kingdom are not to be taken in a legal way. This is not a performance. If Jesus speaks something to you, then what He speaks to you He also gives you the ability to do.

God's Purpose in Man

"The burden of the word of the LORD for Israel, saith the LORD, which stretcheth forth the heavens, and layeth the foundation of the earth, and formeth the spirit of man within him" (Zech. 12:1).

The above verse is one of the verses that reveal God's purpose for creation. There are three main items mentioned: the heavens, the earth and the spirit of man. This is a miniature picture of creation. God created the heavens and earth so that He could then create man and have a body through which to express himself on the earth. God's people have been deceived for years, thinking that the best thing for them was that they would go to a place called heaven when they die, when all the time the revelation of Scripture is that God wants to come to earth and live and be expressed in His people. God created the earth and then man, so that He could have a dwelling place. *"In whom all the building fitly framed together groweth unto an holy temple in the Lord: In whom ye also are builded together for an habitation of God through the Spirit"* (Eph. 2:21-22).

God is Spirit, His substance is Spirit, and He formed His substance in man. When God regenerates our spirit, His very substance comes alive within us. The Scriptures call it waking up. *"And that, knowing the time, that now it is high time to awake out of sleep: for now is our salvation nearer than when we believed"* (Rom. 13:11).

"Wherefore he saith, Awake thou that sleepest, and arise from the dead, and Christ shall give thee light" (Eph. 5:14). There is a sleeping giant within us that needs to awake.

There is a substance in you that is not natural. There is a substance in you that has nothing to do with the fall of Adam. Everything in your human intellect and natural understanding and interpretation is a part of the Fall. However, there is something deep within your being called spirit. The Apostle Paul says, *"He that is joined unto the Lord is one spirit"* (1 Cor. 6:17). Your spirit has been regenerated, and is the very substance of God. You were formed out of the very substance of God. His divine essence, His life and nature, is within the core of your being. That is why it is said in Revelation 14:1, *"And I looked, and, lo, a Lamb stood on the mount Sion, and with him an hundred forty and four thousand, having his Father's name written in their foreheads."*

"And they shall see his face; and his name shall be in their foreheads" (Rev. 22:4). The name represents the character. These are they who have been renewed in the

spirit of their mind. There are people of God on the earth today who are having the name of God written on their foreheads. They are being transformed into His character and nature, and are becoming the fullness of God on the earth. They are having their minds renewed to see the difference between the natural and the spiritual life. They realize that Adam must be swallowed up by the Christ within.

There is no amount of self-seeking or works that we can do to make this happen. It is a work of the Spirit within us. When we get our eyes off of Adam and onto Christ within us, then from the very center of our being arises the ascended, transcendent, Spirit of the living God. *He* begins to live in you, instead of *you.* You begin to experience what the Apostle Paul said, ***"I am crucified with Christ: nevertheless I live; yet not I, but Christ liveth in me: and the life which I now live in the flesh I live by the faith of the Son of God, who loved me, and gave himself for me"*** (Gal. 2:20).

That is the good news of the gospel. The gospel is not about what you have to do after you are saved. It is not about making the natural life better. You work out your salvation not by natural means and methods but by sitting at His feet and learning to hear His voice and then doing what He says. God wants to saturate and permeate your being with His life and nature.

If you have been quickened by the Spirit of God, He is in

you. It is not enough just to know this, you must experience it. Jesus said, *"Abide in me, and I in you. As the branch cannot bear fruit of itself, except it abide in the vine; no more can ye, except ye abide in me. I am the vine, ye are the branches: He that abideth in me, and I in him, the same bringeth forth much fruit: for without me ye can do nothing. If a man abide not in me, he is cast forth as a branch, and is withered; and men gather them, and cast them into the fire, and they are burned"* (John 15:4-6).

I spent many months seeking God as to what these verses meant. It became evident that if I learned how to abide in Him, His life and character would be produced in me. I so desperately wanted to know as a young Christian how to abide in Him. I knew that this was the answer to all my frustrations of trying to live the Christian life. If we abide in Him, we will bear much fruit. I was told that to abide in Him I *must not do* certain things and that *I must do* other things. In other words, if I kept the Law by natural means, if I could make Adam a better person, I would be abiding in Christ. Actually I would just be making Adam a better person. The Scriptures say that *"If any man is in Christ, he is a new creature"* (2 Cor. 5:17). We are a *new* creation, not an old creation made better.

Jesus said, *"I am the vine, you are the branches."* The same life, the same spiritual substance that I am, you are, not in Adam, but in Christ. In Christ you are complete. The Apostle Paul said, *"For in him dwelleth all the fulness of the Godhead bodily. And ye are complete in him, which is the head of all principality and power"* (Col. 2:9-10).

You are complete *in Him*, not in your natural personality, not in your carnal understanding, but you are complete *in Him*. He does not need processing. He is complete. The more our eyes are opened to the truth of His abiding in us, the more we will live by His life. The thing we have to discover for ourselves is how to abide in Him.

How to Know If You Are Abiding in the Vine

"I am the vine, you are the branches." If you look at a vine with branches, they are all one. The branch is connected to and a vital part of the vine. If you cut a branch from the vine, it will dry up and die. God and man are not two separate entities, they are one. You feel separated in your consciousness because of the Fall. The branch and the vine are one. The life that flows through the vine flows through the branch. So Jesus says that if we abide in Him we will bear much fruit.

Your fruit is not all the people you witness to and get saved. Your fruit is the nature and the character and the reproduction of God growing within you: love, joy, peace, longsuffering, goodness, meekness and self-control. These attributes will flow from you, and you won't have to try to be this way. The only way to know if you are abiding in Christ is by the fruit that you are producing. If you are still producing unforgiveness and bitterness, and you are still holding resentment against someone, if you are bringing accusation against a brother or sister in any form whatsoever, you are not abiding in Christ. If you are worried and in fear about tomorrow, you are not abiding in Him. These things are in Adam, not in Christ. So when these negative things come up in us, we must turn away from Adam and to Christ within us.

If you are holding resentment against someone, you can't help it, but you can make a choice to forgive them and turn to Christ for His life supply in you to swallow up all resentment. You can choose, regardless of what you are feeling. You may have rage inside of you for a person. You can look at that rage and stand against it and make a choice to forgive them and to be longsuffering with them. Your feelings may be going wild, but you can choose to turn away from those feelings and look with the eyes of faith and choose to forgive.

I may not like you in the natural, but I must make a choice, knowing that God is love and so I choose to love you. I must stand against my feelings of dislike for you. I must understand that on the Cross of Calvary every act of transgression was forgiven. Through Calvary I must see Christ in you. I have practiced this for many years, and I can testify to you that I have learned to love everyone. Through practice and application, you will begin to see with the eyes of the Spirit and experience the love of God for all of creation.

"If a man abide not in me, he is cast forth as a branch, and is withered; and men gather them, and cast them into the fire, and they are burned" (John 15:6). The first time I ever heard a message on this verse, I was told that the branches which didn't bear fruit were cast into the fire of hell for ever and ever.

It would be very good for everyone to do a study on the word fire in the Scriptures. The word fire in the original language is the word *pur,* Strong's #4442. We get our English words pure, purity, and purify from this word.

If you are a Christian and you are not abiding in the vine, if you are producing bitterness and hatefulness, criticizing one another and producing the works of the flesh, then God will throw you into the fire. He will raise up tormentors to torment you, and you will have no peace day or night until you understand that you are not to bring condemnation on anyone at any time.

"Then his lord, after that he had called him, said unto him, O thou wicked servant, I forgave thee all that debt, because thou desiredst me: shouldest not thou also have had compassion on thy fellowservant, even as I had pity on thee? And his lord was wroth, and delivered him to the tormentors, till he should pay all that was due unto him. So likewise shall my heavenly Father do also unto you, if ye from your hearts forgive not every one his brother their trespasses" (Matt. 18:32-35).

To abide in the vine is to abide in His presence. In His

presence we experience the love of God. We turn from the presence of Adam (our natural life) to Christ within. When you touch the love of God, it becomes your nature to love everyone and to believe the very best of every person. You can see all of their faults and yet realize that you love them and want to minister the love of God to them. Whenever I see someone and I have a tendency to bring judgment on them, I am immediately confronted with the Cross of Calvary.

"To wit, that God was in Christ, reconciling the world unto himself, not imputing their trespasses unto them; and hath committed unto us the word of reconciliation" (2 Cor. 5:19).

If God is not holding you accountable for your trespasses because of the Cross, then I have no right to hold you accountable either. I must continually minister to you and intercede for you, that your eyes would be opened to see that you are a spiritual being. Most of us are more natural than spiritual. We are not natural beings but spiritual beings living in a body. God will take that fallen nature into death so that you will manifest everything that He is to a lost and dying world.

The Apostle Paul said, *"What agreement hath the temple of God with idols? For ye are the temple of the living God; as God hath said, I will dwell in them, and walk in them; and I will be their God, and they shall be my people"* (2 Cor. 6:16).

When you realize that you are the dwelling place of God, you no longer criticize and condemn anyone. You do not know you are the temple of God when you display such a character. You may know it intellectually, but you have no reality of it when you are manifesting the character of Adam. The character of God being formed in you does not act unbecomingly. You may have to bring correction to someone, but it will be in love. If you are really bringing spiritual correction, your heart will be breaking for that person and you will have a burning compassion to help them and to relieve them of their wrongdoing. If you do not have that kind of an attitude, then no matter how wrong someone is, you have no right to correct them. When God's people begin to understand these things, we will have people running to our meetings, because there will be unconditional love and acceptance.

Do you know that it is not our job to change anyone? There is only one person in all of creation that can change anyone and that is God. God's leaders are not to try to control and manipulate and try to change people in an outward way. Leaders try to control what others do if they do not have the power of the Spirit of God to speak life to them. If someone is disobedient and has problems and hangups, you can minister and speak life into them. However, if you go to them and try to correct them in an outward way and try to get them to conform to what you feel is best for them, you are taking the place of the Spirit of God in their life.

There Are Two Seeds:

The Seed of the Serpent/The Seed of Christ

The Adamic life produces the seed of the serpent, which is the fallen human nature within us. The Seed of Christ produces the nature of God within us.

"And the LORD God said unto the serpent, Because thou hast done this, thou art cursed above all cattle, and above every beast of the field; upon thy belly shalt thou go, and dust shalt thou eat all the days of thy life: And I will put enmity between thee and the woman, and between thy seed and her seed; it shall bruise thy head, and thou shalt bruise his heel" (Gen. 3:14-15).

The seed of the serpent produces the fallen human consciousness which is separated from God. When Adam was created and God breathed His life into him, he was only conscious of God's life flowing within him. He was the image and expression of God on the earth. When he was lowered into the flesh realm, he felt separated from God and hid himself.

After the Fall, it is said in Genesis 5:3, *"And Adam lived an hundred and thirty years, and begat a son in his own likeness, after his image; and called his name Seth."* So all of us are born into this world in the likeness and image of Adam. We all have the serpent seed within us. I know this will not be a popular teaching for some, but Scripture bears this out. For instance, when Jesus was telling His disciples He was going to the Cross, Peter began to rebuke him, and Jesus said, ***"Get behind me, Satan!"*** He said, ***"You do not have in mind the things of God, but the things of men"*** (Mark 8:32-33). This Scripture shows that whenever we get into the natural mind and thinking, we are functioning in the satanic realm.

The seed of the serpent grows in the natural mind. This seed produces a life that is both good and evil. Living by the knowledge of good and evil is what keeps you alienated and separated from God in your consciousness. The seed of the serpent is growing in the consciousness of the masses of this world, both Christian and non-Christian. This is why the Apostle Paul said, ***"For to be carnally minded is death; but to be spiritually minded is life and peace. Because the carnal mind is enmity against God: for it is not subject to the law of God, neither indeed can be. So then they that are in the flesh cannot please God"*** (Rom. 8:6-8). They that live according to the natural mind are living according to the flesh. You cannot please God, no matter how good you make your flesh. We must be renewed in the spirit of our mind and live according to the Spirit.

Paul also said, ***"Now then it is no more I that do it, but sin that dwelleth in me. For I know that in me (that is, in my flesh), dwelleth no good thing. But I see another law in my members, warring against the law of my mind, and bringing me into captivity to the law of sin*** *which is in my members"* (Rom. 7:17-18,23).

The satanic life is one with our carnal nature. As long as we focus on the Adamic life within us, we will never overcome the flesh. The more you try to live according to good and evil, the more you become separated in your consciousness from God. We must learn to turn from the Adamic consciousness to Christ consciousness within us.

The Seed of the Serpent Produces the Antichrist

The seed of the serpent produces the carnal human nature, which is the antichrist spirit. I know this is hard for some to receive, so let's look at some Scripture.

Antichrist means one who is against Christ. The word is Strong's #500 - (an-tee'-khris-tos); from 473 and 5547; an opponent of the Messiah.

"Because the carnal mind is enmity against God: for it is not subject to the law of God, neither indeed can be. So then they that are in the flesh cannot please God" (Rom. 8:7-8).

"But the natural man receiveth not the things of the Spirit of God: for they are foolishness unto him: neither can he know them, because they are spiritually discerned" (1 Cor. 2:14).

The natural man with the carnal mind is the Adamic life and consciousness that we received at the Fall. This Adamic life is an antichrist spirit that is against the Holy

Spirit living His life in us. Antichrist is self life—the natural man with a carnal mind sitting in the temple of God (which temple you are), declaring himself to be God. Many have missed this, not realizing that the antichrist is growing in human nature, producing the tree of the knowledge of good and evil.

"Little children, it is the last time: and as ye have heard that antichrist shall come, even now are there many antichrists; whereby we know that it is the last time" (1 John 2:18).

"And every spirit that confesseth not that Jesus Christ is come in the flesh is not of God: and this is that spirit of antichrist, whereof ye have heard that it should come; and even now already is it in the world" (1 John 4:3).

"For many deceivers are entered into the world, who confess not that Jesus Christ is come in the flesh. This is a deceiver and an antichrist" (2 John 1:77).

The Seed of Christ Produces God's Nature In Us

A seed of corn contains everything that is needed to reproduce the corn kingdom. The seed of corn is "predestinated", or you might say "pre-programmed", to bring forth the corn kingdom. The seed has a program, like a computer, and in the seed is the program to reproduce the corn kingdom. You can take a seed of corn and plant it into the ground, and then you can take your Bible and try to teach it how to grow.

This is what Christendom has done for 2,000 years. We get people regenerated–the Seed of God becomes regenerated on the inside of them–and then we take out the Book, and we begin to teach the seed in the ground how to grow. For instance, we tell it that it has to go out and witness, it has to clean up its life, it has to do all sorts of things. And so we produce multitudes of people with itching ears, ever learning and never able to come to the knowledge of the truth, because the truth is not in all the intellectual understanding and knowledge that you can pull to yourself. All the teaching you need is to have a basic understanding of the basic principles of God and His Kingdom, and then seek Him.

So you put the seed in the ground, and all it needs is water (Jesus said, *"You are clean through the Word that I have spoken unto you"*) and the sun, which brings heat (God will throw you into the fire). The heat produces pressure on the seed (the shell of the outer man). The heat and the pain and the pressure of everything you are going through in this life breaks the shell of the outer man, and the Seed begins to grow.

Now you can teach me about how I am supposed to act, but if the Seed of God in me never grows, I will never, in reality, be able to walk in all of the truths that I know. But if the Seed is watered, if the Seed is nourished, and if I understand that the covenant God made is with the Seed, then I will grow to maturity. ***"And if ye be Christ's, then are ye Abraham's seed, and heirs*** *according to the promise. Now to Abraham and his seed were the promises made. He saith not, And to seeds, as of many; but as of one, And to thy Seed, which is Christ"* (Gal. 3:29,16).

God's Promise To the Seed

It is very, very critical, in what God is doing in these days, to understand the covenant. Because, although God gave Abraham a covenant, the covenant was not with Abraham, the covenant was with the Seed, Christ (Gal. 3:16), and that Seed is in you. So Gary Sigler, the natural character and makeup, the fallen being that I am, has no covenant with God. He is guaranteed that he will never under any circumstances be able to enter into the Kingdom of God or die and go to some place called heaven.

It is impossible for Adam to enter into the Kingdom. Flesh and blood cannot enter into the Kingdom of God. Adam, the fallen nature, is simply the shell of the seed that holds in captivity and presses down, due to blindness and religious tradition, the very life and substance of God that is within you. So what you need is not rules and regulations, what you need is not people telling you that now you are saved you need to keep the Law. What you need is water. And how do you get water? You get water by God coming to you bringing the bread of His Word and the wine of His enjoyment. And that may be through a teacher, it may be through a preacher, it may be through an apostolic or a prophetic anointing, or it just may be God speaking to you. But the Seed in you, that is what the covenant was made with.

You must know that you have the regenerated Seed within you. Do not settle for just the knowledge of regeneration. You must experience the quickening power of God. Your spirit will bear witness with His Spirit that you are a child of God. You get regenerated when the Spirit of God quickens you, and you cannot even explain it.

When I first realized that I was regenerated, and the presence of God filled me, I literally wept for three or four days. I couldn't believe the love, the acceptance, the preciousness of His Spirit toward me. I was a mess. And you know what? That didn't completely change me overnight.

Don't think that because you have run to an altar that everything is OK. Have you been regenerated? Have you experienced the God of Abraham, Isaac and Jacob? I can assure you that for 99% of the people, if they have experienced God, religion has shut it down, and they are no longer experiencing Him, because they are listening to the traditions of the elders and the traditions of our forefathers. And they are not producing Seed for the Kingdom, they are producing Baptists and Pentecostals and Lutherans and holiness people. They are producing seed after their own kind, but God produces Seed after

His own kind. So for God to work this in you, you must understand that God doesn't have anything for you (your carnal man).

Adam is a fallen creation, and Adam must die. There is no hope for you, in this life or the next, of escaping death to your flesh. And even Paul said that the promise was to the Seed. How can I be a failure? I have the Seed of God. God made a covenant with that Seed, and that covenant is, *"I will never leave you or forsake you."* I could take you through the Old Testament and show you that God will never, ever give up on you or on anyone else until you are fully manifesting His glory. Do you know what God's glory is? It is His nature. But you cannot manifest the glory of God through Adam. The glory of God comes through Christ. Hebrews 1:3 tells us that Christ was the brightness and the express image of the glory of God, which simply means that Christ, as Paul says, was the embodiment of God. Jesus said to His disciples, *"Have you seen me? Then you have seen the Father."*

The Debt Has Been Paid

I look at Calvary, and I really believe what Jesus said from the Cross. He said, "The debt has been paid." And then Paul says that God was in Christ, reconciling, not the Christian, not those who have run to an altar, but He is reconciling the whole world unto Himself. So at the Cross, the debt was paid for all of humanity. Now not all of humanity is experiencing that salvation. That is why we preach the good news of the gospel. We need to let them know the good news, that they have in their being the very substance of God. You may be a homosexual, you may be a prostitute, you may be one of the most despicable persons on the earth, but the Scripture says that God formed the spirit in man. John 1:9 says that Jesus was the true light that lights *every man* that comes into the world. Proverbs 20:27 tells us that ***"The spirit of man is the candle (light) of the LORD, searching all the inward parts of the belly."***

What we have out there in the Christian world is modern-day Pharisees. The best way to define religion, is man's performance. Man, in his carnal nature, trying and wanting to become godly. That is what caused the Fall in the first place. Religion will always dress and clean up the outward, and through intellectual processing, people believe they have what they think they have, but they really don't. We have Christians all over the world who believe that Jesus lives in them, yet very few actually have Him living in them in reality. We know we do intellectually, but it is not an experience.

Living In the Reality of the Kingdom

Paul gave us many illustrations of what it would be like to live in the reality of the Kingdom. One of them is that you are seated with Christ in heavenly places. We can quote that and we can say that it is such a nice Scripture, but what is the reality of it? Christ is seated at the throne, and the heavenly places are not another planet somewhere. If you are in heavenly places, then you are living out the character of God within you.

Living in the Kingdom is having the awareness of living in the Kingdom. When you are persecuted, you don't hurt for yourself, you hurt for the one persecuting you. That's Kingdom. I could tell you story after story of how I have walked through these principles. If someone is hurting you or despitefully using you, and you are walking in the realm of the Kingdom of God, you will hurt for the one who is hurting you.

If you are walking in the Kingdom and someone is coming against you and hurting you, sure it hurts, but your attitude is such that you will hurt for the one who is hurting you. That's turning the other cheek.

True Forgiveness

People do things because they don't understand. This will help you understand how Jesus, at the Cross, could look at the very men who crucified Him and say, "Father, forgive them," because He knew the Adamic race. He knew that they were only doing what they could not help doing, because they were identified with their Adamic nature. That's why He could say, "Father, they really don't know. So, forgive them." Do you think that after He said, "Father, forgive them," that they will ever be held accountable for nailing Him to a cross? They won't. It will be as if it had never been done. That's forgiveness.

Forgiveness is not forgiving someone who comes to you in repentance. Forgiveness is knowing the heart of God and that the other person is in ignorance, and they just don't understand. This is illustrated through Stephen and Paul. Paul stood and watched while Stephen was being stoned, and Stephen said, "Father, lay not this sin to their charge." Stephen understood the Kingdom. He understood that if the very men who were stoning him had the same vision and understanding that he had, if their eyes were opened as his had been, they would not be stoning him, they would be cheering him. And so he could say, "Father, forgive them."

Dying Daily

This is what God is raising up today. It is the Seed of His life. But you can't experience that until Adam dies. Paul says, "We die daily." Daily we die to our wants and needs, to what we want our spouse to be. My wife and I have been together for 30 years, and she can tell you that I have never corrected her in an outward way. I have never said, "Carol, don't do this," or "You shouldn't do that," or "You shouldn't say this." She will tell you that if she gets into the flesh, she can sense my intercession for her. She can literally feel the prayer and the covering of God over her, and she will change. That's what we need to do with one another.

Do you know what happens when you criticize someone? You are actually saying that you are better than that person. But you must understand that we are all cut from the same mold, that we all have the Adamic nature, we all have that horrible, ugly disease called sin, and it's going to manifest in all of us. We look at sin in degrees. We look at homosexuality as being horrible, and some of the other sins are minor, but what we don't understand is that the root is the same. There is no degree. The knowledge of both good and evil come from exactly the same tree. So the homosexual, in the eyes of God, is no different than someone who is very good. Neither one of them experiences the life of God.

Now, God is good, but good is not always God. Good can be a natural characteristic of Adam. The tree that Adam partook of was both good and evil, but we need to eat from the tree of life. Jesus said, *"If you eat me, you will live by me."* What does it mean to eat Jesus? We need to assimilate Him. We need to look in the Scriptures and look into all the principles that He taught, and feast upon them. We need to meditate upon them and have them consume us until we become what they are. And that only happens through death, but it is not you killing yourself. That doesn't work. But if we, through the Spirit, put to death the deeds of the flesh, we will live.

How does that happen? Paul says in Romans that if when we were enemies we were reconciled to God by the death of His Son, much more being reconciled, we shall be *saved by His life.* Not by our actions or conduct, not by our trying to walk in a certain way or use certain methods or walking the 7 Steps to Divine Healing, or any number of other things. We are only saved *by His life.*

That is why Jesus said, *"I come that you might have life, not a new set of rules and regulations. I didn't come to raise the standard of the 10 Commandments to the Sermon on the Mount. I came that you might have life, so that you might walk in and fulfill the Sermon on the Mount."* But it has to be by the Spirit. It has absolutely nothing to do with the natural makeup of Adam. Adam must die, and every time that you fellowship with the Spirit, every time that you enter into the presence of God, there is a killing aspect, a transmutation of God's Spirit that kills your flesh.

You cannot fellowship with God and not have something of His divine essence permeate you. That's why Paul said that it is day by day that we are being transformed from one degree of glory to another. It's not that today I'm a sinner and tomorrow I'm manifesting the glory of God, but it develops day by day. Day by day we have choices to make, and day by day we are being transformed into the image of God. The Seed reproduces in us the God-kind of life.

Peter said that we have received His divine life and nature (2 Peter 1:3), and we do that through the promises of God, not through self-effort. Naturally, if you hear this word, and you think, "I'm just going to go live it up," you can do that, but remember that if you abide not in

Christ, He just throws you into the fire. So don't think it's a free ride. You may be a wonderful person, but unless you have full confidence and faith, and you understand that it is only through grace and by the power of God that you will be kept as you are, there will come a day when you may fall away. And if that happens, if you don't understand that the covenant that God made is with the Seed that is within you, you will fall under condemnation, and God will turn up the fire.

God has a covenant with the Seed, to bring it into maturity, but it has nothing to do with Adam, except that Adam will fall into the ground and die. And you can do it the easy way, or the hard way. There are multitudes of verses that can substantiate what I am telling you. You were chosen in Christ before the foundation of the world, that you should be holy and without blemish before Him in love. Is that true? If it is true, if God chose you before the foundation of the world, and made a covenant with the Seed, that He would present you holy, and unblameable, and unreproveable in His sight, if that is His choice, and you were chosen and predestinated for that destination, how could that not happen?

God makes no promises your carnality.

If you believe these things, and you get into disobedience, and you believe the tradition that we have been taught for years, and you fall away, and you believe that because you have made that choice, that God can't help you, you will be in a whole lot of trouble. It is so important to understand this principle of the Seed, because God has no promises for you in your Adamic nature. The only thing I know for a surety is that Gary Sigler, that Adamic person that was born into this world and came into the Fall and was blinded, the only promise he has is of dying, and if he doesn't die, he will never experience the Kingdom of God. The only way you can truly die to the flesh is to have Christ rise up within you.

But you know what? Death always produces life. So, as much as the Spirit of God within you can bring you into death, that is how much life you will manifest in resurrection. That is what Paul meant when he said that death works in us, but life in you. If death works in me, then that produces life for you. I hope I don't sound boastful, but some of what I teach, I have never with my ears heard another human being teach in the way I do. Why is that? Because we are all unique. I didn't get this message from a book, I didn't get it from listening to tapes. I have been a hungry person for the Kingdom, but I didn't learn these principles from all the intellectual knowledge that I tried to accumulate. I learned them through revelation. That's why I say, don't take my word for it, you must have a revelation of the truth of what I teach.

Many people tell me that although they have never heard some of these things, they have the inner witness that they are true. Others say that God has spoken this to them but they were not sure they were hearing right. I can promise you that these words will germinate in your life. If you don't like this message, I feel sorry for you, because the seed has been planted. God seals people in blindness until the appropriate time. We don't like to hear that, but the Word says that *God* hardened Pharaoh's heart. Pharaoh couldn't have let the children of Israel go if he had wanted to. It is very plain in the Scriptures. God hardened Pharaoh's heart, in order that His glory might be revealed to the Israelites. So do you think that God is going to judge Pharaoh harshly for what He caused him to do? How would you have liked to have been Judas? Think about it.

The words Jesus spoke from the Cross, ***"Father, forgive them, for they know not what they do,"*** if you can hear this, were words for humanity. The debt has been paid. We really have good news. We have been *told* that the gospel is good news, but we haven't *heard* the gospel of good news. We have heard a gospel of performance. Performance-based Christianity.

Coming Out of Darkness

Chapter 10

The Revelation of Christ Within

One of the greatest needs that we have today is to have revealed to us a revelation of Christ within us. I understand that we all know that Christ is in us, and we even experience it more in these days than ever before. However, we still need a fuller, broader vision and revelation of what Christ is producing in the very center of our being. We must learn to identify with the Christ within us, rather than the Adam that is so predominantly prevailing in most of us even in this present day.

Unless we learn to not identify with Adam, and instead begin to turn and focus all our attention on Christ within, we will always be in a warfare with Adam. I don't believe that battles are won by the typical warfare consciousness that we have been taught. And we certainly know that we cannot, with Adam, crucify our flesh.

I pray that God will impart to us a revealing of the Spirit of the Word. If we can just understand some of these basic, simple truths, our lives will change forever. We can begin to have a fuller experience of turning to the resurrected spirit of Christ that we all know is within us, and we can learn not to identify with Adam.

I was taught 30 years ago that the old man was crucified with Christ. We have had that knowledge for many years. Now that is not our experience, but that is the truth, and as God unveils and reveals to us the truth that our old man *was* crucified with Him, the struggles and the warfare are pretty much over.

One glimpse of the revelation that Adam no longer has dominion over us will bring a lot of freedom to our lives. There are so many distractions in the church, and we have been taught so many things that hinder our spiritual progress, our inward journey, and one of those teachings that has really caused a lot of confusion and has caused a lot of saints a horrendous amount of difficulty is the teaching about spiritual warfare.

We have taken one or two Scriptures and built the whole concept of spiritual warfare and fighting with devils and demons. For instance, we have been taught that there are principalities and powers, that there are demons over our cities. When I first came to the Northwest, I was told that the demonic principalities and powers in the Northwest are stronger than anywhere else in the United States, and that's why there is such darkness prevailing in the Northwest. This teaching is predominant.

Have you ever attended spiritual warfare classes? I have. You are taught how to fight and how to do warfare with all these demonic influences, and I want to tell you, that is one of the greatest distractions that you can get into. The demonic influence in Christianity has been so perpetrated, that most Christians are always in a defeatist attitude, thinking that Satan is out to get them. For instance, we are taught that we must pray for our children before they go to school, we must bind all the demonic influence. We have built, in people's consciousness, a God who is so limited and so powerless that we have to constantly be on guard and be in fear that the demons will get our children.

The biggest problem with spiritual warfare is this: We get our attention on an enemy that is outside of us, and we set our goals on praying and binding, and doing all of this warfare out in the airwaves, and we totally miss the enemy that is tearing us up on the inside. Your enemies are not devils in the airwaves. In fact, your enemy is not Satan himself. Your enemy is all of those things in your natural man, such as anger, bitterness, hatred, and lust. All of those things are your enemies. And so if you are taught spiritual warfare and all of your warfare and your prayer is toward an enemy outside of you, you can imagine what happens. The only place the enemy has any jurisdiction and control is right between our ears. That's why Paul admonishes us to renew our minds.

The Treasure in the Earthen Vessel

"For God, who commanded the light to shine out of darkness, has shined in our hearts to give the light of the knowledge of the glory of God in the face of Jesus Christ. But we have this treasure in earthen vessels, that the excellency of the power may be of God, and not of us" (2 Cor7. 4:6-7).

That's a powerful statement. The treasure in the earthen vessel. I once read a statement that Watchman Nee made, and he said that there is no vessel so earthen that it cannot contain the treasure. Every one of us has the treasure, which is simply the Seed of God, and no matter how earthen we are, or no matter how earthen we see each other, we must know that in that earthen vessel is the treasure. We need to constantly minister to one another with the thought in mind of ministering to the treasure in the earthen vessel, that the power may be of God. The power to live godly is by the power of the Spirit of God. The power that we need to live the Christian life is simply the hidden treasure in the earthen vessel.

In the Seed of God is everything that you need to live godly. A friend of mine found some old seeds that had been around for a long time, but as soon as they were planted and watered, they began to grow. Some of us have had the Seed of God inside of us for many years, and we have been very religious, but we have not had a lot of spiritual growth. The moment that you begin to have an understanding of some of these simple things, that you have the treasure regardless of the earthiness of your vessel, you can then begin to learn to turn to God in the midst of any situation, and you don't have to feel like it, you just have to do it, and you will find that the more you learn to turn to the treasure in your very own being, the treasure in you will begin to shine brighter and brighter.

God Has Called Us Out of Darkness

"But you are a chosen generation, a royal priesthood, a holy nation, a peculiar people, that you should show

forth the praises of him, who has called you out of darkness into his marvelous light" (1 Peter 2:9).

We saw in the earlier passage that He has caused the light to shine out of the darkness. The very light of His presence shines out of our darkness. And He has called us out of darkness into His marvelous light. As long as we are having anything to do with Adam, we remain in the darkness. However, the moment we turn to the Spirit of Christ within, we begin to get light, we begin to sense the peace, we begin to sense the flowing of that light.

God has called us out of darkness. I started this series, *Coming Out of Darkness,* based on what Paul told the Ephesians, *"This I say therefore, and testify in the Lord, that ye henceforth walk not as other Gentiles walk, in the vanity of their mind, having the understanding darkened, being alienated from the life of God through the ignorance that is in them, because of the blindness of their heart"* (Eph. 4:17-18).

To walk in the vanity of our mind is to walk according to the Adamic nature, which is alienated from the life of God within us. Coming out of darkness is simply a matter of understanding the treasure in the earthen vessel and knowing that you, moment by moment, exercise yourself to turn away from Adam to the treasure within.

"For this cause we also since the day we heard it do not cease to pray for you, and to desire that you might be filled with the knowledge of His will, in all wisdom and spiritual understanding, that you might walk worthy of the Lord unto all pleasing, being fruitful in every good

work, and increasing in the knowledge of God, strengthened with all might, according to His glorious power unto all patience and longsuffering with joyfulness" (Col. 1:9-14).

I always love to find verses that put the responsibility and the initiation upon God. It is *His power* that causes us to be godly. It is *His power* working in us that causes us to begin to walk in holiness. *"Giving thanks unto the Father, which has made us able to be partakers of the inheritance of the saints in light"* (Col. 1:12).

There is so much in Scripture about darkness and coming out of darkness and being filled with His light. Jesus said, *"You don't light a candle and put it under a bushel"* (Matt. 5:15). I used to think that meant we had to go out and preach the gospel to everyone so that they could see our light, but no, the light of God just shines from us wherever we go. Without you ever preaching the gospel, people can sense the love of God. In a market, on the street, on the job, wherever you go, people sense the light of God.

I worked at NASA for about six years, and I used to go in about an hour before any of the other people got to work, and I never bound any devils, I never cast out any demons, I simply went there and began to release the anointing of God, the light of God. I used to walk up and down the hangar every day for about an hour, and I would just pray in the Spirit, and I can't tell you the change that took place, first in me, but then even in the people that I worked with, without me ever preaching the gospel.

"Who hath delivered us from the power of darkness, and hath translated us into the kingdom of his dear Son" (Col. 1:13). That's a powerful statement. Do we really believe it? If we have been delivered from the power of darkness, then why do these demons in the airwaves have so much power over us? How can they subdue our cities? Do you know how that can be? If you get a group of people to strongly believe in anything, do you know what's going to happen?

Whether we realize it or not, we are created in the image of God, and whatever you strongly believe in your heart and you confess with your mouth, that is going to become your experience. And if you are taught and you believe that the devil and the satanic influences have so much power over you, and you have to be in so much fear, then that is going to be your experience.

But the Scripture plainly says, *"He has delivered us from the power of darkness, and has translated us into the kingdom of his dear son."* I used to read that, and yet my experience was totally the opposite. However, I found out that believing is not faith. Believing is a choice, and when you find out the truth, you don't have to feel that it's the truth, but you can believe it and act accordingly. /***Experiencing God's Word**

I read some of these verses, that I had been translated out of the power of the darkness, and then I looked at my experience and it was totally opposite of that. I seemed to be full of all kinds of darkness. The truth is, that God, by the power of His Spirit, has quickened us, and we have been translated, transferred out of that kingdom of darkness and placed into the Kingdom of His Son. Now you can choose to believe that, or you can choose to believe your experience, and if you continually believe your experience, it will always be your experience, but if you choose to believe what the Scriptures say, and what God speaks to you, then you will experience His Word coming alive in you.

God has to speak these things to you. And if you really believe that this is God's Word, and you read or He speaks to you, *"You have been delivered from the power of the darkness,"* then faith comes in simply by choosing to believe what God has said, regardless of what you experience. You can know that your experience is a lie, and you can begin to believe, to meditate, and to walk and to talk according to what God has said. I have experienced this time and time again.

I have not, for years, had to fight a devil outside of myself. The devil gives me no problems. Absolutely none. The only problems I have are those areas in my flesh that still rise up. The only place the devil has in me is those areas in my soul that have not yet been transformed. The devil outside of you is not the problem. You overcome simply by believing and by talking to God, by confessing what God says (this is not the old name-it-and-claim-it, but in a sense it is, because what you believe, you are going to talk about, you are going to confess).

One day God said to me, "Gary, what do you believe?" I said, "Well, God, I believe you." He said, "No you don't. Listen to how you talk." I used to say, "Lord, when you come back, I know I'll still be doing this, I know I'll never change." I used to tell people that I can't do it, that I know I'll never change. He said, "You don't believe me, because if you did, you wouldn't talk like that." This is why we need to be still. You need to take the time to be still, and God will begin to speak some things to you. And so He revealed to me that if I really believed Him, I would think and talk like it.

I stopped talking negative, and without feeling it, still having the problems and some of the habits, I started talking like this: "Father, I am so thankful that you have transferred me out of the Kingdom of darkness. God, I am so thankful that the power of your Spirit is operating in my life. No, I don't see much yet, but I do believe, because belief is not a feeling; belief is a choice. Choose this day whom you will serve. It is not a feeling; it's a choice. And so I say Lord, I choose to believe your Word."

That's when He began to take me through Scripture and reveal some simple things that changed my life. We sometimes read the Word and it just kind of goes right over our head, because it is not our experience, and what is not our experience is very hard to relate to.

God Has an Inheritance In Us

The Apostle Paul says, *"We cease not to give thanks for you, making mention of you in my prayers; that the God of our Lord Jesus Christ, the Father of glory, may give unto you the spirit of wisdom and revelation in the knowledge of him: the eyes of your understanding being enlightened; that ye may know what is the hope of his calling, and what the riches of the glory of his inheritance in the saints"* (Eph. 1:16-23). What is the hope of His calling? The hope of His calling is that He might fill every area, every avenue of my thought and brain. God wants to totally possess me.

God has an inheritance in us. Paul told the Corinthians, *"You are God's husbandry."* The word husbandry actually means a farm, a place to plant and to grow things. Paul said, *"You are God's husbandry. I planted, Apollos watered."* We are simply a garden. Remember where Adam was placed in the very beginning? We are a garden within ourselves, and in our garden, God is producing all of the loveliness of His attributes. Everything that He is, He is producing from that Seed of His life. Everything is there in the Seed. It's predestinated, and it's pre-programmed to reproduce The Kingdom of God within us.

If you have a grain of corn, you can set it on a chair for 20 years, and then plant it, and it will grow. The only reason we haven't grown is that we have been fed religion rather than life. We haven't understood that we walk according to faith and not by sight. Faith is not a feeling. It will become a feeling. I have some wonderful feelings in the Spirit of God, but faith always precedes feelings. You don't always feel like something in order to make the right choices and go for it.

"And what is the exceeding greatness of his power to us-ward who believe, according to the working of his mighty power, which he wrought in Christ, when he raised him from the dead, and set him at his own right hand in the heavenly places" (Eph. 1:20).

Now again, these verses are telling us that we should know the *exceeding greatness of His power,* and it is the same power that He wrought in Christ when He raised Him from the dead. So what this is telling us is that when Jesus breathed on His disciples on the day of resurrection, and when He breathes upon us, we receive everything that He is, but it is in seed form. This is why Peter said that as newborn babes, we desire the milk of the Word, the pure nourishment of the Spirit.

"And hath put all things under his feet, and gave him to be the head over all things to the church, which is his body, the fulness of him that filleth all in all" (Eph. 1:22). I like the way the Amplified version says this. It says that the Church is His body, who fills everything, everywhere, with himself. Can you believe these verses? You can't, if you keep looking at Adam. If I look at Adam in you, I'm not going to believe these verses, but there is a real key here. We have to stay in God's presence until we see Christ in us, because until we do, we can't see Him in anyone else.

Once you really see Christ in you, and you begin to walk in that experience of Christ not only being in you, but beginning to grow up, and you begin to sense the love that He has for humanity, then everyone you look at, you can see Christ in. You can see past Adam. God never looks at Adam. God has said some of the most beautiful things to me, such as, "I don't see you where you are; I only see that which I am producing in you. I only see the garden in you that is growing all the lovely things of the Spirit." It is by His power; it is not by ours.

The Power of Christ's Spirit In Us

"For this cause I bow my knees unto the Father of our Lord Jesus Christ, of whom the whole family in heaven and earth is named, that he would grant you, according to the riches of his glory, to be strengthened with might by his Spirit in the inner man" (Eph. 3:14-16).

That's the key: *His Spirit in the inner man.* You will never experience the life of God in Adam. We have to stop identifying with that part of us that does not have anything to do with God. We must turn and look into the face of Jesus and meditate in His Word. The best thing that you can possibly do is to meditate on the words that He speaks to you. Stay in the quiet every day, and listen for His voice.

Real prayer is really a quiet, peaceful listening. God has so many things that He wants to say to you, but if you have the concept that prayer is always vocalizing your wants and your needs and your desires to God, you will waste a lot of time. The only prayer God answers is the prayer He initiates within you. There are multitudes of people who spend an hour talking to God every day, and get up and leave without ever sitting in the quiet to see if God might have something to say to them. We have had a wrong concept of prayer.

"That Christ may dwell in your hearts by faith; that ye, being rooted and grounded in love, may be able to comprehend with all saints what is the breadth, and length, and depth, and height; and to know the love of Christ, which passeth knowledge, that ye might be filled with all the fulness of God" (Eph. 3:17-19).

We are to become the fulness of Him who fills everything everywhere with himself. That's why we have to stop looking at Adam, because it does not matter how bad Adam is, if you get a hold of what God is doing in your life. If you understand that the Spirit of the resurrected Christ lives within you, and if you will begin to make the right choices, then your experience will line up with the desires in your spirit. It won't be a quick operation, it will be gradual. You will fail many times, but as you continue to forgive your mistakes and walk in the right direction, you will experience transformation.

"But we all, with open face beholding as in a glass the glory of the Lord, are changed into the same image from glory to glory, even as by the Spirit of the Lord" (2 Cor. 3:18).

"Now unto him that is able to do exceeding abundantly above all that we ask or think, according to the power

that worketh in us, unto him be glory in the church by Christ Jesus throughout all ages, world without end. Amen" (Eph. 3:20-21).

It is amazing how much emphasis, throughout the Word, is placed upon *His power within us,* His working in us, His Spirit in us. This whole deal is God's; it has nothing to do with our effort. The only thing that we can do with our self-effort is prolong the working out of what God wants to do in our lives. *We need to rest.* We are so tired of being harassed by the flesh, and we need to rest. But you can't rest as long as you are trying to make that ugly thing better. You need to rest and be quiet. *"Be still and know that I am God"* (Psalm 46:10). That is not a New Age teaching, that is the Word of God.

When we pastored a church in Oregon, we were there about three years, and we never promoted this, but there were times when we would come together as a church, and a hush, a silence, would come over us, and we would sometimes sit for 20 or 25 minutes in total silence, and it wasn't boring. Sometimes people would begin to weep or laugh. We had the presence of God in our meetings in a marvelous way.

The organization we were with eventually sold that property to a couple that came up from California, looking for a place to retire. Our church and home were on five acres of beautiful property with a nice creek running through it. These people saw the For Sale sign and stopped, and bought the place. I still had some equipment there, so after they bought the place, I went back and the man let me in to the church building to get my equipment out, and I asked him how he happened to buy the place. He told me, "The moment I stepped on the property, I began to weep, and I told my wife, 'We have to buy this place; God is here.'"

We heard that testimony time after time from people who would come into that assembly and walk onto that property. Why? Because a few people had learned the secret that Adam could not stop them from gaining God, unless they focused their attention on their failures and weaknesses. This is very difficult not to do. That's why you have to make a choice. We are at a critical time in the Church, and we need to decide whether or not God is able to work in us His will, and if He isn't, we may just as well give up. But if He is, if it is God that works in us, it is not something we have to do. His Word clearly reveals from Genesis to Revelation that He is doing a work. ***"According as he hath chosen us in him before the foundation of the world, that we should be holy and without blame before him in love"*** (Eph. 1:4).

How can that be? Because you have the Seed. His covenant is with the Seed. God had a covenant with you before you ever came to this earth, that the Seed would be brought into maturity.

"Now unto him that is able to do exceeding abundantly above all that we ask or think, according to the power that worketh in us" (Eph. 3:20). If we discover this power, if we really understand that we have been delivered from the power of darkness, and we are now in the Kingdom of His Son, you won't have to worry about demons. You won't even have to pray over your children out of fear that the devil is going to get them. I'm not saying not to pray for them, but you have to understand where I am coming from. *God is able to keep us.* God is able to keep our children. When they walk out the door, all we have to do is have a thankful heart to God. "I'm so thankful, Father, that you are guiding and directing my children." We don't have to chase demons off of them.

"For by him were all things created, that are in heaven, and that are in earth, visible and invisible, whether they be thrones, or dominions, or principalities, or powers: all things were created by him, and for him" (Col. 1:16-17).

We need to spend time meditating on these verses. **All** of the principalities and power, **all** things in heaven, **all** things in earth were created by Him and for Him. God does not have an arch-enemy. He has a tool that He uses to perfect the saints, but He doesn't have any enemies. He created all things, and all things are for Him, whether they be thrones or dominions or principalities or powers;

all things were created by Him and for Him, and He is before all things, and by Him all things consist.

Walking In Christ–Right Now

"As ye have therefore received Christ Jesus the Lord, so walk ye in him" (Col. 2:6). How did you receive Him? Walking in Him is so easy, you can't believe it if you haven't experienced it. How do you walk in God? There is only one time in which you can do that, *and that is right now,* in this present moment. Right now, in this present moment, you can live, move, and walk in the Spirit. You can't do it yesterday; you can't do it tomorrow; but you can do it right now.

This is an example of how I walk in the Spirit now. *"Father, I am so thankful, right now, that I have the blood of the covenant. I am so thankful that right now I stand in your presence without any sense of guilt, and without any sense of shame, I can come boldly right now into your presence. I don't have to look at my failures or shortcomings or habits. I don't have to look at Adam, because I have the blood of Jesus. Father, I am so thankful that even as your Word says, as far as the east is from the west, you have removed the transgressions of your people. And I believe that not only for myself, but I believe it for the human race. I so strongly believe that Jesus is the Lamb of God, that takes away the sin of the world. I am so thankful that right now, in this present moment, I can enjoy you, I can walk in you and fellowship with you. I can sense the flowing of your life."*

Right now. That's the only time you can do it. And if you fall, in the next instant you can start fellowshipping with God again. That's how easy it is. But the moment you fall, and you look at Adam, the more you concentrate on the fall, the bigger it becomes and the more it will happen. You have to stop looking at Adam. There was a time when God said to me, "Gary, stop confessing your sin to me." And I'm very well aware of Scriptures and what they say, but God said to me, *"Gary, if you really believe my Word, stop confessing your sin. I don't look at it. I don't see it. I only see the preciousness of my life that I have placed within you. And I'm going to feed you, I'm going to nourish you. Yes, I'm going to raise up the fiery trials that will bring you through, but don't continually come into my presence confessing something that has already been dealt with and put away."* I found that when I stopped confessing my failures and focusing on them, they started leaving, just like a vapor.

You see, we are fighting with a dead enemy. Adam is dead, and we don't know it. He is only alive because we, being created in the image of God, keep him alive with our belief. Whatever we believe, is real to us. That's why we have to have our minds renewed. We have to understand that at the Cross, Adam was taken into death, and the more we see that and the more we choose to walk in that direction and not look at Adam, the quicker he will fade away. You will never be able to deal with him. Please, stop it. You don't have to deal with Adam, but you do need to be very, very intimate with the Christ within.

"According to my earnest expectation, and my hope, that in nothing I shall be ashamed, but that with all boldness, as always, so now also, Christ shall be magnified in my body, whether it be life or death. For to me to live is Christ" (Phil. 1:19-20).

This wasn't just for the apostle Paul. For **you** to live is Christ. For me to walk on this earth is Christ. You have to see this for yourself. What does Christ means? Christ means "the anointing". The Spirit of God is the anointing. For me to live is the anointing of God, to be loosed in the earth. For me to live is Christ to be revealed to the world. And the more you choose to believe what God is doing, rather than your experience in Adam, the more you will experience Christ arising within you.

The people of God have been failing for 2,000 years. We have not been able to see that what Adam does is to no avail, because religion is ingrained in us; it's in our DNA. Every religion in the world was created out of man's desire to get back to God. That's why I say it doesn't matter what you believe intellectually, what matters is that you have a heart that seeks after God.

If you don't hear anything that I am saying, yet you have a heart for God, you will spend time in His presence. And as you spend time in His presence, seeking Him, He will reveal these things to you. That's why I say it doesn't matter where you are. Anywhere in the world, in any culture that you may be in, if you have a desire for God, and you cry out from the depths of your being, God will quicken His Seed within you.

I use the illustration of a man in India who has experienced God. There is a hunger for God within him, and he knows that there must be something greater than he is, so he cries out to God, and God quickens his spirit. And the same thing happens to that man in India that happens to you in the United States. This man in India has never heard the name of Jesus, and he knows nothing of our doctrines, he knows nothing of the Crucifixion, he knows nothing, but his heart cries out for God, and God meets the cry of a hungry heart.

Would you believe that God is not insulted if you don't know His name? Yet this man in India, after he meets God, he might meet a Buddhist monk, or a Hindu, and that Hindu will then introduce him to the Hindu religion. And so this man will become a very confused man, and may spend the rest of his life in the Hindu religion and never get to know the God that has quickened his spirit.

This type of thing happens in our country day after day after day. People meet the God of Abraham, Isaac, and Jacob, and they start going to church, and they are taught religion instead of following Christ by a living guidance within their very own being.

The Living Star

One of my favorite verses is 1 John 2:27, ***"But the anointing which ye have received of him abideth in you, and ye need not that any man teach you: but as the same anointing teacheth you of all things, and is truth, and is no lie."*** We haven't been taught that we don't need anything but God. Remember the story of the wise men from the east? Isn't it funny? They would have been considered Gentiles or heathen by the Jews. The wise men from the east saw the star, and came to worship Jesus. The star guided them, but when they got to Jerusalem, instead of following the star, they got into their minds, and they knew that Jerusalem was a place where His people were, so they went into Jerusalem, and that caused an awful stir. And the result of that was a horrible slaughter. But the moment the wise men left Jerusalem, the moment they left religion, the star went before them again. You can read the account in Matthew 2:1-9.

When you meet Jesus, you experience that living star. You experience a feeling that you can't explain; a living guidance has been turned on inside of you. And if you are like I was, the only thing I knew to do was to go to church, because that is what I had been taught all of my life. And the moment I went into church, I lost that living guidance, and I was fed all the doctrines, and got into the mind trip, and into gleaning all the knowledge I could get, thinking that was going to make me godly. And the moment I understood what the problem was, and I came out of all that confusion, guess what happened? The living star began to appear within me again.

A lot of people don't like this kind of teaching, but you do not need anyone to teach you. We all need to fellowship together, and it is wonderful to have teachers and listen to them, but what you need is teachers to teach you that you can hear God for yourself. I love to listen to the great teachers of today. They have and still do help me tremendously. The Kingdom teachers we have today are the best ever, but none of them are building their own kingdom. I sometimes sit for a couple of hours with J. Preston Eby's Kingdom Bible Studies and get ministered to richly. When I read the Kingdom ministers I am not fed from man's carnal theology.

You need people who can help impart to you the truth that you, just in the quietness of your meditations with God, can sense that living star. You do not need anyone but the living guidance of the living Christ. And He will guide and direct your life. We need to learn to listen to our intuition. How many times do you go to do something, maybe something very good, and you will just have that sense, *"Maybe I shouldn't."* This is your living guidance, and you can learn to be very, very precise and perceptive of that living guidance. You know, when God first started teaching me these things, I thought it was the devil, because He would reveal things to me that the church absolutely could not handle. We haven't been taught to listen.

People are so afraid today of getting into deception, because in the last days, seducing spirits will come. Listen, the only way that you can stay in deception is if you can't hear God speak to you. If you can't learn to follow and trust the anointing that is within you, you will always get into deception.

You know, it's not a matter of being deceived. For 2,000 years, most of the Church has been in deception. We are coming out of deception. We are coming out of that falling away, and we are coming into that glorious light of the wonderful gospel and manifestation of His presence within us. *God will speak to every one of us.* The most important thing that you can have is a heart that wants nothing but Him, and if you don't have it, God will give it to you.

Focusing On Christ Within

There have been times in my life when I got so tired of fighting with Adam that I just felt I didn't have a heart for God any more. I used to drive out in the desert in Lancaster, and I would say, *"God, I just don't even have a desire for you anymore. I need help."* And guess what would happen? The desire would come back.

His whole design, intent, and purpose is to fill us with Himself. The very purpose for bringing you into being was so you could be filled with His life and His character and His nature. Our world is in such a mess, and people, especially Christians, are so disappointed and so heart-sick. Multitudes of Christians have hearts that have been shipwrecked. We have something to offer them that they have never heard. We have a gospel that is so far surpassing anything that they have ever heard, that they just absolutely love the revelation of the love of God, who loved so much that He included all of creation in His redemption.

If you could only be in my office. We get phone calls and letters every day from people who are so excited, because God has been speaking these things to them. We are reaching a lot of people who have never heard this message before, and they are so excited because they can say, "We knew this was true. God had been saying some of these things, but we just couldn't believe that we had been hearing right." It is so wonderful, preaching the gospel of good news. And the only thing that is going to keep any of us from that is if we focus our attention on Adam rather than Christ.

Christ is in you. Everything that He is, all of His attributes, all of His loveliness, His kindness, His longsuffering, you have everything that He is in the Seed of His life within you. And by sitting in His presence and feasting at His table in the midst of your enemies, you will discover the greatness of His power that is in you. Paul said that the same power that resurrected Christ from among the dead dwells within us. *"If the spirit of him that raised Jesus from the dead dwell in us, he that raised Christ from the dead shall also quicken our mortal bodies"* (Rom. 8:11).

Begin to focus on Christ within. If you try sitting in the quiet and you fall asleep, so what? Keep doing it. God will deal with you in your sleep. The main thing is that our heart's desire is to know Him.

If there was any advice that I could give anyone, it would be to learn to sit in the quiet. Sing songs to Him, worship Him, but by all means, sit in the quiet, and just see if He doesn't start speaking to you. And you know what? Here is a real key: In His speaking is the ability to do that which He speaks.

Several times, my wife and I have experienced hearing Him and doing the impossible, yet having Him meet our needs. When He speaks to you, in His speaking, His authority, His power, and even His willingness are imparted to you, to do that which He wants you to do.

Everything hinges upon you hearing God. Many people tell me that they have never heard God speak. They may have been a Christian for 40, 50, or 60 years, and never heard God speak. How do you hear God speak? The number one thing is time. We have to have time in our busy schedules to worship God and to listen to what He has to say.

I often feel sorry for people who get caught up in spiritual warfare, because the more you do it, the more real it becomes. I took a spiritual warfare class, and I have literally fought demons. I'm not saying that there is no such thing. I know what it is like to get into spiritual warfare, but I also know that it is not necessary, because there is no demon in hell that has any power or authority over God's children. None. But because we believe they do, and even get into combat with them, they become a distraction. There is no such thing as demonic power overpowering God's people. Not if the Scriptures are true. Not if we have been taken out the kingdom of darkness and placed into the Kingdom of light, in the Kingdom of His Son. If that has truly happened, then we are not under the authority of any demon, and neither can any demon harass us.

If we are having problems, we can't blame it on the devil. It doesn't work. The problem is right between our ears. That's the only problem we have. And that's why we need the Scriptures. We need the time in worship, and we need to hear God speak. That will renew the mind.

I used to get up every morning, thinking, "Oh God, another day to live in defeat and failure." And now I get up in the morning and I don't even think about it. I don't even think about trying to live godly today, it's totally effortless. Am I perfect? No. Do I still have problems? Absolutely. Do I still sin? Yes I do, but I never get up in the morning with a consciousness of "Oh God, another day of failure."

It is wonderful to get up with the awareness that God in you is sufficient to meet anything that comes your way in the day, and we can only have that as we begin to focus on Christ within. Take the time to discover the treasure that is in your earthen vessel, and you will find that He is really there, and He will absolutely fill every area, every avenue of our thought and brain. Every cell of our body is being permeated with the Spirit, and when that happens totally, Christ will appear within us. Hallelujah!

Coming Out of Darkness

Chapter 11

God's Concept of Reconciliation

I have heard it asked by many recently why no one has done a message on the basics of reconciliation. I was surprised to find out that there has not much been much spoken about it that I could find, even among the Kingdom speakers. It is woven all through their messages, but there is no single message that covers the basic concept. I do not want to reinvent the wheel in sharing this, especially in book format, because there have been a lot of deep writings about the subject already, but I feel that a simple explanation of the topic would be helpful to many people who are genuinely seeking the heart of God on this matter. This chapter came from a spoken message that was given in Colville, Washington, in July of 1998.

The Present Day Religious System

Before I get into the subject of reconciliation, I want to share a few things about the condition of the present day religious system. It is very hard for some to hear about the magnificent all-inclusive love of Father towards His creation, because of what we have been taught in the past. I beg of you to prayerfully consider what is here presented as God's eternal plan and purpose for all of creation. If you are steeped in the "traditions of the elders", you *must* look deep into your heart and spirit to sense the utter joy of God's wonderful love. Your mind may tell you, because of what you have learned in the past, "No way could this be true," but your spirit will bear witness with His Spirit. Listen with your heart and not your head.

The religious system of today is mostly one of performance and entertainment. We go to a building that we call a "church" and sit down and get entertained, both by music and preaching. Some of it touches our emotions somewhat, but there is almost no impartation of the Spirit to bring change to our lives.

If there is anything that we need today, it is to be ushered into the presence of our God. We need the power of the Spirit in our gatherings that will carry us into His presence. And you know, where that takes place you really see church meetings.

The Old Testament type of this is the working of the good land. Are we not the precious land of Christ, in which His seed has been planted? In our land grow all of the beautiful aspects of the Spirit of God. We must enter into His presence on a daily basis and learn to feast at His table. Then when we come together we bring that which we have worked in our land and we present it to one another.

David said many years ago, *"My heart overflows with a goodly matter; I speak of the things which I have made touching the king: my tongue is the pen of a ready writer"* (Ps. 45:1). When we practice the presence of God in our daily lives, this verse becomes our experience. When we come together, our tongues become the pen of a ready writer. Oh, that we could get the people of God to understand these concepts!

Religious meetings, as most people know them today, are absolutely unscriptural. There is no place in the Bible where you can find a senior pastor or an associate pastor. We recently visited a church where they had a senior pastor, an associate senior pastor, and then some associate pastors. It's so sad! After two thousand years of going to religious meetings, look at what we have produced. I've seen large religious organizations of five and ten thousand people that have been built upon a personality. When that personality, for one reason or another, resigns or goes somewhere else, after ten or fifteen years they have not reproduced themselves in someone else who can step into their shoes and continue the ministry.

The very fact that someone can sit under your ministry for years and you not reproduce Christ in them is an indictment against your ministry. We as ministers are responsible to minister life to the saints and cause the seed of Christ in them to reproduce sons of God.

The concept of God that has been given to us through the system of Christianity and other religions of the world is very sad indeed. In their teaching is a God who unconditionally loves His creation and desires to save them but eventually will lose the majority of them to endless suffering in eternal torment.

A lot of people ask me, "What are you?" I'm not a Baptist. I'm not a Catholic. I'm not a Lutheran or Pentecostal, and I'm definitely not a Christian, according to their understanding of what a Christian is. *I am simply a member of the Body of Christ.* I know that's confusing to a lot of people, but I don't want to be associated with a false image of what God is. Don't tell me about the love of God and then display to me what I see in religion. Don't tell me that God teaches, "Love your enemies, do good to them who despitefully use you. Bless them who curse you," and then tell me that He is going to leave endless numbers of people in agony for eternity in hell. I don't know that kind of a God.

I know a God who reaches down into the very depths of my despair. I know a Father who loves me so deeply that I can turn my back on Him—and I've done it. I can look at Him and say, "Enough, I can't take it any more! I can't take the pressures! I can't take the rejection! I can't take it!" and I can turn and walk away and He just says, "Gary, it's too late. I'm looking for an inheritance. And, to be honest with you Gary, it really doesn't matter how you feel. I have an investment in you. I have placed the very seed of My Life within you."

"Listen to this My people, I have placed the very seed of My Life within you. Everything that I AM, everything that you desire in your heart of hearts, everything that you could possibly imagine that I can do through you, is in the Seed of Life that I AM—hidden deep within the consciousness of who you are.

"Can I forsake Myself? Can I forsake that of Myself that I have placed within you? Think not that I have come to destroy you. Oh yes, I have come to destroy that false concept of yourself. I've come to destroy that Adamic nature—that false sense of a self life that causes you to feel separated from my presence. That was destroyed at Calvary. Some of the sweetest words in the universe are that death produces life. That which dies brings forth life. There is a very hard shell around the seed of My Life that's within you. That hard shell is simply the Adamic life. Oh, I speak to the seed. Can you not hear? Can you not sit in the quiet and listen and hear Me speak to you?"

We Will All Experience Death to Adam

I guarantee you that all of us will experience death— death to the Adamic life. You may not want it. You may fight it. You may have given up, as I have in the past, saying that it's too hard and I can't make it; however, I know a God who is big enough and loves you enough that He will perfect that which concerns you. I don't know a God who is not able to finish that which He has started.

Too long have our Christian leaders and teachers taught us our responsibility as believers. I have no responsibility as a believer to perform. *He* is responsible to perfect that which concerns me. It is not my responsibility to make Gary godly. I tried.

I often say to people now when they come to me in such despair and despondency, "You don't have to worry about it." I know that it's hard. Death is not an easy process. Death is horrible, but death produces life. You see, what makes it so horrible is when you feel like you have to perfect that which God is trying to kill. You try to keep it alive. You try to make it holy. You're reading ten chapters of Scripture a day. You're praying for an hour or more each day. You're doing everything possible to make that ungodly thing holy, and you can't. Give it up! Adam will never be holy. He was crucified at the Cross.

We've had 2,000 years of performance-based Christianity. If you believe right—run to an altar—say it right—do it right—you're going to go to heaven when you die.

In the consciousness of most Christians is the idea that heaven is a place to go to when you die. There is not one verse anywhere that says that when you die you're going to heaven. Heaven is not out there somewhere on a planet waiting for you to die to get there. Saints, if you die right now, you'll simply cross over from one dimension to another, and you'll be no different. Don't think that dying perfects you and that when you die everything is okay. Don't be deceived.

Our concept of death is wrong. Death is not when your body falls down and is put into a grave. Death is being separated in your awareness and consciousness from the presence of God. Millions of people are walking around in bodies, but they are dead. When your body dies, it is simply a crossing over from one realm of life to another. Whether you're a Christian today or not, if you're full of lust, resentment, hatefulness, bitterness, and division, death is not going to change that. That's why the Apostle John said, ***"And now, little children, abide in him; that, when he shall appear, we may have confidence, and not be ashamed before him at his coming"*** (1 John 2:28).

Death has absolutely no power to change you. All the Christian teachings and principles in the world have no power to change you. There is only one thing that will change you and it's called impartation. Only God, through His Spirit, can impart Himself unto you. You can be a Christian for 90 years, and without the impartation, without the transforming power of His Spirit, you'll be no different when your body falls over than you are today. Again, look at the situation after two thousand years of religious teaching.

Christianity The Jewish Religion with a Face Lift

When I heard about the Baptism of the Holy Ghost, I thought that it was the answer. I was told that if you receive the Holy Spirit and speak in tongues, it gives you the power to live the Christian life. I ran to find someone who could help me receive the baptism. Again, I was disappointed. Not in the experience—I had a wonderful, marvelous revelation of God when I was baptized in the Holy Spirit. And, indeed, imparted into me *was* the power to live the life—*but, I didn't come out of religion.* Religion began to tell me that now you have the Holy Spirit you can't do this and you can't do that, you have to walk like this. So, I never learned to rely on and tap into that resource of His Spirit that was within me. All that was given were concepts of what I (Adam) must do, and how I must perform so that I can be blessed.

Christianity has only taken the Jewish religion of the Law and the prophets and put a new face on it. It is still for the most part a Jewish religion that has been made to look a little bit better. We have never been given a true concept of a God who loves us and will live His life in us, instead of our trying to make our Adamic life godlier.

You can try to put the responsibility on Adam (the carnal nature) to live godly, but he can't do it! You say, "But Jesus said that He came to fulfill the Law." Indeed He did, and today I am living by the grace of God. I am experiencing the fulfilling of that Law flowing from the very essence of my being that has absolutely nothing to do with my natural character, the Adamic life.

There is such a clear division between the spirit and the flesh in my consciousness in these days. Why is that? I quit performing. There came a day when I said, "God, I can't perform any more. I can't do it." I quit listening to preachers and I quit going to religious meetings where my ears were polluted and I began to listen to God.

Christianity's False Image of God

Most Christians worship a false image of God given to them by the religious systems of our day.

What is an idol? An idol is a false image of God, whether it's something you carve out of wood or stone or whether you carve it out of your imagination. An idol is something that you worship that is not really God. You may think it is. You may be convinced that it is. You will worship God as you perceive Him, even if it is a false image. That's why I don't want to be called a Christian. I cannot accept the false image of the God of today's Christianity, yet Christ lives in me. I experience the love of God for all of His creation. I don't have to try, in order to love you. Nobody has to teach me to love you. God is love, and when we experience His life in us, we love as He loves.

Religion tells people that God is love, and then begins to teach them that they have to love one another, yet inside they may be full of rage. We've never been taught how to deal with these feelings. All we know is what we're supposed to do, but when we can't do it, we come under condemnation.

There are multitudes of Christians on the scrap heap because they have never understood the love of God which surpasses all. They've never understood the simple basic concepts of the teachings of godliness, one of these being, *"Jesus is the author and finisher of our faith"* (Heb. 12:2). Do you believe that? You may say, "Well, yes I believe that He's the author, but I have certain responsibilities . . ." With that concept, you do not have the assurance that Jesus can perfect in you that which He designed to do.

If you take on the false responsibility of making Adam

perform in the likeness of God, you have just replaced godliness with the serpent's lie. Whenever the serpent nature—the Adamic nature—tries to perform and tries to make himself godly, he causes you to walk into the abomination of desolation, which is self trying to become like God—the Adamic nature sitting in the temple of God trying to make himself God. For the most part, the teachings I hear in Christianity are on how to make Adam more like Christ. Now, they're not said in that way, but that is the message we receive. Whenever you listen to teachings that make you feel responsible to perfect that in you which God began, you are making a big mistake. You're in for a lot of hurt, a lot of disappointment, and a lot of condemnation. Adam cannot make himself like God. *This is the abomination of desolation.*

The Seed of God Needs Nourishment

You don't have to make yourself like God. When you begin to see as God sees, you can look into the eyes of all humanity and see the treasure in the earthen vessel. As Watchman Nee said many years ago, *"There is no vessel that is so earthy that it does not contain the Treasure."* You have the Treasure. However, when you try to walk out the Christian life by performance, you miss the Treasure. You bury it under the Adamic consciousness.

Do you think you have to teach Christ how to grow? Yet,

that's what we do! If you take a seed of corn and plant it into the ground and water it, then do you need to get the book out and try to teach that seed how to grow? No, yet that is exactly what we've done. We take baby Christians as soon as they are regenerated and we start getting them into works, saying, "Now, if you really want to grow in Christ, you need to go out into the streets and witness. You need to read ten chapters a day in the Bible, and you need to pray an hour a day." We get them into works, never allowing them time to rest, never allowing them time to just soak in the presence of God. You see, most teachers do not trust the Spirit of God in their followers. If they did, they wouldn't have to try to teach them about all of the things that *they* have to do.

A seed does not need teaching. A seed needs water. What causes the seed in you to grow? There are several things. One is teaching, of course, but not just intellectual knowledge. A true minister can impart to you the very words of the Living God. The word of God, flowing from their lips, coming from the Spirit and Presence of God, can transfuse into the hearer and make those words come alive. We need teachers who can speak to the seed and *cause* it to grow—not just teach it *how* to grow!

I am so tired of religious teachings. I don't want to just teach—what I want to do is worship. When we worship, or are with folks who worship, and we get into that atmosphere and are drawn into the presence of God, we then begin to share one to another, and our church meetings come alive. God has jewels everywhere, all around us. You don't need someone who is a "preacher" to drive for hours to teach you something. God has treasures right among us. Because we have the concept of a one-man ministry, we miss hearing from those around us who have much to share concerning their fellowship with the Lord.

The Ministry of Reconciliation

I believe that the price that Jesus paid on the cross of Calvary is big enough and all-inclusive enough to bring all of creation to their knees—not by force, but to bring all of creation to the place where they voluntarily give glory to God for who He is. I believe that with all my heart.

The Bible starts in the very beginning to teach reconciliation. You know how it is, when you see a truth in the Scriptures, you can find it everywhere from Genesis to Revelation. This revelation on the reconciliation of all of humanity you can find in both the Old and New Testaments. In fact, we have a book that lists over 600 verses that have to do with God restoring all of creation back to Himself. The Scriptures are absolutely full of it.

Let's begin at Colossians 1:19-20, *"For it pleased the Father that in Him should all fullness dwell; and, having made peace through the blood of His cross, by Him to reconcile all things unto Himself; by Him, I say, whether they are things in earth, or things in heaven."* Notice the two words "all things", not just "some things". Not just the things on the earth, but all things—both in heaven and on earth.

"Wherefore remember, that you being in time past Gentiles in the flesh, who are called uncircumcision, by that which is called the circumcision in the flesh made by hands, that at that time you were without Christ, being aliens from the commonwealth of Israel, strangers from the covenants of promise, having no hope, and without God in the world. But now, in Christ Jesus, you who sometimes were far off are made nigh by the blood of Christ. For He is our peace who has made both one (the context of this is the Jew and the Gentile, the saved and the unsaved), *and have broken down the middle wall of partition between us; having abolished in His flesh the enmity, even the law of commandments contained in ordinances; for to make in Himself of two one new man, so making peace; and that He might reconcile both unto God in one body by the cross, having slain the enmity thereby"* (Eph. 2:11-16).

So he took two classes of people, the Jew and the Gentile, the Christian and the non-Christian, the saved and the lost, and through the Cross He took all of humanity and reconciled them into one body in Christ, having slain all the enmity. There is absolutely no enmity between man and God, and we will see this as we go on. There is no enmity between you and Christ. There is no enmity between any man or woman on the earth today and God—there is nothing standing between them that can stop their accessibility to walk boldly into the presence of God to receive grace to help in time of need. There is no barrier between man and God.

Saved By His Life

"For if, when we were enemies, we were reconciled to God by the death of His son, much more being reconciled we shall be saved by His life" (Rom. 5:10). This verse is a key to what I've said previously and to what I've already written in the *Coming Out of Darkness* series. How are we supposed to live this (so-called) Christian life? Either we have to find out how to make Adam walk this road or we have to discover that Christ within us is more than sufficient and will enable us to walk this way.

This reminds me of what Jesus said, *"I am come that you might have life"* (John 10:10), not that you would discover the teachings of Christianity and then try to live according to this Christian concept. The word "life" in this scripture is the Greek word *zoe,* which, in essence, was telling them that He was come that we may have His life *within* us. Not our Adamic lives made over. Not

Adam being born again, but there is a brand new creation life birthed within you.

If you come away from all the religious concepts and all the teachings and just come into His presence, you will discover the life that is really Life. You'll discover a love that knows no bounds and no limitations. You'll experience the well of living water that will unceasingly flow from the very innermost depths of your being, and that will produce life everywhere that it goes.

"Much more, being reconciled, we shall be saved by His Life." Now do you understand why He is the author and finisher of our faith? *It is His Life.* It is His operation by the power of His spirit *in* you, **"for it is God who works in you both to will and to do His good pleasure"** (Phil. 2:13). In a little plainer English, that verse says, "It is God working in you who both wills and does His good pleasure." It has nothing to do with Gary Sigler trying to make himself godly. *I am saved by His Life.*

So, what happens when my flesh rises up? What happens when I get angry? What happens when I find all of the works of the flesh rising within me? I turn to the Life. I don't reach out to a God way up there somewhere and cry for Him to come and touch me. I simply turn to His Life that is in my innermost being and I say, *"I'm so thankful that Your Life floods my consciousness. Father, I'm so thankful that in the very presence of the enemy called anger that I can feast at your table. Lord, I'm so thankful that I have the flowing of your Life within the very center of my being."* You know what? When I do that, my anger just dissipates. You can't stay angry and talk to God for very long.

All Things Are of God

"And all things are of God" (2 Cor. 5:18). The great majority of Christians do not believe that all things are of God. I hear all the time that the devil beat me up, and the devil did this and the devil did that. The reason we experience those things is that our teachers have given us a devil consciousness. Our teachers have built into our consciousness this awareness of satanic powers. For instance, they say, "There are principalities and powers in the airwaves, and over the cities there are demonic principalities who keep all of God's creation in that city in darkness. These powers are so powerful that we can just barely get people to understand the Gospel. And, your enemy, the devil, is so strong that you have to be on guard every moment of your life or you're going to be deceived. Don't ever let your children go out of the house in the morning without putting your hands on them and praying for them or the devil might get them."

We have built a devil consciousness into God's people. *God help us and forgive us!* All things are of God.

Anything that the devil does is only done by the permission of God. Now, until you begin to understand that, you'll always fear the devil. And until you understand the perfect, complete, love of God, you will always have some fear in you—fear of failing, fear of living the Christian life, fear of backsliding, fear of being deceived. Until you understand and can rely fully on God's ability to bring you through all things, you'll always have some fear. Fear is the exact opposite of what God desires, which is faith. Perfect love casts out all fear (1 John 4:18). God is able. Gary isn't able, you aren't able—GOD IS ABLE!

All things are of God. We need a revelation to understand this. What do you think God means when He says "all things"? Does He mean some things? Just those things that have received Christ? Just those who walk a certain way? Can you see that absolutely all things are of God? The more you have the revelation of this understanding, the less problems you're going to have. What causes us problems is the darkness and deception.

The Gospel of Reconciliation

What do you think the Apostle Paul meant when he wrote, *"To know, that God was in Christ, reconciling the world unto himself, not imputing their trespasses unto them; and hath committed unto us the word of reconciliation"* (2 Cor. 5:19)? Do you think he meant that God was in Christ, reconciling a few people to Himself, or God was in Christ reconciling those who went to an altar and received Him, or reconciling all those who believe certain things and who adhere to certain doctrines and fundamental teachings? Of course not!

"God was in Christ, **reconciling the world** unto Himself, **not imputing** their trespasses unto them." There is nothing in here talking about saved people, He is talking about the *world.* The word "impute" means to hold accountable. Not holding them (the world) accountable for their sins. You're hearing the Gospel of Good News! God is not holding anyone accountable for their sin, because sin was inherited from Adam. *"Wherefore, as by one man sin entered into the world, and death by sin; and so death passed upon all men, for that all have sinned"* (Rom. 5:12).

The only gospel the Apostle Paul told us to preach was the gospel of reconciliation. Not telling people how bad they are—they already know that. Not telling them that they have to change and God will bless them, but telling them that God is not holding them accountable for their sin, so they can instantly enter into His presence and begin to fellowship with and get to know Him. This so far surpasses the religious mindset of the modern day Pharisees.

Do you know that if you are a prostitute, a homosexual, a pervert, that God is not holding you accountable for that? Why is that? Because that is the Adamic life. Adam was the one who introduced the Fall to humanity. So death, through Adam, was passed to all of creation. If you are a homosexual, lesbian or prostitute, it is simply the fruit of the Adamic life—or, you could say, the fruit of the Tree of the Knowledge of Good and Evil.

The Adamic Nature

The Adamic life produces either good or evil, or a combination of both, and that's what we are. The human consciousness is basically a mixture of good and evil. If I am a Christian and I'm taught certain principles, I try to be like that. So, at times I can be very lovely and just love you. However, when you do something that's not right or you abuse me, I immediately cry out to God asking how this can be. Then instead of loving you, I become filled with resentment, because I was good to you and you hurt me. I hear this from the lips of Christians all over—resentment, bitterness and divisiveness. That is Adam.

God, more than anyone else in the universe, understands the Adamic nature. He knows that you are not responsible for that which you inherited through your father Adam. Jesus understands you can't help it, so He provided the Cross. By His death on the Cross, He has brought all of creation back into fellowship, reconciliation with Him. He is not holding us accountable for our sin, because He realizes that we inherited that nature from our father Adam. If you understand that you are not responsible for displaying the Adamic life, you will walk in freedom.

Now, you may think that this gospel going to give you liberty to sin, you think your flesh is going to go wild. But not if you understand Romans 7, where Paul was saying that if he did things that he didn't want, it was the sin principle that was dwelling in him. We don't try to make that thing better, we get into the presence of God. Now, I'm going to make a statement, and as hard as it's going to be for some to accept this, you'll find out later on that it's the truth. *God will never bring you before His throne and remind you of your Adamic nature and your sin.* I know that's hard to accept. I'm not saying you won't be judged. (Chapter Eight in *Coming Out of Darkness* dealt with "Understanding Judgment".)

God will never bring you before the presence of His glory and remind you of your Adamic life. He's not holding you accountable for that. If He is, we've got to tear a lot of verses out of the Bible. He has made it so easy for you to enter into His presence, and His presence will deal with that Adamic life. As you're in His presence, He transfuses His very nature into you, and you cannot remain the same.

When God first began to reveal some of these truths to me, I was a mess. I didn't change overnight, but I understood the concept that God was not holding me accountable, and then I read in Romans 4:3 where it said that Abraham believed God, who justifies the ungodly.

You Are Not Adam

God very specifically said to me, "You don't believe the Scriptures. You say it is my Word, you confess it's my Word, but you don't believe it. Why? Because you're looking at Adam. In Adam you'll never understand these truths. They're not found in Adam. They're found in Christ. You are not Adam, you are Christ. The Word is living and operative, even to the dividing asunder of soul and spirit. You need to look at Adam only to recognize that he is not you.

You are the new creation. **"Whosoever is born of God does not commit sin,"** indeed **"he cannot sin, because he is born of God"** (1 John 3:9). Every one of us needs to realize that in the deepest part of your being there is that substance of His life that is incapable of sin. That's who you are. You are not Adam, you are Christ manifested in the flesh.

God Took Away the Sin of the Whole World

It's good to ask ourselves questions. It's good to ask God questions. Did He or did He not take away the sin of the world? We have been taught to put everything off into the future. For instance, most people are looking only for a future judgment, not realizing that we're in judgment now. There are multitudes of Christians who have been cast into outer darkness. They can't see revelation. They can't hear revelation. All they have is the old religious things, and you can't put the new wine into the old wineskins. If you do, they are going to burst—and that's okay too. Some of those wineskins need to get burst.

I'm not saying that if you have old concepts we can't help you and feed you, but it's hard to grasp the love of God with the religious mindset. In many areas, we've been taught just the opposite of what the Scriptures say.

"The next day John sees Jesus coming to him and says, 'Behold the Lamb of God that takes away the sin of the world!'" (John 1:29). Did He take away the sin of the world or didn't He? Even in the Old Testament there are verses like, *"As far as the east is from the west, so far has he removed our transgressions from us"* (Ps. 103:12). *"God so loved the world that He gave"* (John 3:16), and He didn't give a new set of principles, He didn't raise the law to a higher standard, He simply gave what He is—and that is Love. That love is committed to itself to bring all of creation back into harmony with Him. That's how much He loves. His love will never stop until every knee bows—not forcefully, but in adoration and love, confessing Him as Lord.

Most preachers read Romans 3:23 and stop there. ***"For all have sinned and come short of the glory of God."*** They can take that verse and preach you right under condemnation with it. But, the next verse, ***"Being justified freely through the redemption that is in Christ,"*** puts a totally different light on that Scripture.

We've all sinned and come short of the glory. What is the glory? The glory of God is the expression of God—His beauty, His loveliness, His longsuffering, His joy. We've all come short of the glory of God, but we have been justified freely through the redemption that is in Christ Jesus.

You don't have to feel bad again because of Adam, you just have to realize that Adam will always be Adam. God is authoring His work in you, and Adam is going to die. That is what judgment is for—to put Adam to death. So God will throw you into the fire and raise up any kind of circumstances that He needs to raise up to cause you to know that He is Lord. He's not angry and He's not vindictive; He loves you enough to do anything that it takes for you to bow the knee and recognize that everything that's ever happened to you—from your very inception until right now—has been designed by the hand of God to bring you into reconciliation and experience His love.

The devil has no power over your life except that which

you believe and submit to. People are all the time trying to pull down these strongholds instead of dealing with what's inside of them. The only power that Adam has is those concepts which are between your ears. The devil has his power through the Adamic mindset, through the carnal mind. That's why the Scripture says that the natural man, the carnal man, is at enmity with God.

The Adamic nature will never be reconciled to God. You see, God didn't reconcile Adam to Himself, He reconciled the Seed that He has planted in you. That's why it is called re-generation. That seed of God in you has been regenerated. That seed is incapable of doing anything except pleasing God. So, we need to discover His life within us and learn how to abide in His presence within us and stop being religious.

God took away the sin of the world, and in Hebrews 9:26 it says, *"But now once in the end of the world has he appeared to put away sin by the sacrifice of Himself."* This is powerful! Did He put away sin, or didn't He? You may say, "Well, I know that the Scriptures say He did, but I'm still sinning and I'm still displaying all the works of the flesh." All you need to do is turn to the Christ within.

You say you don't know how to do that? Then, just talk to God. Turning to Christ is simply talking to God. I used to say things like, "Lord, I'm so full of this junk and I'm not anything like I know a Christian should be, but I'm so thankful that I know I've been regenerated. Lord, I'm so thankful that deep in the recesses of my being I have experienced the God of Abraham, Isaac and Jacob. Therefore, I must not look at Adam, I must turn and look at Christ. I must fellowship with Him who is able to save me to the uttermost." Sin is no more. He put it away and when we come into a revelation and understanding of that, it will be put away in our lives.

All Creation Will Bow the Knee

"Wherefore God also has highly exalted Him and given him a name which is above every name: that at the name of Jesus every knee should bow, of things in heaven, and things in earth, and things under the earth; and that every tongue should confess that Jesus Christ is Lord, to the glory of God the Father" (Phil. 2:9-11).

Another verse that we need to read along with this one is 1 Corinthians 12:3, *"Wherefore I give you to understand, that no man speaking by the Spirit of God calls Jesus accursed: and that no man can say that Jesus is the Lord, but by the Holy Ghost."* We see in these verses that every tongue shall confess that Jesus Christ is Lord, and then it says that no man can say that except by the Spirit of God.

There's going to come a day when all of creation will

bow the knee and say that Jesus Christ is Lord. What happens at that point? Everyone will have been brought back into harmony with God. *"No man can come to me, except the Father which has sent me draw him: and I will raise him up at the last day"* (John 6:44). Do we really believe that? Do we really believe that no man can come to Jesus, except the Father, who has sent Him, draw him?

We go out sometimes and preach condemnation and hellfire and brimstone to the whole world and condemn them for not coming to God. We say that God loves you, but if you don't accept what He has provided for you, then as much as He loves you, He is going to allow you to spend eternity in an unending agony and torment. We have to know God better than that! There's something wrong with that concept. *"No man can come to me except the Father, which has sent me, draw him."*

John 1:11-13 says, *"He came unto His own, and His own received Him not. But as many as received Him, to them gave He power to become the sons of God, even to them that believe on His name: which were born, not of blood, nor of the will of the flesh, nor of the will of man, but of God."* Do you understand what that simple verse is saying? You see, if you're not born by the Spirit of God, if you have not been regenerated, you can forget the Christian life. Forget it—it's not for you (yet). These were born, not of blood nor of the will of the flesh nor of the will of man, but of God.

Another verse is, ***"Him that cometh unto me I will in no wise cast out"*** (John 6:37). The door is open for everyone. This is why you have to see that God's plan is for all of creation. It's not just for you because you ran to an altar. It's not just for you because you said, "Jesus I receive you," it's not because you believe everything right intellectually. It has nothing to do with that. *This is God's idea. This is God's plan.* This is God's purpose, and it includes you. It includes all of creation. All creation will be brought back into harmony—that was the reason for Calvary.

"For therefore we both labor and suffer reproach, because we trust in the living God, who is the Savior of all men, especially of those that believe" (1 Tim. 4:10). You sure will suffer reproach if you pick up *this* gospel. We don't trust in our flesh. We don't trust in Adam, we trust in the Living God who is *the Savior of all men.* We need to think on these things.

God revealed this gospel to me over 25 years ago. I was such a horrible person in Adam. There was no hope for me if God didn't give me some revelation of His ability and His power to deliver me. He is the Savior of all men, but especially of those that believe. Our relationship with Him is so wonderful because it's not based on our performance.

We know we were hopeless. We know we can't be that little goodie Christian. We know our flesh rises up from time to time. However, there is the most precious essence of His being within us. I know that and I love it, but I hate the Adamic side of me. Thank God, it is being put to death. Nevertheless, we are all in the same boat! Some of us a little better, some of us a little worse, speaking of Adam. However, we're being transformed every day from one degree of glory to another, into the essence and presence of what God is. In Adam, we're dying. In fact, Adam is dead, and we're just finding out about it.

All Men Will Be Saved

"For this good and acceptable in the sight of God our Savior; who will have all men to be saved, and to come to the knowledge of the truth" (1 Tim. 2:3-4). Well, the gospel I heard in church is directly, diametrically opposed to this truth. Oh yes, God wants all men to be saved—but He's not able to deliver them, because some choose not to serve Him. Therefore, He wills that they would be saved, but He can't help them because of their choice. What does that do? That produces the modern day Pharisee. If God's desires me to be saved, I can guarantee you that His Will will prevail over my will.

The teaching in Christianity (you'll need to investigate it for yourself) regarding free will is absolutely unscriptural. There is no such thing taught in Scripture as you having a free will. It isn't there. You can challenge me on it, and if you find it, write me and I'll publicly repent. In fact, I can prove to you through Scripture that you don't have a free will, and I'll give you one illustration.

God came to a man by the name of Jonah. He said, "Jonah, I want you to go to Nineveh and preach the gospel." What did Jonah do? He jumped on a boat and went in the wrong direction. He said, "No, God." What did God do? Did God go against Jonah's free will? Did God have a desire for Jonah to go to Nineveh? Did He let Jonah's will interfere with His desire for Nineveh?

Well, God desires that you will be saved. God desires that you will display, from the very essence of your being, everything that He is. He has a desire in His heart that you display His love, His joy, His peace, His longsuffering, His goodness, His temperance, His meekness and His self control to all of creation. Do you think that your will can stand against that?

"This is good and acceptable in the sight of God our Savior, who will have all men to be saved and come unto the knowledge of the truth. For there is one God, and one mediator between God and men, the man Christ Jesus; who gave himself a ransom for all, to be testified in due time" (1 Tim. 2:3-6). There will come a day in your life and mine, when every word of God will

come to pass and be fulfilled. *". . . who gave himself a ransom for all, to be testified in due time."* This is a very powerful verse.

"For since by man came death, by man came also the resurrection of the dead. For as in Adam all die, even so in Christ shall all be made alive, but every man in his own order" (1 Cor. 15:21-23). It can't be any clearer than this. *"As in Adam all die."* You see, you were born into death. Death isn't when your body falls into the ground. Death is being born into this natural realm and feeling separated and alienated in your consciousness from the Living God. That's death.

We All Experience Death

In Adam, we all experience death. We all experience the knowledge of good and evil, some to one extreme and some to the other, but, it's all death—it's a death realm. Carnal man lives in a realm of death—an illusion. However, *"in Christ shall all be made alive."* I've heard teachers say that the "all" in Christ is not the same "all" that is in Adam. They say that those in Christ are only those who have said the words, "Jesus, I receive you," or they've run to an altar, or they live a certain way. But these verses do not say that. *All that died in Adam will be made alive in Christ.* Everyone, without exception, and without fail.

Do you have loved ones who have died without ever

knowing Christ? There is still great hope. I can't imagine the agonies of a mother or a father who has a teenager who dies, thinking that they're going to be eternally separated from God, suffering in an endless agonizing hell. Jesus said hell was created for the devil and his angels. (There is more about this in the next chapter.)

We are not saying there is no hell. However, if you believe that God created a place where there is unending, agonizing torment for ever and ever without any hope of release, you are wrong. If he created a place like that, knowing that billions of people would suffer in unending agonizing torment, then He's not God, he's a devil. I don't know a God like that. I know a God who is able to save me to the uttermost.

I have been in some of the most awful places as a Christian, because in my Adamic life I couldn't make it. And because of the revelation God gave to me, I've always known that the prodigal can simply turn and say, "Jesus, help me." Every trial that comes to my life is to cause me to realize that in the midst of the trial, in the midst of the storm, in the midst of the suffering, God is saying, *"Come unto Me, all ye that labor and are heavy laden, and I will give you rest"* (Matt. 11:28).

Grace Never Ends

The following question always comes up when teaching reconciliation: If this is really true, that God will save everyone, what about the people who have died without accepting Christ or died with unconfessed sin in their life? We all know from our Christian teachers that as long as you have breath in your lungs, you can repent. But once you die, they say there's no more hope for you. God loves you—but you have to have breath in your lungs, because once you die His love for you is gone, it's over, you're hopelessly lost eternally. This isn't the kind of God we have. Grace does not end when the body falls over. God's mercy and grace never end.

If there is no hope for us after we die, please explain these verses. *"For Christ also has once suffered for sins, the just for the unjust, that He might bring us to God, being put to death in the flesh; but made alive by the Spirit: by which also He went and preached to the spirits in prison; which were disobedient, when the longsuffering of God waited in the days of Noah, while the ark was preparing, wherein a few, that is, eight souls were saved by water"* (1 Peter 3:18-20). No hope after death? Do these verses not say that Jesus went to those who were disobedient, those who rejected the gospel in the days of Noah, those who were shut up in prison?

When Jesus died on the Cross, one of the things He did was go to where the spirits were in prison, those who were disobedient in the days of Noah, and to bring them the message of their deliverance. Can you imagine Jesus walking into this realm of the dead and saying, "Look here, folks, look at my hands and look at my feet, you dirty rascals you! You rejected the preaching of Noah, so I can't help you." We have to rewrite the Bible to fit what our teachers have told us.

Paul made the statement, *"If in this life only we have hope in Christ, we are of all men most miserable"* (1 Cor. 15:19). That might be taking that verse out of context, but nevertheless, it's true. It's not just in this life that we have hope in Christ, but He is going to perfect that which concerns us. And yes, we might enter into His presence, fall at His feet and be ashamed, but restoration will come. The foolish virgins will still have the opportunity to buy the oil and be perfected in the glory of their Lord. This is the good news of the gospel.

Ephesians 4:8 says that when Jesus ascended on high He led captivity captive and gave gifts to men. (This is a direct quote from Psalm 68:18, which adds, *"Yea, for the rebellious also, that the Lord God might dwell among them."*) Who were the captives he led? Could it have been those spirits in prison that He went to preach to? When he ascended, it says that He took a host of captives with Him. At the end of that statement, it says, *"He that descended is the same also that ascended up far above all heavens, that He might fill all things"* (Eph. 4:10).

If any of you have a computer with a Bible program on it,

just key in the words "all things", "all men", and "reconciliation", and see what you come up with. It's fun!

Now that you've heard all of this, you will have to go to God and get a revelation on it, because information alone will not help you. Truth doesn't help you unless you get into the presence of God and see it for yourself.

God's Purpose

"Having made known unto us the mystery of His will, according to His good pleasure which He hath purposed in Himself" (Eph. 1:9). He purposed His will within Himself. What that means to me is that it doesn't depend on me to fulfill His purpose. He purposed something in Himself.

The next verse tells us what He purposed: *"That in the dispensation of the fullness of times He might gather together in one all things in Christ, both which are in heaven, and which are on earth; even in Him."* That's the divine mystery of His Will—that in the fullness of times He would gather together *in one all things in Christ.*

"And to make all men see what is the fellowship of the mystery, which from the beginning of the world hath been hid in God, who created all things by Jesus Christ" (there's those words "all things" again): *to the*

intent that now unto the principalities and powers in heavenly places might be known by the church the manifold wisdom of God, according to the eternal purpose which He purposed in Christ Jesus our Lord" (Eph. 3:9-11). This is the message, this is the mystery, this is the word that the Church of the Living God should be bringing to the peoples of our world—the message of God's love, not the message of God's vindictiveness, of His hatefulness.

One of the most horrible doctrines ever perpetrated by the church is the idea that there is going to come a day when those who have said the proper words and tried to do the best they can are going to be suspended in the air while God pours out His anger and wrath and His horrible judgments upon creation. Again, that's a false God.

Am I saying that judgment is not coming? Of course not! Even God's anger toward you is His love perfecting you. He raises up circumstances in your life to purify you. There will come a day when you'll come before Him and you will be judged according to whether or not you have built with wood, hay, and stubble, or gold, silver, and precious stones. It says that some of us will have everything burned up, yet we will be saved so as by fire.

No one is totally lost, although you may lose all that you've worked for in this life. You may have had a church of 10,000 people. You may have had accomplishments beyond measure in the realm of religion in the natural life. On that day, you'll stand bare, and everything you've done will be burned up. There's only one thing in judgment that God is looking for and that's Christ. Christ in you is the hope of glory. Adam hasn't a snowball of a chance. He will be melted in the fires of tribulation. You may lose everything, but you shall be saved, yet so as by fire.

"Who has saved us, and called us with a holy calling, not according to our works, but according to His own purpose and grace, which was given us in Christ Jesus before the world began" (2 Tim. 1:9). I like this verse because it shows us when and where we received what we have. When you realize how big and how wonderful God is, it will destroy all of the idols that have been built up in your consciousness—all of the fear of missing God.

I can guarantee you that you're going to miss God. That's not to be feared. I miss God every day of my life. I miss God in Adam. But, every day of my life, I turn to the seed of His life, to the presence of His life, to the substance of who He is. I've discovered that within the essence of my being. That is what I look at, not Adam.

Is God big enough to perfect His will in your life? I'm not saying that your will does not come into play here, because we know we're certainly not puppets on a string.

People hear this message, and because they're not much into God anyway, they say, "If this is true, if God is going to save me anyway, then I'm just going to go do what I want to do." Well, then that's what you need to do. Because then you're being honest, and God is able to raise up the fires and the trials that will cause you to bow the knee. However, as long as you're pretending and suppressing those desires in you and being religious with it, you're just becoming a Pharisee.

No one is hopeless in God's plan of the ages. He will bring all of creation into a marvelous expression of His life. No one loses anything except their old Adamic life. God will be "All in all".

Coming Out of Darkness

Chapter 12

God's Concept of Hell

I find it so sad that two of the most wonderful revelations in the Bible (salvation and hell) are not understood by most Christians. The understanding of the salvation of all, when seen in the light of the revelation of the Spirit, will absolutely change forever your carnal thinking about salvation. Discovering that salvation is entirely a work of God through grace and not human intervention is one of the most wonderful experiences you will ever have.

The proper understanding of hell is also a wonderful thing when understood with the mind of the Spirit. Hell is certainly real and not something we would like to experience. However, when you understand God's concept of hell, even though your natural carnal Adamic mind says, "No way," and greatly fears the fires of God, your inner man rejoices, knowing that when the carnal man is thoroughly purged and is no more, then Christ in all of His glory will be revealed and manifested in His temple, which temple *you* are.

The teaching of hell, as the traditional religious systems teach it, has caused much torment and sorrow in the hearts of God's own people. How many have lost loved ones who never accepted the religious teachings and think they are going to suffer in torment throughout all eternity? How sad to think that there is no hope beyond the grave for those who have never submitted themselves to God.

Daddy, What If . . . ?

Our dear friend Charles Slagle recently wrote a little booklet we published called *Daddy What If . . . ?* In it, he shares how fear of hell was implanted on him as a child. He writes:

It was the year 1958.

"Daddy."

"What, son?"

"After we die, do we all really have to stand before God?"

"Yes, son. The Bible says all of us will have to stand before God and answer for all we have done."

My heart pounded. I was nearly twelve years old, the "age of accountability". At least that was what most people in my church believed. But we were often told it could be far younger.

I shuddered inside, staring straight ahead as my dad and I drove down the highway. As the telephone poles, the fields and trees whizzed past us at sixty miles per hour, I hardly noticed them.

I glanced at my dad. As he steered the pickup he seemed . . . cheerful? He was whistling again. It was one of his favorite gospel songs, "Victory in Jesus".

"Daddy."

"Yes, Charles?"

"What if we do something wrong and get killed all of a sudden before we can ask forgiveness?"

"The Lord has to send us to hell, son. For no sin will enter heaven."

"But what if we fall on our knees and beg and plead for mercy and tell Him we're really sorry and we'll never do it again?"

"Nope. It won't work, son. After this life, if you aren't ready for heaven, you'll have to spend eternity in the lake of fire. God loves you, son. But he hates sin, and the only time for forgiveness is now."

My dad continued whistling and I stared at the highway rushing toward and beneath us.

"Daddy."

"Yes, son?"

"Is Jesus coming soon?"

"Oh yes, I really believe He is, son. Don't you remember that newspaper headline I showed you back at the cafe where we ate? It said in big bold print: PEACE AND SAFETY. The Bible says that when men begin to declare 'peace and safety', sudden destruction will come."

"I wish I had never been born."

(Charles & Paula Slagle, PO Box 211447, Bedford, TX 76095)

Saved By Grace, But . . .

I was taught in the Pentecostal religion that you were saved by grace, but if you backslid and died without forsaking your sin, even though you had been saved by grace you would have to spend eternity in unending torment in hell. I was in a Pentecostal holiness meeting one time and the preacher, making an invitation to come to Jesus, said, "I know that there are some of you here, that as you come to receive Jesus you will be saved. But some of you will immediately go outside, light up a cigarette and be right back more a child of hell than you were before you came to the altar." This is the doctrine taught by Arminianism.

Arminianism teaches that although you are genuinely saved, if you are not careful, you can lose it. And it doesn't matter the reason. You can be entrapped by the devil. We all know we have an enemy. Most Christians use the devil as a fall guy, but we do have an enemy. We have a mind that is anti-christ and we have no guarantee, according to Arminianism, that once we are saved we are really saved. We really don't know our destiny until we die. Because even though we are saved, and we've experienced God, we always have to be careful, because if we die in a backslidden condition, if we die with any unrepentance in our life, then God will throw us into hell and we will burn eternally forever and forever in unending torturous agony. Even if you are filled with the Holy Ghost and speak in tongues, you always need to be on your guard, because if there comes a day when you backslide, then you may spend eternity in hell. You may be a Christian for ninety years and have this happen to you. You have no guarantees with the doctrine of Arminianism. (Some people refer to this as "once saved, hardly saved".)

Once Saved Always Saved?

The other side of the doctrine of Arminianism is the doctrine of eternal security, called Calvinism. This is the Baptist doctrine of once saved, always saved. Calvinism says that once you are saved, you are eternally saved and there is absolutely nothing you can do to ever lose that salvation. However, the back side of it is, that if a Calvinist backslides and gets into sin and unrepentance and dies, then Calvinism says they weren't really saved in the first place. So there goes your eternal security right out the door. If you're really genuinely saved, you are eternally secure. But if you ever backslide, and get into sin and die, you weren't really saved in the first place.

The thing about Calvinism and Arminianism is that there is a thread, a grain of truth in them, but there is a bridge that should be built between Arminianism and Calvinism because there is some truth in both of them, as we shall see as we go on in this message. The good news of Christ's total victory cannot be found in the doctrines of Arminianism or Calvinism.

Absolute Assurance

I would like to quote from another book by Charles Slagle called *Absolute Assurance in Jesus Christ*. He says,

Christ brought us ALL back to God through his own blood shed at Calvary. He came to earth for this purpose, to destroy the devil's deceptive works and to save that which was lost. Eventually our Lord will fulfill His purpose and inherit all that he paid for. That is because God is holy love, and love means commitment. God's commitment is stronger than our weaknesses, our foolish choices, our stubbornness, our sin. For if God's commitment to us is only as strong as our commitment to Him, perish the thought, that means He is no better than we are. God's fires of purifying judgment are unrelenting, though not of endless duration. Contrary to tradition but not Scripture. So He persistently and patiently corrects us until He succeeds in redeeming us. For our heavenly Father's judgments are not from vindictive rage but from His loving mercy. He loves us too much to let sin and death destroy His dreams for us. Christ's death on the Cross demonstrates the depth of God's love as well as His commitment to destroy sin and death. It shows us that through His own hurt and agony, the Lord is absorbing all the death dealing abuse of our sin and will swallow it up into His life as He saves us.

The Lake of Fire Purifies

Let's look at some of the Scriptures that theologians have used to put the fear of eternal hell in people. I simply want to say here that the Scriptures in the original language did not teach eternal or never-ending punishment. (An excellent booklet on this subject, *Just What Do you Mean . . . Eternity?,* can be ordered at no charge from J. Preston Eby, PO Box 371240, El Paso, TX 79937-1240.)

I think nearly all of us are surprised when we find out

that we will all go through the purifying fires of the lake of fire. Jesus said, *"For every one shall be salted with fire, and every sacrifice shall be salted with salt"* (Mark 9:49).

Revelation 21:7, *"He that overcomes shall inherit all things; and I will be his God, and he shall be my son."* What is an overcomer? An overcomer is one who has overcome. We are now in the process of overcoming, but most of us have a long way to go. We can't judge people who are overcoming because we see faults and blemishes and hang-ups in them, because they are still in the process of overcoming. So he speaks here to those who will overcome. This is when the books in heaven are opened. Do you remember what Paul told the Corinthians? He said, *"Forasmuch as ye are manifestly declared to be the epistle of Christ ministered by us, written not with ink, but with the Spirit of the living God; not in tables of stone, but in fleshy tables of the heart"* (2 Cor. 3:3).

Do you realize that you are an epistle, you are a book, right now being written, and someday the books will be opened, which simply means that everything that you are will be opened and will be exposed?

What is the book of life? We are living epistles, written in the book of life, which means that the Spirit of God in me has written His covenant on the tables of my heart.

Ezekiel 26:36 says that God will take away your stony heart and give you a heart of flesh, and will cause you to walk in His statutes.

All Will Go Through Fire

Let's continue with Revelation 21:7, **"He that overcomes shall inherit all things and I will be His God, and he shall be My son."** Verse 8 says **"but"**, and this is a big "but", **"But the fearful . . ."** I would ask you if you are ever fearful, because the above verse says that overcomers have overcome all things. They are no longer in any kind of defeat or failure, but they are walking as those who have overcome all things and they inherit all things.

Are you ever in fear over your future? Are you ever concerned or in fear over what might happen to you when you are not able to work any longer? That's fear. Any kind of unbelief, or having no confidence in God's ability to keep you and save you is fear. **"The fearful, the unbelieving."** Do you ever have doubts and unbelief? If so, you may be in the process of overcoming, but you are not yet an overcomer. Therefore, you are going through the fire. **"The fearful, the unbelieving, the abominable, the murderers, the whoremongers, the sorcerers, the idolaters and all liars shall have their PART in the lake which burns with fire and brimstone, which is the second death."** So, if you have any of these areas in your life that you have not yet overcome, you are going into the fire. Some are going through it now and some will go through it later. That's exactly what it means. Everyone is going to be salted with fire until there is nothing left of their carnal Adamic nature.

The root word of fire is *pur,* from which we get our English words pure, purifying, and purge. Each will have their part in the purification process. So if you are an overcomer, you will inherit all things. You will have no part of the second death. You'll be walking fully in the glory and the manifestation of your God. But if you have not overcome, if you have fear, if you have any unbelief, if you have anything in your life that is not according to godliness and holiness, you will have your part in the lake which burns with fire for purification.

Fire Burns the Dross

You have to understand God's concept of fire. The fire of God, as far the New Testament is concerned, began on the day of Pentecost. It says that they were baptized in the Holy Ghost and they saw tongues of cloven fire. The day of Pentecost was when the fire of God began. The fire of God has one purpose, and that is for purification and cleansing. That's what the word *pur* means—purify, cleanse, make pure.

If you throw precious metals into the fire, gold, silver and precious stone, and they have anything connected to them such as wood or dross, the fire will simply purify the gold, the silver and the precious stones. Are we not told over and over that we are living stones and that we have the redemption of God, representing the silver, we have the gold, representing His divine life, and the precious stones, representing transformation?

So when you are judged, if you stand before God and still have fear and unbelief and you still have not overcome, the only thing that happens is that you will get salted with His fire. You have your part in the lake of fire. The Bible calls it a lake of fire because in the beginning the disciples were baptized in the Holy Spirit and fire and that fire grew from the day of Pentecost until it became a lake of fire in the book of Revelation.

Have you ever heard these words: *"And of the angels he saith, Who maketh his angels spirits, and his ministers a flame of fire"* (Heb. 1:7)? His ministers are a flame of fire. The Lord told Jeremiah, *"Wherefore thus saith the LORD God of hosts, Because ye speak this word, behold, I will make my words in thy mouth fire, and this people wood, and it shall devour them"* (Jer. 5:14).

Once we understand that the fire of God is for correction, purging, and purifying, we can see that the lake of fire will only destroy that which is not of God. Right now, we are all in the fires of purification. I have felt this fire many times and I am sure I will again. Whenever your heart turns away from the Lord, He turns up the fire. We are so blessed to be going through the fire now. *"And I will bring the third part through the fire, and will refine them as silver is refined, and will try them as gold is tried: they shall call on my name, and I will hear them: I will say, It is my people: and they shall say, The LORD is my God"* (Zech. 13:9).

"As the fire burneth a wood, and as the flame setteth the mountains on fire; so persecute them with thy tempest, and make them afraid with thy storm. Fill their faces with shame; that they may seek thy name, O LORD" (Ps. 83:14-16). You can see in this verse that the fire of judgment is to cause men to seek the Lord.

The purifying fires of hell are taking place in me right now, and you can be sure that you also will go through the fires of purification. Jesus taught torment. If you have an unforgiving heart, you will be turned over to the tormentors. I believe in torment. I believe in horrible torment, but it is not eternal, because God's judgment and His heart toward me is for correction, for reproof, and for purification, but He is never vindictive, hateful or vengeful.

A lot of misconception and misunderstanding has come from the mistranslation in the book of Revelation that says that the punishment in the fire is for ever and ever.

I'm not going to explain that to you in this message, but I will say this, if you read J. Preston Eby's book called *Just What Do You Mean . . . Eternity?,* it will do a much better job than I could ever do to explain that the word in Revelation which is translated "eternal" does not mean everlasting and unending. Preston proves to you by taking you through the Bible that that word always means a period of time, with a beginning and an end, although in some cases it can be of a long duration, even ages upon ages.

One of the examples that is used is that in the Old Testament, Jonah said when he was in the belly of a fish, ***"The waters compassed me about, even to the soul: the depth closed me round about, the weeds were wrapped about my head. I went down to the bottoms of the mountains; the earth with her bars was about me for ever"*** (Jonah 2:5-6). There are more illustrations in Eby's book that will fully reveal to you that the word eternal is a mistranslation by the translators of the Scriptures.

The Doctrine of Eternal Torment

The eternal torment doctrine became ingrained by means of the Catholic church. Most of you have heard of the horrible degradation and the darkness when the whole world went into Catholicism. The teaching about eternal torment was brought into the church to keep the people in bondage to their religion.

My wife, Carol, was in a convent about thirty years ago. She wanted God desperately and she thought that because she was raised a Catholic, then to be really godly, she needed to be a nun. So she was in a convent and she prayed and sought after God every day, and one day she heard the audible voice of God say to her, "You need to leave this place." So she went to her mother superior and told her that she had heard God speak and that she was leaving the convent and they immediately told her, "If you do this you will go to hell."

This teaching of eternal torment was never in the mind of God and it was never in the original language of the Scripture. However, it is in almost all of the translations, and the concordances. Most of them, including Strong's, will tell you that the word *aion* means eternal, but that is not true. You have to understand that most of the translations that we have today, including the concordances, have come out of the religious influence of Catholicism.

Do you realize that every denomination today is a descendant from Catholicism? Revelation talks about Mystery Babylon who has many daughters, well, they are all a result of coming out of Catholicism.

God started with Martin Luther to bring some truth and revelation, and separated a group of people and brought them out of Catholicism. That was the very beginning of

God recovering His people back to some of the truths that you are hearing today. So if you were alive on the earth when Martin Luther came on the scene and you weren't a Lutheran, you were flat out missing God if you were not listening to and accepting the doctrine of justification by faith. In those days, if you did not leave the Catholic church, you were not hearing God, because Martin Luther fully exposed all of those dark, dreadful teachings.

Today it's not so good to be in a traditional Lutheran church, because God has gone far beyond the scope and vision of Martin Luther, yet the traditional Lutherans have not advanced beyond what Martin Luther gave them.

So generation after generation, God would call people out of Catholicism, and then He began to call them out of Lutheranism, and then out of Calvinism. Now He is beginning to call them out of Pentecostalism, and the final call is to come out of all religions, all denominations, all carnal religious ideas, and come to Him. We are in the closing of one age and the ushering in of a new.

The Age of Laodicea

Most of Christianity today is in what Revelation calls Laodicea. This is the church that says she has so much, but actually has very little. She says, "Jesus lives in me," and yet she lives like the devil. She says, "I love you, but only as much as you love me. I love you and I'll help you, but the moment you are a little bit ungrateful, the moment you say something I don't agree with, I no longer like you."

That's the Christian system of today. It's the fruit of the Tree of the Knowledge of Good and Evil. I can be very good. I can be very loving to you, until you do something against me, then all my love for you and all the good things I've done for you turn to resentment. Then I say, "Lord, how could they ever do that to me?" The thing of it is, the person who mistreats you, they will get the fire, but when you judge them and when you are critical and you can't love them regardless, then you get the fire too.

God is going to purify our heart motives and our attitudes. If someone does you wrong and you are resentful and unforgiving toward them, even if you are 100% in the right and they are 100% in the wrong, if they cause anger, bitterness and resentment to rise up in you, that is simply a sign to you that you need the fire.

Making Right Choices

We must learn forgiveness. These things are not a matter of feeling, because if you have resentment, you can't help it. If you hate someone, that's Adam. You can't help it, but you can make the choice to not do it.

We get faith and belief all mixed up. You do not have to feel like forgiving someone to forgive them. Forgiveness is a choice and a decision you can make. If you will make that from the heart, even though you don't want to, if you will make the right decisions, you will find that eventually your emotions will follow your decisions. That's what real faith is.

Believing something is not faith. Believing is to be able to look at the promises of God and just believe Him regardless of how you feel. Maybe you are in a miserable, sinful condition, but you believe with all your heart that God justifies the ungodly. I came to a point in my life where I really believed that, and I was still very ungodly, but I believed it. I heard it with my spiritual ears, not just read it with my intellect, but I believed that God justifies the ungodly, and I began to speak like that and I began to think like that, I began to meditate in the wonderful ability of God to justify me, the ungodly, and guess what happened? My emotions, my feelings, and my experience lined up with what I believed. I made the choice to believe what God said, rather than what I experienced.

This is how you experience genuine faith. Only God can give you that. You can't work it up, but you can make right choices and right decisions. You can choose to forgive someone that has wronged you and tomorrow the hate and resentment will rise up again, but you make the choice to disagree with these feelings and stand against the Adamic nature that is rising up in you, and choose to forgive them. In the magnificent name and nature of Jesus, you forgive them and command the feelings of resentment and bitterness to die at the root. Guess what happens? You are speaking to the rock. This is how you overcome.

Revelation says about the overcomers that they overcame by the blood of the Lamb and the word of their testimony. What are you testifying to? For years as a Christian, my testimony was this: "I love God, but I'm full of lust. I love God, but I love cigarettes. I love God, but my experience is this." I was sowing mixed seed, but then I realized that overcomers overcome not by doing, but by seeing.

It takes a revelation to become an overcomer. You have to see that you overcome by the blood of the Lamb and by the word of your testimony. Well, what is your testimony? I stand justified before God, not because of my conduct, but because of what He did. When He said, "Father forgive them," I just need to understand and include myself in His forgiveness. I overcome by understanding that the blood that was shed absolutely annihilated my sin.

Here's another good point about eternal torment. Most people would agree that Jesus suffered the penalty for our sin. Is that not the Christian teaching? Well then if He suffered the penalty for our sin and that penalty was eternal torment, then He would have to be eternally tormented to pay for that sin because He is bound by His word. We overcome by revelation, by the blood of the Lamb and by the word of our testimony.

Speak to the Rock

I don't always feel victorious. Things still rise up in me that are not godly. You know, once in a while, I even get angry with my wife. Those things are from Adam, but when that happens, I very quickly speak to the rock and I am thankful that though I get angry, it dissipates in a split second. Sometimes it takes longer than that, but the point is this: No matter how deep into the throes of anger and resentment you get, you must learn to speak to the rock, speak to the seed of God that is on the inside of you. Have you ever thought of that? You have the seed of God on the inside of you and you need to water that seed. We're always wanting someone else to water the seed, but *you* need to learn to speak to the seed.

I know that the seed of God is in me. Therefore, by all the authority and the power of the Spirit of God, I command the seed of God in me to arise and to take dominion over the works of the flesh. I bow myself and I give the seed of God, the Spirit of God in me, permission to do whatever it takes to transform me into a child of

God, into a son of God. I don't agree with the anger. Even if I have it, I don't have to agree with it, but you know what, I don't have to feel bad when it's there either, because that's Adam. I never feel bad when I miss God. I never feel bad when I'm angry with my wife, but I am quick to repent and I am quick to speak to the rock. There is no way that you can enter into the presence of God and be angry with anyone. If you do, then you are fooling yourself. Anger and God's presence do not mesh. So whatever arises within you, learn to speak to the rock, speak the truth to the rock, and make the choice to forgive and drop the resentment, and have the eyes to see, and know that as you believe and as you confess, so shall it be.

Believing and Confessing

God's principles always work without fail. One of God's principles is this: Romans 10 says that if you believe in your heart and confess with your mouth, you will be saved. That's how you know that you are saved. You believe in your heart and confess with your mouth and what happens? You are regenerated and you begin to experience the Spirit of God energizing and quickening you. Faith works, whether it is positive or negative. If you believe in your heart that you are a failure, you'll never make it.

I often said that I would have a cigarette in my hand

when Jesus returns. That was my confession. I believed it with all of my heart, so what I reaped from that was that I smoked for 13 years as a Christian. I knew that I could never stop on my own, but when I began to grasp hold of what I am telling you, I began to believe in the overcoming power of God, and I began to speak to the rock and I began to take dominion over the power of nicotine my life. It didn't happen overnight, but by speaking to the rock and believing in God, and believing those things I could not see, believing in them anyway, there came a day when that desire absolutely dissipated. After 13 years, my struggles ended.

This is one example of many in my life that took place by believing in the power of the blood and the word of my testimony, regardless of my experience, that brought to me the reality of all of those things that I had wanted for years. Whatever you believe, you will speak, and whatever you speak, because you were created in the image of God, will happen. Because you are from the very substance of God, therefore whatever you believe, you speak, and that will be your experience. Positive or negative, it works. That's why people use positive confession in the wrong way to reap all kinds of material gain. If they really believe that teaching and confess it, guess what happens? It works for them. It doesn't necessarily mean that they are godly, because the principles of God can be and are misused by the majority of Christians.

The key is: God, purify me. At any cost, purify me. The cost is very severe at times. That principle is also applied in Matthew 11, where Jesus told His disciples that if you say unto this mountain, "be thou removed," and do not doubt in your heart, but believe that that which you say shall come to pass, you shall have whatsoever you say. That's what the doctrine of the word and faith movement was built on. Name it and claim it. You set your hope and belief in God and that causes faith to be built in you. Faith is the evidence of things not seen. Because of the age that we are being ushered into, we will have all of the realities of these things.

A lot of the things that Jesus said, are not to be taken literally. I don't believe that He meant that the mountain would be picked up. I believe He was talking about the insurmountable problems in your life. Speak to the circumstances in faith, and sometimes without any evidence or feeling, just speak in faith and those mountains will be dissipated. There is no way that a godly person is not going to suffer in one way or another. You are going to suffer continually. Anyone that is godly is going to be hurt and going to suffer, but it's okay to be hurt. I'm not saying that you should not have these feelings, just know that it is okay and that you need to make the choice of unconditional love. If you can love unconditionally those who are hurting you, they will be your dearest of friends, but it takes some time.

We are taught that we should not resent, and that we should not harbor bitterness. We know that, but what we haven't known is that our feelings do not matter, but what does matter is our choices. I choose to forgive you, I don't feel like it, I'm so angry with you, but I know that God's heart is to restore you and for me to forgive you, and I make that choice. Eventually your feelings will line up with your choices.

Calvary Is All-Inclusive

There is no way really that you'll come to an understanding what I've shared with you here without seeing the magnitude of Calvary's victory. If you do not understand that Calvary paid the price for every act of disobedience, you cannot love unconditionally. You cannot love yourself unconditionally and you cannot love anyone else until you understand that God loves that way. You will portray whatever you believe God to be.

God is big enough. Calvary's price covered all of mankind, and when you really understand and have that revealed to you, you will enter into the heart of God and then you'll be able to have the same unconditional love for everyone that He has. If you don't see the extent of Calvary's victory, you won't have that kind of love. You will no doubt hear a lot of things contrary to what I have just written, but I believe that there is a solid enough foundation laid here that even though it may get covered up, the seed will be sure to grow. It is done. Other people will come in and they will have a limited scope and a limited forgiveness and you'll be able to pick it up right away. That doesn't mean that you shouldn't listen to them, just realize that they don't understand, and it's okay. Only God can unveil and reveal His heart to humanity. He will, but not everyone can see it yet, it's just not time. I know that this is one of the reasons God is sending me out today.

Jesus said a wonderful thing to His disciples: He said that it has been given to them to understand the mysteries of the kingdom. God has a people on the earth today who are prepared and who will understand what His ministers speak. They have already been prepared and they have ears to hear and understand. That's why the word today is being released across the world, because you have been prepared to hear it. Your mind may tilt and you may try to run this through your mind for a long time, but it's okay. When we understand that this whole thing is God's responsibility and it's His workmanship, and that He is the author and He is the finisher, we begin to put all of this stuff together and we understand that the steps of a righteous man are ordered by the Lord. You begin to see this whole picture. When you begin to see the scope of this thing and the intricacies of the details that He works out, it's awesome. Everything is in God's hand.

I would like to end with a quote from the anointed pen of

J. Preston Eby in his December 1996 Kingdom Bible Studies. He writes:

It seems wonderfully significant to me that in the closing pages of the book of Revelation, when the Spirit of God reveals the final and ultimate revelation of God to creation through the glorious city of God, the very last message proclaimed is this. "And the Spirit and the bride say, come. And let him that hears say, come. And let him that is thirsty say, come. And whosoever will, let him take the water of life freely."

Remember before these words were spoken there was a great white throne judgment. Multitudes were cast into the lake of fire. Our God is a consuming fire. The fire of God is God's glory. Only the Holy Spirit can make this real to us, but a person under deep conviction is tormented. Tormented with what? He is tormented with the fire of God's Holy presence, the fire of His penetrating, burning word. He has no peace or rest day or night. His conscience troubles him continually. When you and I were under deep conviction for our sins and past life, we were tormented by the Holy Spirit, the presence of God. And we had no rest day or night. I have seen men literally run out of meetings to escape the convicting presence of God. When we were finally broken by the Holy Spirit's dealing and repented and came to Jesus for mercy, we cried and shed many bitter tears of remorse and regret.

The smoke of their torment rises day and night. The fiery dealings of God are upon the proud, the rebellious, the blasphemers. Is judgment the last word? Is the lake of fire the concluding word? Is the torment of the damned the final word? No! Is there no escape? **"Whosoever will, let him come and take the water of life freely!"** That, my beloved, is the last message. That is the final word. And for how long shall this cry continue? For as long as the torment lasts. "And they shall be tormented day and night unto the ages of the ages." "And the nations of them that are saved shall walk in the light of it: and the kings of the earth do bring their glory and honor into it. And the gates of it shall not be shut at all by day: for there shall be no night there." Those gates shall always be open. The day of grace never ends! Should grace end it would mean the destruction of God himself, for he is all goodness. God's goodness and grace and glory shall follow...and flow until the last poor hungry and thirty soul has marched out of the lake of fire and come through the portals of the city to partake of the GREATEST GLORY OF GOD—HIS GOODNESS, HIS CHRIST, HIMSELF.

Coming Out of Darkness

Chapter 13

The Power of the Gospel

"For I am not ashamed of the gospel of Christ: for it is the power of God unto salvation to everyone that believeth; to the Jew first, and also to the Greek" (Rom. 1:16).

Isn't it amazing that we live in America and people have not *heard* the gospel of Jesus Christ? The Apostle Paul says that the gospel of Christ is the power of God. So if you haven't really heard the gospel and you don't understand the gospel, that is the reason that you don't have the power to live a godly life.

The word "salvation" means a *complete* redemption from the Fall, which is basically poverty, sickness and death. The power of the gospel when heard with your spiritual ears will begin to deliver you from the effects of the Fall.

You may have heard or read what J. Preston Eby declared last July (1998) at a meeting in Alamogordo, NM. He said, "The work is finished." We are now waiting for the unveiling of Christ within us. The Apostle Paul said many years ago that *"In him* (Christ) *dwells all the fullness of the Godhead bodily. And you are complete in him, who is the head of all principality and power"* (Col. 2:9-10). Once we have the revelation that Christ in us is complete, we then we grow in our awareness of Him. It is not that we have to do something to make Christ complete, but that we know that in Christ *we are complete,* and able to do all things that God would have us to do. It is a matter of shifting our attention and focus away from Adam (the carnal nature) to Christ.

You may love God with all your heart. You may spend time reading ten chapters of the Bible a day. You might spend an hour praying every day. Maybe you've experienced the baptism in the Holy Ghost and speaking with tongues, and spend hours every day speaking in tongues. But yet, for some reason you just don't have the power to live the life that you know you should be living. If that's the case, you haven't *heard* the gospel of Jesus Christ.

We live in America, where there's a church building on almost every corner. There used to be a gas station on every corner, now there are places where Christians meet on almost every corner, and in all varieties. No matter what flavor, no matter what doctrines you like, there is a place out there where you will fit. And you may be in agreement with the pastor or the elders or the people that teach, but you still won't have the power to live the life, because you really don't know by experience that Christ is in you. You are perfectly convinced that you cannot possibly live as a manifestation of God on the earth, because of the experience of failure you have had at trying it. You must turn away from your failures of the past and realize that Christ in you is complete, and He certainly knows how to manifest Himself through you. Paul said the gospel of Jesus Christ is the power of God unto salvation. We've missed something. We've all heard a *partial* gospel. We've heard a gospel that has caused many of us to go to an altar, and many of us to say the words, and in many cases we have experienced something that we call regeneration. We're born again, but because we haven't heard the full gospel, we don't have the power to live the life.

Our Substance Is Spirit

"The burden of the word of the LORD for Israel, says the LORD, who stretches forth the heavens, and lays the foundation of the earth, and formed the spirit of man within him" (Zech. 12:1).

The people of God definitely need to have an understanding of this verse. Do you know that your body was made from the very dust of the ground? And that the land that God is really interested in is *not a parcel of dirt in Israel?* That was only the type. The real land of inheritance is you and me. We are the good land. *"The earth is the Lord's and the fullness thereof"* (Ps. 24:1) and you were created from the very dust of the ground. The Scriptures use that in typology to show you that you are the land that God wants to inherit. He wants to infiltrate you. He wants to possess your ground.

So Zechariah 12:1 is a mini picture, it's like a flash of lightning, it doesn't give you very much explanation. But the first time I saw this it was like lightning. I just saw a flash of something! Zechariah 12:1 says, ***"The burden of the word of the Lord."*** That's important. That's saying that this is the burden of the word of the Lord. Then it goes on to list three things of creation:

1. **The Lord stretched forth the heavens.**

2. **He laid the foundations of the earth.**

3. **He formed the spirit in man.**

God is *spirit*, and he formed *spirit* in man. Oh, I hope you can see this. You are not just a carnal human being with a natural personality, but *you are spirit.* Deep within the recesses of your being, far past what you can think or know by natural methods, YOU ARE SPIRIT. That's why Jesus said, *"If you want to worship me, you must worship me in spirit."* That means for you to really understand God, for you to really worship God, for you to enter into the presence of God, is not a matter of your intellect, it's not a matter of your mind, it's not a matter of your conduct, it's not a matter of how good you are, it's not a matter of how bad you are, it's a matter of understanding that you are spirit. And to contact God is simply a matter of contacting spirit.

God wants to fully infiltrate, permeate, and saturate your being. You see, your problem is not your conduct, your problem is not your habits. The problem is you haven't understood that you are spirit, and that God, regardless of your condition or conduct, wants to, from the spirit person you are, infiltrate and possess every area, every avenue of your thought and brain. The Spirit of the living God wants to permeate every cell so that, as the Scripture says, ***"If He that raised Jesus from the dead dwell in you, then He that raised up Jesus shall also quicken, shall give life even to your mortal bodies"*** (Rom. 8:11). So to worship God is a matter of spirit. And if you think it's a matter of conduct, you will never, ever feel worthy enough, you'll never make it into genuinely living in His presence.

There used to be a time when I would touch God by accident. I'm sure you all experience times when you're in the Scriptures, or in prayer, or you're singing with the Lord, and He just fills you up, and it's glorious. It's almost like, "I don't know how I did it, but God touched me." So we make up these songs about God, "He Touched Me!" But I'm telling you, our experience is to be that we absolutely live in His presence. Not only do we live in His presence, *we are His presence in the earth.* You must understand that you are not a carnal human being, but *you are spirit.* And when you understand you are spirit, then you begin to understand how you could be His presence in the earth. You'll also begin to understand some of the deep mysteries like Paul wrote about in Ephesians 5:23. He said that you are bone of His bone and flesh of His flesh. Paul told the believers, *"You are the fullness of Him who fills everything everywhere with Himself"* (Eph. 1:23, Amp.).

You cannot receive the gospel of God with the carnal mind. You can't try to figure out how this could be, because it will never happen according to your intellect. Aren't we all well experienced in the failure of trying to be and live as Jesus lived on the earth? Do you have a problem when someone really upsets you, when someone does you wrong? Do you have a problem with resentment? Do you ever have a problem with anger? As you begin to enter into the reality of the Kingdom, you find yourself with the nature of forgiveness instead of resentment. As you begin to feel resentment rise up within you, you realize that those feelings come from the carnal realm, and you learn to turn to and release the spirit within you, and your resentment dissipates.

Awake, You Who Are Sleeping!

You have to know that you are not a carnal human being, you are spirit. God is spirit. What are you saying Gary, I am God? Not in the sense that I am my Father God, no! But let me ask you something, are you a human? Why are we human? Because we had a natural father, and he was a human. And so we are a product of the first human man, Adam and we have a human life because we are human. If you begin to understand that you are spirit and God is spirit, then you begin to understand that you have

His divine life and nature. The apostle Peter teaches this in his epistles.

People all across the world are beginning to wake up and hear the truth. As Paul said so many years ago, "Awake, you who are sleeping." *Wake up!* You see, Adam is sleeping and is in a dream state. But when you begin to wake up, the spirit man realizes who he is. In the very core of your being, *you are spirit,* and when you begin to wake up, you realize *God really is my father.* I do have His life. He created me. What did He have to create with? What kind of life does He have? The God kind of life, for lack of a better terminology. So what kind of life has He given you? Jesus said, ***"I am come that you might have life, and have it more abundantly"*** (John 10:10). In the original language of the New Testament there are basically three descriptions for our word life. In Greek you can use the word "bios", which is biological life. You can use the word "psuche", which is your soulish life, your mind, emotion and will. And there's also the word "zoe", the highest form of life, which is God's life. When Jesus said, "I am come that you might have life," He used the word "zoe". In essence He said, *"I have come to give you my life. The same life that courses and flows through my being, I am come that you might have that life, the life of almighty God! The life that knows no bounds and no limitations. The life that has never tasted of death. The life that has never been tainted by sin."*

You have, within the very core of your being, the life that

is really life, because it's *spirit.* Your spirit man, the real person that you are inside, has never really known what sin is. The Adamic nature has covered over your true nature. And when your spirit is regenerated and wakes up, guess what happens to you? That wretched person that you think you've been begins to fall away from you, *the seed breaks forth within you and produces once again on the earth God manifested in the flesh.*

You don't have to be good to experience this. You can be bad and have this happen to you. The modern day religious folks can look at you as the scum of the earth, but God will speak life to you. You may feel there is no hope for you, but I could speak just a few words to you and bring life and restoration because when I speak to you the seed of Christ within you will begin to stir. And your heart will begin to burn, and your ears will hear life, and your inner man will begin to rise, and the outer man will begin to fall into the dust. You don't have to be good. *The gospel of Jesus Christ is the power of God.* And we haven't had the power of God because we haven't had the full everlasting gospel revealed to us.

Where Should We Worship?

Religion has said that if you (meaning the human personality, your Adamic nature) want God, you must stop sinning, you must change your life, you cannot live this way and be godly, so you must change your ways to enter into His presence and to be favored by God. If this were true then none of us would qualify to enter in. If you want to worship God, *you must worship Him in spirit.* The woman at the well in John chapter 4 said to Jesus, *"Lord, where should we worship? Should we worship in Jerusalem or should we worship on this mountain?"* We are always looking for the right place to worship. Where is God? *Where is He?* For years I wanted to know, "God, what church are you in? Where do I go to find a place to worship you?" People have all kinds of different doctrines and theologies. You could run here and run there. "God, where do I find you?" I was looking for Him in the wrong place. The only place you can find Him is in spirit. You are spirit, and that is where you worship Him.

I knew years ago that the answer, of course, is walking in the spirit. But to me the spirit was the Holy Spirit. And the Holy Spirit to me was out there somewhere. I was told that the Holy Spirit was within me, but I didn't know how to get to Him to experience Him. So I was trying to walk in something that was confusing to me. The only way that you can overcome Adam is by understanding that you're not Adam *you are spirit.* And as you learn how to enter your spirit, you find that your spirit is one with the Holy Spirit. If you learn how to live and function from your spirit and release your spirit, you are walking in the spirit. That's why Jesus told Nicodemus, **"You must be born again,"** for that which is born of *flesh* is *flesh.* The physical Gary that was born from my natural father is flesh, it's a carnal, human personality. Flesh and blood cannot, and will not ever, no matter how good it gets, enter the Kingdom of God. You must enter in through the spirit, for he told Nicodemus, ***"That which is born of spirit is spirit."*** That which is born of the Holy Spirit is your human spirit. Paul says, ***"He that is joined unto the Lord is one spirit"*** (1 Cor. 6:17). What does that mean, he that is joined unto the Lord is one spirit? It is so simple, but because of our religious teaching we haven't understood it. He that is joined unto the Lord is one spirit. So if I have been joined to the Lord, if I have been quickened, if I have been regenerated by His spirit, then that means *my spirit and His spirit are one spirit.*

If I learn how to enter into my spirit, and I learn to speak from my spirit, and I learn how to function from my spirit, then God once again is manifesting Himself in humanity. But if I take my carnal nature and clean it up, and I go to Bible school and learn homiletics and hermeneutics and how to prepare sermons, I can then graduate and begin to teach you all that I have intellectually learned about God, but I'm dead and you're dead, and you'll never have anything of real spiritual substance with just intellectual learning. Everywhere I go, I tell people, listen, we've had nothing, and I mean almost nothing, more than a performance-based Christianity. I'm talking about the systematized thing that we have out there calling itself Christianity, and denominations calling themselves the Church. For the most part, we have nothing but 2000 years of just dry, dead, theological teachings, with no power to give you life. You've got to understand that flesh and blood does not count in the things of God. All the wonderful sermons and all the soulish prayers and the demon chasing mean nothing when it comes not from the Holy Spirit in your spirit.

You're going to see what the religious system considers the scum of the earth arise in a mighty awakening. When they find out that God loves them and that they can turn to Him and enter into His presence, then that will bring them change. *You do not need to be good to change, you just need God.* When God begins to arise in you in reality, all your old habits and way of life begin to just disappear. The more you fellowship with God and enjoy Him, the quicker you will see yourself change.

Religion Tries To Find God Through Effort

If you're set in religious theology and tradition, you can't hear this word. It's going to take a mighty shaking and a mighty stroke of lightning for you to see what I'm saying. I'm telling you that in God's eyes a prostitute is no different than a man in a suit and a tie holding down a good business job.

In the Garden, in the very beginning, what caused the Fall was man eating from the tree of the knowledge of good and evil. That's why we're in this mess, because we're partaking of the knowledge of good and evil.

We're trying to figure out with our intellect and with our mind how by being good we can once again enter into the presence of God and be acceptable before Him. Every religion, whether it's Christianity, Buddhism, Hinduism, Taoism, basically teaches you the same thing, that you must, by different methods, make yourself acceptable to God so that when you die you can go to heaven. And, I'll tell you what, if you're the traditional Christian of today, you are no better off than the Hindu, no better. *Believing in an intellectual Jesus does you no good. You must be born again!* Yet, if you have the awakening and begin to enter into the presence of God, you begin to look through the eyes of God, and you will see that the Hindu, the Christian, the Moslem, the Jehovah's Witness, some of them have a deep longing and heart cry to know God. Some of them have been told that Hinduism is the way, some have been told that Hare Krishna is the way, some have been told that Christianity is the way, and all of them are lost, trying to figure out how to make Adam acceptable before God. It has never worked.

Christianity has produced a lot of good people, and it's certainly good to learn the good, ethical, moral teachings. You are much better off to be a good person than a bad person, but you have to understand that in God's eyes the tree of the Adamic nature is both good and evil, and there's nothing you can do to make that nature acceptable so that your human personality, that carnal nature, can enter into the Kingdom of God. *It cannot be done.* But if you understand that you are spirit, then you understand that when God created the heavens and laid the foundations of the earth, He also formed your spirit. There are all kinds of verses in the Bible that indicate that God knew you even before you were born. Do you think He just kind of knew you, like, "Oh, I know that someday he will be coming along"? I don't believe so. Before you ever came into physical form, you were spirit. You're made out of the God stuff. And no, you're not a god in yourself, but listen, you get a few of us together, you get the body together, which we are going see in the days to come, then people are going to begin to arise out of these old, dead, theological places, and we're going to begin to unwrap the grave clothes as they come out of the death places. And they're going to stand up and shine with the glory and the manifestation of their God.

It Is God Who Works In Us

Years ago I used to cry and cry over my sinful, wretched condition. We all want to be like Jesus, but we have had this concept that we must do something to make it happen, and all the time all we had to do was realize that we are spirit, that God brought us into being, He is our father, and as our father it is His responsibility to bring us into glory. It is not Adam's responsibility to perfect himself, but as long as you're trying to do that God has to let you see what a failure it is. You have to come to the total end of yourself and realize that you don't have to perfect yourself, there's nothing you can do to make yourself acceptable in His sight, because the fact is, *you already are.* You see, God doesn't look at a prostitute or a homosexual as a prostitute or homosexual. He looks right through the Cross that obliterated sin. Do you believe what John said when he saw Jesus? He said, **"Behold the lamb of God who takes away the sin of the world"** (John 1:29). We know that He did, and we know He resurrected from the dead as proof of what He said. If He truly was the lamb that took away the sin of the world, do you think He's condemning the world for their sin?

If only they knew the heart of God, if they only understood the grief and the pain of God who made this sacrifice for humanity, yet they don't understand and they're still trying to perfect themselves by their own works, when all the time all they have to do is stop and rest and just begin daily to fellowship with Him. You can be a homosexual and fellowship with God. Just talk to Him, "God, you understand my condition. I know I can't hide from you. And I also know that there's absolutely no hope for me except that You begin to stir in me." Just begin to talk to God like that. He says, *"I have a robe of righteousness for you."* Oh, you may feel so dirty, and you may have unholy desires that you can't control, but He said, *"I place around you the robe of my righteousness. When I look at you I see my righteousness. I don't see all of the sinful things; in fact, My eyes are too holy and pure; I cannot look on sin. And you know what, I really don't have to because I took it away."* And you say, "Well if He took it away why am I still sinning?" If you understand what I'm telling you, you won't be sinning much longer. Because coming out of Adam, coming out of sin, coming out of all the horrible, lustful things, coming out of that is a matter of growth and transformation.

Nobody ever told me this. I've never heard one preacher, ever, in my life, tell me that coming out of sin is a matter of growth and transformation. The only thing I was told was that you've got to stop it or God can't help you. And again I have to say, if God can't help you, you are never going to come out of it. If He's not willing to help you, you'll never stop.

The only people who feel that they deserve to have what they have are the people that Jesus most strongly rebuked in His day, the self-righteousness Pharisees. He never condemned one person. We all know that the classic example is the woman taken in adultery. What He said was, *"He who is without sin, let him cast the first stone."* There was only one person in the universe at that time that had the authority to stone that woman. He was the only man standing there at that time in the consciousness of having no sin. So He said, "Any of you who is without sin, let him stone her first."

Jesus came to show the heart of God, because somehow the Jewish religion had become so twisted that everything was a matter of keeping outward laws and regulations. So Jesus came to reveal the heart of His father. And He said, *"It is written, an eye for an eye and a tooth for a tooth. But I say to you, love your enemies, do good to them who despitefully use you."* That's why they wanted to kill him. He said, *"I know you search the Scriptures because, in them, you think you have eternal life. But God is standing in front of you. Here I am in all of His fullness and you won't even come to me that you might have life. You cling to your old concepts of the Scriptures."* The Christian movement has done the very same thing. It has taken a word that was meant to give us life and has put bondages and laws upon us, and weighted us down with rules and regulations trying to make Adam godly. That's why we don't have the power of God in the gospel, because they don't understand the gospel. Just look what Jesus did with a handful of men. And then look what a few men did right after that. They were so full of the power of God that just walking by them, people were healed. There was such a reality in that day of God being manifested on the earth. Paul said, ***"I live, yet not I, but Christ"*** (Gal. 2:20).

Jesus taught his disciples who they really were. He taught them that they were descendents of almighty God, that they weren't just mere human beings, but that they were godly men and were made of the same substance as He was. You see, we've taken the humanity of Jesus and we've elevated it and worshiped Him in His humanity, never receiving the word that He gave to us. Christianity the world over worships a man called Jesus, but has never understood and received His word. It's pitiful. The apostles understood it. And that's why the gospel of God that they received produced the power in them to live the life.

We have had a doctrine for many years in the Pentecostal church that said, "If you want to be full of the Holy Ghost, you just come up front here, let us pray for you, and you'll speak in tongues, you'll be full of the Holy Ghost." It hasn't worked, has it? Tell me how it's unified the church. Tell me how it's brought unity and oneness among the believers. Jesus said, ***"A house divided against itself cannot stand."*** That's why one of the most important things you can learn to do is to not throw the first stone. The problem isn't the people who are trapped in bondage. The problem isn't people who fill the churches that are dead and have no life. You can't throw stones at anyone. You throw life at them. *"Let he who is without sin cast the first stone."* The moment you begin to open your mouth in critical judgment of another, you've lost sight of who you really are. You've once again slid back into the Adamic nature, because God condemns no man. Even in the Old Testament, before Jesus came along and sacrificed Himself, the Word says, ***"As far as the East is from the West so far have I removed the transgressions of my people."*** You see, your problem in not having the power of God is because you still believe you're an old sinful creature, and all the time the word and the spirit of the living God is grieved and crying out in deep intercession, *"I am come that you might have life."*

The gospel really is good news, because it's for everyone. Paul shared in 1 Cor. 15, *"For as in Adam all died."* Now we know that's true because we've all experienced it, haven't we? What does that mean, "As in Adam all died"? Well, death to God does not mean when your body falls over. Death to God means that you are separated from Him in your consciousness and awareness. You have no awareness of God in your life. That is a walking dead man. That's why Paul said in Ephesians that even when you were dead in your sins, He made you alive in Christ. The gospel isn't for the dead man, it is for the spirit man. And when you begin to understand that you are a spirit and not a carnal human being, behold the messenger shall surely come to His temple, *which temple you are.*

So much of the Christian world, even right today, has their eyes focused on Jerusalem, and is looking for a temple in Jerusalem to be rebuilt, totally missing almost every word that Jesus and the apostle Paul taught. *You are the temple of the living God.* And let me tell you something, the temple that is being rebuilt is not a structure in Jerusalem, but it's a re-establishing and a rebuilding of the tabernacle of David. In the tabernacle of David, there was no separation between the outer court, the holy place, and the most holy place. In David's tabernacle, you walk directly into the presence of almighty God. And when Jesus hung on the Cross and said, "It is finished," if you look it up in the Strong's concordance, when He said "It is finished", what He really said by the word "finished" is, ***The debt has been paid.*** And when He said, "The debt has been paid," the veil in the temple was rent from top to bottom. That meant that no longer was there any barrier between man and God. No longer was it just one man once a year who entered into the most holy place and experienced the awesome, almighty presence of God. But now every believer has that ability to enter, any time, any place, in any condition, directly into the presence, and feast upon almighty God. Let me tell you something folks, that will take care of your natural disposition and your character. Then you begin to experience being a carrier of His presence. Again, you don't just enter His presence, you *are* the presence of God in the earth.

The Feast of Tabernacles

This is what is known as the final feast, called the Feast of Tabernacles. You see, in the Feast of Pentecost there was still the mixture of flesh and spirit, because in Pentecost we get the baptism in the Holy Spirit and we begin to experience God *in* us. We begin to experience His quickening power. We begin to hear His voice. But it's still a mixture, it's still me and God in this temple. It's still Adam and Christ. At one time I'm in Adam, the next moment I might be in Christ. Pentecost is a mixture. The very best it can be is a mixture of Adam and Christ in one temple. As you know in typology, in the most holy place there was absolutely nothing there but the Ark, the presence of God. Now, what was in the Ark? The main item in the Ark was the tables of stone, or the Ten Commandments, along with the golden pot and Aaron's rod.

The Ten Commandments were not ever to be taken as ten laws. The Ten Commandments are simply an expression of God's life. That's why they were in the Ark. And that's why Christ was a type of the Ark, because the very essence of His being emanated the character of God, the expression of God, the life and fullness of God. When you enter into Tabernacles, you begin to experience times when you enter in and you realize there's absolutely nothing here but God. Adam isn't here anymore. I don't feel weak anymore. I don't feel the inability anymore to do what God says. I don't feel any lack, I just sense God is filling me. Do you know what it is like to stand in His presence and sense no guilt and no shame and no condemnation? You can only experience that when you realize that God isn't condemning you, nor is He condemning anyone else. We are entering experientially into the Feast of Tabernacles where there is nothing but God reigning in a people.

Do I experience this all the time? No, but more than not. You see, nothing with God is instant. People like instant food today, like a quick hamburger. Things of God are not instant. There are a lot of people waiting and thinking that there's going to come a day when, presto!, we're going to be changed into His likeness. I'll tell you what, that's a deceiving lie. Because *you are being changed.* Paul says you are being transformed from one degree of glory to another degree of glory, day by day. You'll never experience a quick, instant, one day I'm fully in Adam, and the next day I'm showing forth nothing but Christ. It doesn't happen that way. It's a matter of His life taking root, growing within us and producing the fruits of His life. It's not the *works* of the spirit, it's the *fruit* of the spirit. Most all that we've been taught pertains to making Adam acceptable to God. And that's not fruit, it's flesh. Fruit has to grow.

Well, what is fruit? We can see in the book of Galatians that it is love, joy, peace, longsuffering, goodness, gentleness, meekness. These things are the fruit of the spirit. And as you understand who you are, you understand that you and God are one, not in your mentality, not in your intellect, not in your emotions, you are one in spirit. Then you begin to seek God to give you revelation of that spirit within you that's one with God, and you'll begin to experience that oneness. God says, *"My glory I will not give to another."* If you are trying to get something of God in your Adamic nature, that's something other than God. You are not one with God in your Adamic nature. You are one with God in spirit.

That's why Jesus said in John 17, *"Father I have given my disciples your word, they believed my word, they have been purified through my word."* Isn't that different, purified through a word? You don't have to do anything. I used to tell people, if you will come and listen to the word, and if you will keep coming and listening to the word, you will be changed. I absolutely know that when I speak, it will change your life, not because Gary is anything, but because I have words of life. Jesus said, *"The words that I speak to you they are spirit and they are life"* (John 6:63).

Listen, life is quickening, life is changing. That's why you can prove beyond a shadow of a doubt that out there in the religious world, in the denominational system, there is no life, because life is always changing, life is always improving, life is always growing. And whenever you are in a place that never changes from year to year, and everything is set, there's no life. I can go down to the local Christian bookstore and get a book that will give me outlines and full written messages that I can learn so that I can preach every Sunday a different message. There's no life in that folks. We must have life. When you get a hold of this, then the only thing you have for people when you go out on the streets is *good news.* You don't have a word of condemnation, you don't have a stone in your hand to throw at them, you don't have to tell them they're going to hell if they don't repent. *You bring them the gospel of   Jesus Christ.*

10 Commandments Become 10 Promises

God doesn't even look at your sin. He said, *"I took it away."* Ezekiel 36:26 was a prophecy concerning the New Testament covenant, *"I will take away your stony heart, I will give you a heart of flesh, and I will put my spirit within you, and I will cause you to walk in my statutes."* You can't do it, but you must understand that it's His job. God is saying to you, *"I have already given you that new heart. I've given you a heart of flesh, I've put My spirit within you, and now I am going to cause you to walk in my statutes."* And then all of a sudden the Ten Commandments stop being rules and regulations that you have to try to perform, they become ten glorious, wonderful promises to you. "Thou **shalt** have no other gods before me, thou **shalt** honor thy father and thy mother, thou **shalt** not covet," because God has written it upon your heart. That's why the apostle Paul said that you are epistles written not with pen and ink but by the spirit of the living God. When a man of God speaks to you, he does not speak to your mentality, he speaks to your spirit, who he knows you really are. And as he speaks his words, his spirit mingled with the Holy Spirit begins writing on the tables of your heart, and you begin to change. It's so gradual sometimes that it takes awhile for you to realize that you have really begun to change, but it's all because you've come in contact with the living spirit of the living God. And I'm telling you, there are men and women all over the earth today carrying the presence of God who will literally speak reality into your being. They will speak life; you will sense a quickening, an enlivening, a refreshing, when you listen to these people speak.

God has raised up a leadership on the earth today that cares for nothing at all. They care for no glory, they care for no names, they care not whether they minister or someone else does. The only thing they desire is to display the loveliness of God to His creation, with no selfish motives, no selfish ambition, and they will recreate that in you. It's a great gospel, the power of God. But as long as you are sitting under a ministry that is trying to convince you that you have to make Adam godly, you can't hear this message. It's too easy. Brother, are you telling me that I can be a prostitute and still enter the presence of God? Absolutely, I'm telling you that! I'm telling you that you can be the scum of the earth, and as you begin to turn your heart, you begin to understand that in the deep recesses of your being, you are spirit. As you begin to fellowship and to cry out to God for an unveiling and an understanding of His love for you, it will absolutely transform your life without any effort at all on your part.

I never thought there would come a day in my experience when I wouldn't have to try to be godly. I thought that was impossible, but I'm telling you that today I never have to try to be godly, I never have to get up in the morning and determine within myself to walk and to give forth a Christian testimony. I don't have to do that anymore, it's just natural. Just as it is natural for you to live your human life, when you get connected up with God's life then it becomes just as natural for you to live the God kind of life. You see, it's an exchange. It's not you being godly, but it's God in you being godly. It's not you, Adam, becoming God, but it's God filling you and becoming as you. Think of it! There's a song we used to sing about this, in fact several. But one of them says this, "You are what is seen of Him who is invisible, You crystallize the One who has no form, you localize the One who is everywhere." You, **you!** You are the temple of the living God, and God is going to unveil your eyes.

We need to understand some very simple truths, that we are spirit, that we have the God life in us, and as we seek Him we will be transformed into His image. You can't correct yourself, and even if you can you have to understand it is not by making the Adamic life better that we are changed. It is natural for us to try to correct ourselves, but whether you can or you can't makes no difference. What you must do is begin to talk to and fellowship with your Father and get to know Him intimately and experience the power of God that will enable you to live the God kind of life on the earth. I had habits in my life as a Christian for 13 years, and when God revealed this truth to me that my true nature is spirit I began to be transformed. I had been taught for years and years that Jesus lived in me. I knew I had experienced God, I knew I had been regenerated, but I did not know that deep within the recesses of my being I was spirit and I had the God kind of life. When I began to have some unveiling and some understanding of this, there were habits that I had struggled with for 13 years that just absolutely vanished out of my life with no effort on my part whatsoever. The thing that keeps you in bondage to sin is your concentration on it. If you want to stop something's power over your life, don't give thought to it. The minute it comes to your mind, get rid of it by centering your thoughts on God, centering on what you really want deep inside. Focus everything on Christ within you. Do not look at what you are today in Adam. You have to stop thinking of yourself as you are today.

The reason there is so much bickering and backbiting in the church, the reason there's so much trouble in marriages, is that we focus on the negative. Many times two people are attracted to one another. When they are courting and dating they see all the good traits in the other that attract them, but when they are married and they live together they begin to see the things that they don't like so well. Rather than continuing to focus on "Why did I love this lady in the first place?" I begin to focus on the things I don't like about her, and then I go to her and talk to her about it, and begin to focus on her faults and blow the negative so out of proportion that we can't even live together anymore. We've forgotten what attracted us to them in the first place because we've allowed the negative to overtake the positive. And that's what happens to you in your Christian life. You're more centered on your failures and your inabilities than on God's ability to get you out of it. The more you focus on God, the more you spend time in His presence, the more you turn off everything and begin to center yourself on God, you will find that Adam will just fall into the dust. You'll never do it by trying to crucify the flesh, because that's Adam trying to kill himself, and he doesn't want to anyway and he never would. You are just fooling yourself.

All Made Alive In Christ

"For the creation was made subject to vanity, not willingly, but by reason of Him who subjected the same in hope, because the creation itself also shall be delivered from the bondage of corruption into the glorious liberty of the children of God" (Rom. 8:20-21). The whole creation shall be delivered from the bondage of corruption, not one person will be left out. Now, go back to what I shared a little bit earlier in 1 Corinthians 15, *"As in Adam all die".* Every one of us were born into this human race, descendents of the flesh according to Adam, and we've all entered into a death state of being separated and alienated from God. So Paul says, *"As in Adam all die, so in Christ shall all be made alive."* You see, the gospel is good news that leaves out no one, but you cannot receive it with the traditional Christian mindset. The Christian mindset says yes, Jesus died for

your sins and He went to the Cross, but when it's all over there will be a handful in heaven and the masses of humanity forever in a lake of burning fire. But the Word says, *"As in Adam all died, so in Christ shall all be made alive, but every man in his own order."* I can guarantee you that if you were born into this earth through a natural parent, you were born into death. But I can also guarantee you that on the Cross Christ took the whole creation into death and raised it out of death. You may not be experiencing this now, but as in Adam all died, so in Christ shall every one of you be made alive, without exception. It's good news, folks.

Are you telling me I can live any way I want to and God is still going to get me in the end? Absolutely! But let me ask you this. How much hell do you want to go through? It is no small thing for the judgment of God to come on your life, but if you understand the purpose of judgment, then you understand that God is never angry and vengeful, but His judgments are to correct you and cause you to turn to Him. *"When your judgments are in the earth, the people shall learn righteousness"* (Isa. 26:9). So you may go through hell, you may go through horrible judgments, but as you're going through, it will teach you righteousness. Will you suffer? Absolutely! Jesus taught that if you're not willing to forgive as my Father has forgiven you, you will be turned over to the tormentors. God knows how to get your attention. You throw the first stone and you'll have a handful coming back at you. But if you understand not to cast that first stone and you understand the love and mercy of God, you will have that for every human being on the earth. Oh, if you could only have the eyes of understanding to know the reality of *"He hath taken away the sin of the world,"* and that He will continue to judge the earth in righteousness until every human being bows the knee in adoration and gives glory unto God, and then they too will be manifesting the glory of God.

Yes, judgment is a horrible thing to the flesh. Hell is a horrible experience, but it's not the end of the story. God told Jeremiah, *"I will make my words in your mouth a fire and the people stubble."* In other words, Jeremiah, when you speak to my people, the fire of my word will come out and will begin to burn the flesh. You'll speak and the fire of God will begin to burn away and melt away the dross of my people, and they will begin to understand who I am and who they are. Oh, we have great, great things ahead for us because more and more, day by day, you're going to learn these truths, and you're going to begin to see God in such a light, such a revelation of His love, that you too will never again be able to look at another human being with guilt and condemnation. And if you do, God will quickly rebuke you and you'll repent and say, "Father I'm sorry. I realize that they don't understand." So you'll become just like Jesus, who on the Cross said, *"Father forgive them, they don't know what they are doing."* When you have the eyes of the spirit, you'll be able to look at the most rebellious, horrible, sin-laden creature and say, "Father, forgive them, they don't know what they're doing." They don't understand that they too have the very life and nature of God within them that needs to be awakened. And as you say, "Father forgive them," guess what happens, for God has given you power to remit sin. If you pray over someone and they have sinned, their sins shall be forgiven. You see, we have the power of life and death. We can speak life to God's creation or we can speak condemnation and death. What would you rather speak?

Coming Out of Darkness

Chapter 14

God's Infallible Guidance System

"The burden of the word of the Lord for Israel, saith the Lord, which stretches forth the heavens, and lays the foundation of the earth, and forms the spirit of man within him" (Zec. 12:1).

This verse is a mini picture of creation and God's intent for creation. He stretches forth the heavens, He lays the foundation of the earth, and then He forms the spirit in man. *God is Spirit and He formed spirit in man.* One of the most important revelations you will ever receive is that *you are spirit.* In the very depths of your being, far past your intellect and your natural mind and your will, far in the very deepest recesses of your consciousness, perhaps hidden and covered over by the Adamic life, is the spirit of the living God. The burden of the word of the Lord is to unveil and to reveal Christ to the world. The burden of the word of the Lord is to unveil *your* eyes, that you might know that you, in bodily form, are a manifestation of Christ in the flesh. What a treasure you find within yourself when you discover your infallible guidance system. God today is revealing how we as His heritage can find fullness in Him and be His manifestation on the earth.

"Then the eyes of the blind shall be opened, and the ears of the deaf shall be unstopped. Then shall the lame man leap as an hart, and the tongue of the dumb sing: for in the wilderness shall waters break out, and streams in the desert" (Is. 35:5-6).

Today *the eyes of the blind are being opened.* We are beginning to see that we are more than just flesh and blood, we are more than a natural carnal being. We are beginning to see that our true makeup is *spirit.* For years we could only see the natural person that we *seemingly* were. We have learned by experience that our human nature could never manifest the loveliness of God. Once we see that we are spiritual beings and our substance is spirit, we then become conscious that we have the same life and nature as our Father, who is spirit. To understand that our true identity is spirit, and not carnal, enables us to look away from our carnal nature and focus on our true nature. *"He that is joined unto the Lord is one spirit"* (1 Cor. 6:17). When we look away from the natural carnal life and look to the Spirit of God within us, we find that we are being transformed day by day. *"But to this day whenever Moses is read, a veil lies over their heart; but whenever a man turns to the Lord, the veil is taken away. Now the Lord is the Spirit; and where the Spirit of the Lord is, there is liberty. But we all, with unveiled face beholding as in a mirror the glory of the Lord, are being transformed into the same image from glory to glory, just as from the Lord, the Spirit"* (2 Cor. 3:15-18,

NAS).

The veil is our flesh. Whenever we focus on the natural life, trying to make it godly, we are veiled to our true identity. However, when we turn to the Lord within, the veil is removed and we see ourselves as sons of God (spirit) not sons of Adam (flesh).

The ears of the deaf are being unstopped. We are beginning to hear God for ourselves in this glorious day that is dawning. We have listened to many voices in the past, but now our ears are tuned to hear the voice of our beloved. Any voice that does not line up with our Father's character we shall no longer hear. We listened to men for years who told us God was vindictive and would throw most of His creation into a fiery unending torment, without any hope of escape. We are now hearing the truth about God's judgment and correction. He loves us enough to go to any measure to cause us to realize our need of Him. He is relentless in His judgments, not for condemnation, but for transformation.

The lame are beginning to walk. When our eyes are opened to see the reality of our true identity and our ears are opened to hear the voice of God, we then begin to walk as sons of God on the earth. Some of us heard the gospel for many years and we were lame in our ability to walk in the spirit, but today the lame are beginning to walk in the reality of the Kingdom. Today we are beginning to walk and leap and shout and delight in the spirit of the living God. Now, we know that only the life of God can live as God lives on the earth. We have within us the uncreated, indestructible life of God himself. There is a people on the earth today who are walking in the divine life. The more we turn to the Lord, the more the veil will be taken away. We are being transformed day by day into what He is.

Never fail to remember that *God formed the spirit in man* and *God is Spirit*. If this gets into you, you will reveal Christ wherever you go. It's the burden of the word of the Lord that you would go forth and reveal and unveil Christ to all of humanity. Jesus said, ***"God is Spirit: and they that worship him must worship him in spirit and in truth"*** (John 4:24).

I'd like to share with you about your infallible guidance system. You know, this is a computer age with computer terminology, and so I thought that "guidance system" is a pretty good term to use for the Holy Ghost. This is a message that Jesus delivered to His disciples and they took it to the world, and it's the message that turned the then known world upside down and set it ablaze for a short time in the reality of the Kingdom of God. But the message has been lost, and just as Adam and Eve fell in the Garden, so has the New Testament church of God been deceived by the serpent and has been feeding upon the knowledge of good and evil rather than learning to live by God's living guidance system.

For 2,000 years, the system of Christianity has taught us to live by a knowledge of good and evil instead of hearing God for ourselves. Very few have known about it, because living by the inner guidance system was lost 2,000 years ago. Not to everyone, but to the masses of God's people. Most of us don't know too much about church history, but even before the passing of all the original apostles, this subtlety began to creep into the church. This philosophy crept in, teaching people not to follow the inward sense of the spirit, but to follow the outward code of a written law. Trying to decide what is good and what is evil, and trying to take the carnal human life and make it good and make it godly, it totally missed the kernel of the gospel.

His Going Is His Coming

"Let not your heart be troubled: ye believe in God, believe also in me. In my Father's house are many mansions: if it were not so, I would have told you. I go to prepare a place for you. And if I go and prepare a place for you, I will come again, and receive you unto myself; that where I am, there ye may be also" (John 14:1-3).

In the gospel of John, chapter 14, Jesus began to tell his disciples that He was going to leave them. Just imagine what it would be like to have lived with a man for three and a half years who was literally God on the earth! You had seen every need met. You had been with a man who had walked on the water and stilled the winds of adversity. You had walked with a man who had physically opened the eyes of the blind, and caused the physically lame to leap. You had lived with a man for three and a half years and heard nothing pour out of him but the wisdom and the council and the loveliness of God. Then one day that man begins to tell you that he must go away. Can you imagine the grief? Can you imagine the hopes that they may have had while being with him? For generations our people have waited for the Messiah, and *now here he is*. Not too many recognized him, but his disciples, his followers, knew who he was. And can't you imagine that their hopes had built up to such an extent that I'm sure they thought that this man was the one who was going to establish the Kingdom of God on the earth. What a disappointment it must have been when he began to share with them that *he must go away*. In fact, he said to them, **"Nevertheless I tell you the truth; It is expedient for you that I go away: for if I go not away, the Comforter will not come unto you; but if I depart, I will send him unto you"** (John 16:7).

How could they understand that? A man who could control everything in the universe, a man who didn't need a thing. Anything that he possibly desired, he could speak into being. He could feed five thousand people with just a couple of pieces of fish and some bread. How could it possibly be gain for a man like that to go away? What could the world gain by losing such a one who literally was God on the earth, living in a body? How could that be possible, that it would be more beneficial for him to leave than to stay?

"And I will pray the Father, and he shall give you another Comforter, that he may abide with you for ever; even the Spirit of truth; whom the world cannot receive, because it seeth him not, neither knoweth him: but ye know him; for he dwelleth with you, and shall be in you" (John 14:16-17).

He then began to share with them. He said, *"He that has been dwelling with you shall be in you. You see, if I don't go away, the Comforter will not come to you."* There is something that we have missed in the reality of Jesus going through death and resurrection. He said, *"I must go away so that the Comforter, the Holy Ghost, can come."* The reason that must be is that when he went through death and came out in resurrection, then according to 1 Corinthians 15:45, *"The last Adam* (Christ) *was made a life-giving spirit."* Or, it could be said that *He became a spirit who could give life.* Not a man coming out of death and resurrection to set down a new standard of living or a higher set of values, *but a spirit who could give life.* He told them, *"The Comforter has been with you, but I must go away so that He that has been among you can be in you."* Now most of us know this, at least intellectually, but most of us don't know this as a reality. However, you are going to know this, not just mentally, but you are going to hear the Lord Himself speak to you. *"I will pray to the Father and He will give you another comforter, that He may abide with you forever."*

The whole Christian world is waiting for the second coming of Jesus. Is that not true? I want to tell you something, *He was only gone just a few days.* He who was *among* them on the day of resurrection came *into* them on the day of resurrection. He said, *"I am among you, but shall be in you. I'm here now and I can meet all of your needs. I can supply what the world needs, in an outward sense, but what you really need is to realize that you are not a mere human being with a carnal mentality and a carnal lifestyle. You are not Adam* (the Adamic life), *but you are a manifestation of God in the flesh, and you do not realize that yet, because your spirit at this time needs to be regenerated."*

Why is the word "regenerated" used? According to our natural concept, the proper terminology would be that your spirit needs to be generated. That is because most of us do not know our true nature. You have never understood that the burden of the word of the Lord is that He formed you a spirit, so that *He that is among you now can be in you.* So what did Jesus do? The very first day of resurrection, He appeared in the midst of His disciples and he breathed on them and said, *"Receive ye the Holy Ghost."* At that very instant, *He who had been among them quickened them* (made them alive) *and came into them.* Jesus suffered the pangs of death so that He could become a life-giving spirit to give to you everything that

411

He is by the breath of His mouth.

The first Adam was created by the breath of God, and on the day of resurrection, Jesus came to His disciples and breathed upon them and said, *"Receive ye the Holy Spirit."* At that moment the new creation man came into being. We are a new creation, not an old one made over. He breathed His life into our spirit, not into our carnal Adamic nature.

In the breath of life that Jesus breathed into His disciples was contained everything that He is. Everywhere enveloping you is the Spirit, the breath of God. Every day we can breathe the heavenly air of His Spirit and be enlivened by Him to live the divine life on the earth. Jesus said, *"Receive ye the Holy Spirit,"* and what He breathed out of Him and into them was His divine essence. That breath contained everything that He is. Everything that we need is in the breath of God. Just to breathe His name, "O Jesus," is to breathe in all that He is.

When Jesus breathed into them, His breath contained many elements. I will just briefly comment on them here and the Lord can impart much truth to you Himself.

1. The divine life. Peter tells us that **"His divine power hath given unto us all things that pertain unto life and godliness, through the knowledge of him that hath called us to glory and virtue"** (2 Pet. 1:3). As Jesus breathed upon them, their spirit was quickened and divine life began to flow within them. He who had been among them at that time came into them. No longer was it a matter of rules and regulations, because His life would regulate them from within. The outward law of letters became a law of life written upon their hearts. The law of life is His nature regulating you as your life. What we received when we were born again was the life and nature of God.

2. The divine nature. Godliness is the expression of His character. When He breathed on them, they were infused with the character of God. In the flowing of His divine life is the forming within us of His character. When God breathes on you, His life begins to flow in you. This happens regardless of your condition. Peter denied the Lord before the crucifixion, but he still received the breath of God and became a bold teacher of the Word. On the day of Pentecost, Peter boldly proclaimed the gospel, and three thousand were saved. You can breathe in God every day and in that breath is the power to change you into what He is.

3. Death to self. In the breath of Jesus is His death. The experience of that death is in the life-giving spirit that He breathes into you. You will never die to your flesh and come out of your carnal nature through exercising your natural man. You will never be holy in His life and character until His life begins to well up within you. To come out of your carnality you must begin to touch and experience His life that abides within you. When His life begins to flow in you, you no longer have to try with your carnal nature to be holy. You no longer have to worry about the hang-ups in your life. Every time you get into the presence of God and realize His spirit is within you, something of His divine essence is transmitted into you, and in His presence is the killing aspect to your flesh. Death to self comes through His life rising in you, not through you trying to kill the flesh yourself. This is much simpler than we realize. We just learn to turn to His Spirit within us, and as we do that our flesh is put down.

4. *His human living.* In the life-giving Spirit is His human living. His humanity was the finest example we have of someone who was one with God. His nature was one that only did what His Father told Him to do. His divine, exalted, uplifted humanity is in your spirit. Whenever you turn to His Spirit within, you can live by His humanity. ***"He that is joined to the Lord is one Spirit."***

5. *His Resurrection life.* In the breath of God is the resurrection life. The apostle Paul prayed that the eyes of our understanding would be opened, that we might know that the same power that raised Christ from the dead now dwells within us (Eph. 1:19). Paul also said, ***"If the Spirit of him that raised up Jesus from the dead dwell in you, he that raised up Christ from the dead shall also quicken your mortal bodies by his Spirit that dwelleth in you"*** (Rom. 8:11).

6. His ascension. The breath that Jesus breathed also contained his ascension. In the Spirit, you can rise above sin and death. Paul says in Romans 8 that to set the mind on the flesh is death but to set the mind on the Spirit is life and peace. Whenever you set your mind on the Spirit within, you rise above the law of sin and death. This experience is progressive. The more we turn to the Spirit within, the more we rise above sin and death.

7. His enthronement. Enthronement speaks of His authority. He is the supreme head of the universe and we are seated with Him in heavenly places. Paul says in Ephesians 1:21-22, speaking of Jesus, ***"Far above all principality, and power, and might, and dominion, and every name that is named, not only in this world, but also in that which is to come: and hath put all things under his feet, and gave him to be the head over all things to the church, which is his body, the fullness of him that filleth all in all."*** As we learn to turn to and live in our spirit, His authority grows within us. We soon learn to take authority over our Adamic nature and live in His abundant life.

This is why the first apostles turned the world upside down, and this is why we are going to do it again. He says here, *"I'm going away, but I'm not going to leave you comfortless, I will come to you. It will only be a short while and you will not see me, but I will come to you."* Christians have been waiting for 2,000 years for the man Jesus to come and set up His Kingdom. *It will never happen that way.* Please don't misunderstand me. I'm not saying that Jesus will never come back to earth. I'm saying His Kingdom will not be established by Him coming and forcing His rule upon humanity. He is God, and He does not act that way. *He conquers His enemies from within.* He who has been among you shall be in you. That is what you experienced when you were born again, or regenerated, or saved, or whatever terminology you use. When you had that experience, what happened to you at that very moment is that He whom you had heard about, He whom you had read about and who went to the Cross, *came into you at that instant.* And because you've never been taught about your infallible guidance system, you've gone to an outward form of religion. You've gone to the pastors, you've gone to the priests, you've set up a pope, and you get all of your direction, all of your material, and everything else, from the outward realm of humanity and religion, because you have not known that *everything you need is now on the inside of you.*

He who is among you shall be in you. Second coming? It happened on the day of resurrection. But you see, the carnal human nature never changes. Jesus was rejected the first time because He came in a package that they didn't recognize. We tend to look at the package, and because He didn't do what they thought prophecy said He should do, that is to restore the Kingdom, and because He came breaking their Old Testament law, and He came saying things like, *"It is written in your Scriptures, but I say to you, listen to me. This is what My Father is like. I know what your law says, I know what your scriptures say, they say an eye for an eye, and a tooth for a tooth, but I say to you love your enemies and do good to those who despitefully use you."* And then for two thousand years we've been taught that God does the exact opposite to His enemies. That if you won't submit, there will come a day in His anger and in His wrath and in His vengeance that He'll pour out horrible tortures and abominations upon you and send you to an eternal, agonizing, endless hell. You see, I know what your scriptures say. I know what you've been taught as a Christian, but I say unto you that God will not leave anyone in an endless, agonizing torment, but from the inside, from the very depths of your being *He will arise and deliver you.*

"If you find yourself in the throes of hell, behold I am there. And I am there, not to condemn you, but to restore you." This is the kind of message that Jesus brought to the religious people of His day and they put Him on the Cross. The Lord sent His finest example into His vineyard, thinking that His servants would appreciate His finest being, but wicked and slothful men took the most beautiful man in the universe and nailed Him to a cross. Do you think they won't do it again today? Do you dare to stand up before the religious people of today and say, *"I have come that you might have life"*? They will do exactly the same thing to you that they did to Jesus.

What, you, a man, make yourself as God?

Your True Being Is Spirit

The burden of the word of the Lord to His people is that they might understand that their being is spirit, and that will break all of the human bondage. All of the human beliefs and limitations shall begin to crumble when you understand that He whom you thought was outside of you is within you. You see, Gary Sigler in his humanity is so limited in his ability. Gary in his humanity was one of the most horrible examples of what a Christian should be, 15 years ago. But today, I live, yet not I, but it's Christ. And unless I had somehow come into an understanding of that, I would still be that human creature that was alienated and separated in my mind from a God who lives within my being. Oh, the Apostle Paul said, ***"That I might know Him and the power of His resurrection"*** (Phil. 3:10). He prayed, ***"Oh Father, that the eyes of their understanding would be enlightened, that they might know the hope of their calling, and that they might know that that same life that raised Jesus from the dead now dwells within their very own being"*** (Eph. 1:18-20).

If you are in sin and bondage, if you have habits that you can't overcome, go to God for an unveiling. These are the days when He is unveiling Christ once again. Behold the messenger of the covenant shall surely come to His temple, *which temple you are.* It's almost unbelievable when you begin to walk in the reality of the Kingdom to realize that you could have sat in church and read the Bible for years, listened to hundreds of messages, and yet have never understood that He, the Spirit of truth, is within you. Many still think that they are going to have to die to experience heaven, when all the time, Jesus said, ***"The kingdom of God is within you"*** (Luke 17:21).

The ministry that God has given me is to restore the hearts of his children back to Him their Father. We have been given such a poor concept of our Father's ability to work in our lives. All that we have been told is that we are not worthy. In our religious mentality we feel so unworthy. How could I enter the presence of God the way that I am? Yet Hebrews 10 tells us that by the suffering of Jesus, He has once and forever sanctified you, and that He has taken away the sin, *your* sin, your *every* act of disobedience, *every* habit in your life, the consequences of your actions in His sight. You will never be tossed into an endless torment for your actions. You don't have to be ashamed to walk boldly into His presence with your habits and your hang-ups and your drug addictions and your prostitution. I'm telling you that the veil of the temple has been rent, and as it says in Hebrews 10:16-19, ***"This is the covenant that I will make with them after those days, saith the Lord, I will put my laws into their hearts, and in their minds will I write them; and their sins and iniquities will I remember no more. Now where remission of these is,*** *there is no more offering for sin. Having therefore, brethren, boldness to enter into the holiest by the blood of Jesus."*

Come boldly into His presence *and watch your life change.* If you can believe that God loves you enough to receive you every day just as you are, you can come into His presence and your life will begin to change. Electricity is a good typology to use for God. If you take a cover off of a light socket and you grab hold of a bare wire, that electricity has no concept of your good or evil. It doesn't matter how good you are or how bad you are, that electricity will infiltrate and permeate every area of your body. If you understand the price of Calvary and if you understand the heart of your Father, you can take your prostitution and you can enter into the presence of God, and I'm telling you that as you enter into His presence, there is something of His divine essence that is transfused into you that will bring you transformation. I know how this sounds to the religious mind, but I am telling you the truth, as God is on the throne, that if you stop your prostitution, that is good, but that is not the goal of God. His goal is to absolutely infiltrate, saturate, and permeate every area of your thought and being. He wants to saturate and permeate every cell and every atom in your body. If you could have just a little bit of understanding and just a little bit of faith, you would know that nothing, absolutely nothing, can separate you from the love of a father towards his child. When you enter into His presence, every day you will be transfused with divine electricity.

The Spirit Will Guide You Into All Truth

John 16:13 says, *"Howbeit when he, the Spirit of truth, is come, he will guide you into all truth: for he shall not speak of himself; but whatsoever he shall hear, that shall he speak: and he will shew you things to come."*

The reason each and every one of you today has not been ushered into and understands the whole truth of the gospel is that you have always been taught to listen to another voice which tells you that you must submit yourself to a pastor or priest or to an apostle or prophet. *The priesthood of Aaron ended at the Cross.* You no longer need a man such as Aaron or a pastor to go into the presence of God for you. You no longer need a high priest to enter for you into the presence of God to plead to God on your behalf.

Today the priesthood has been changed into the Melchisedec order. What does that mean? It simply means that God Himself comes to you bringing to you the bread of His word and the wine of His enjoyment. *When He, the Spirit of Truth, is come, He will guide you into all truth.* You see, you are hearing truth from me, *but God will also speak within you.* Don't try to figure this out according to the knowledge of right and wrong. God, is what this man saying right? God, is what this man is saying wrong? You go to God for the infusion of His spirit within you. When He, the Spirit of Truth, is come, *He will guide you into all truth.* For He will not speak of Himself, but whatever He hears, that shall He speak. *He will show you things to come.* Do you really realize that the Spirit within you will show you things to come? You no longer need anyone to tell you what to do.

Most of God's people are still under the old order of the law and the prophets. So many are always trying to get a word from a prophet. Almost everywhere I go, people say they can't hear God and cannot understand when they are told that they can hear God. Stop listening to outward voices. Stop running to the pastor, stop running to the prophet to get a word, and understand that *He, the Spirit of Truth, is in you, and He shall reveal to you all truth.* Folks, this is Bible. When He, the Spirit of Truth, is come, He will guide you into all truth. I'm obviously not against teachers, because I am a teacher, but I am going to share with you what the scripture says.

1 John 2:27 says, ***"But the anointing . . ."*** The anointing is the moving and quickening of the spirit of God within you. ***"The anointing which you have received of Him abides in you and you do not need that any man teach you."*** The pastors and the leaders absolutely gnash their teeth when they hear this word. *The only thing that a teacher is here to do is to teach you that you do not need to rely on the teacher.* The teachers need to teach you how to hear God and then you won't need the teachers. The men who are sharing the word today are not so much

teachers as they are confirmers of the word. What they share with you, you may not have heard before, but something within you will bear witness to the truth. Most of the time, it will be a confirming word that the Lord has already been speaking to you.

"The anointing which you have received of Him abides in you and you do not need that any man teach you, but that same anointing teaches you all things, and it is truth, it is not a lie. Even as it has taught you, you shall abide in Him." You have not been taught that you don't need anyone but God. In fact, there is no person who can help you *but* God, no one understands you but God. Other people can look at you and say, "Look at you, you have been a Christian for years, and look at the condition you are in. Look at the habits that you still display. Look at the carnal nature that you still exhibit." Nobody but God understands you in reality. He knows exactly why you are doing what you are doing. He knows the conditions and environment in which you were raised. He knows the way in which you were taught and brought up. He knows every facet of your being, but most of all, He knows that whatever you are in the natural, you have inherited from Adam, and just as deadly as cancer is to humanity, so sin is that deadly. Just as you cannot help a cancer growing on your body or in your body, no more can you help the disease of sin which you have been born into. It is an incurable disease that has passed to every human who has ever drawn his first breath. Not all of you

will experience the disease of cancer, but all of you have experienced the disease of your father Adam. ***"For as in Adam all die, even so in Christ shall all be made alive"*** (1 Cor. 15:22). ***"Wherefore, as by one man sin entered into the world, and death by sin; and so death passed upon all men, for that all have sinned"*** (Rom 5:12).

No one understands you like God, and that is why His heart is to get you to turn to him, because he understands that you have been born with this horrible disease called sin, that in some people is much more evident than in others, but in everyone, the root is the same. He came not to recreate Adam, not to make your natural life better, but *He came to replace that old Adamic nature.* When you begin to understand your inner guidance system, you then begin to enter into the presence of the Lord, and as you seek Him, you will then enter into reality the realm of Pentecost. *The realm of Pentecost is not just a matter of speaking in tongues, but it is the experience of beginning to hear the voice of God.*

I know many people who speak in tongues who absolutely do not understand when I speak to them about hearing God. I am not downplaying the importance of tongues, I am simply saying that the most important thing you will ever experience in your life is He who you thought was without you is within you to become your inner guidance. You keep praying to a God in the heavens like He is some kind of a Santa Claus, and in your mentality you think that if I fast enough, if I pray enough, if I read my Bible enough, if I don't sin too much, then when I pray, Santa Claus will answer me. But you better watch out, because if you are not living right, if you are not doing right, Santa Claus will not answer your prayers. I know that is offensive to the religious mind, but that is the image of God that we have been given. He is no more than a giant Santa Claus in the sky, and if we do right, He will bless us, and if we do wrong, He will curse us. But He says, *"Behold I make my rain,* (representing the Spirit of God) *to fall on the just and the unjust."* He is not a Santa Claus.

The only prayer God will ever answer for you is the prayer and the intercession that He has birthed within your spirit. I sometimes cry and weep in agonizing prayer for God's people, but I could never work up some kind of a religious feeling that I need to pray for people because they are lost. However, when He rises up within you to speak His word or to intercede, you can be assured His will will be accomplished. Do you think that today He is not weeping over the condition of His people? He weeps within His temple. He lays between the porch and the altar, and *He intercedes in humanity.* That's how God operates. He doesn't operate from some far away planet somewhere, *He operates from within His holy temple, which temple you are.*

You must begin in very simple ways to seek God to introduce you to your inner guidance system. Just speak to Him, "God, I don't know how to hear you. God, this sounds wonderful, because if what this man is saying is true, I have One inside of me who will lead me into all truth." Isn't that what you are seeking? Isn't that what the masses of humanity are running into churches for? They are hungry for truth. Yet that which they are seeking from their pastor, that which they are seeking from their churches, can be found within their very own being.

When you begin to hear God for yourself, you will run to your assemblies and you will speak to one another in songs, in hymns, and in spiritual songs. You won't have to ask if anyone has a testimony. There was a time when I went to church, that if the pastor would ask if anyone had a testimony, I would quiver and shake in fear that he would call on me. Now I can boldly stand before thousands of people and proclaim the gospel without any sense of inferiority or fear or inability to do that which He has called me to do. Gary did not learn that by being a good boy. He learned that through his inner guidance system.

Living Law of Letters, or Law of Life

Most of us have lived our Christian lives according to the principle of right and wrong, good or evil, which is based on an outward code of conduct. When we go to do something, we must stop acting according to right and wrong and look to the anointing within. Our dear friends Bill & Elaine Cook say, "When you go to do something, you wait for the rising or falling of life within you." If there is a positive response within you, the inner life and anointing is saying OK. However, if you sense a decrease of the anointing, if you have an unrest in your spirit, then you stop, even if what you are about to do seems right. Also, if it seems a wrong thing to do and the anointing rises within you to do it, then by all means do it. As an example, when someone on the street asks me for money, I never try to figure out if I should or shouldn't give it to them. I don't think about what the person may do with the money, I go by the inner anointing. If I feel a rise of the spirit, I give the money, if I feel a falling of the anointing, I don't. It is that simple. We must all learn to trust our inner guidance system. We do most things according to the knowledge of right and wrong because we do not check within for the anointing.

There are times when I will go to do something, or I will want something really badly, and I will set my will in motion to go do that very thing, and as I go to do it, I might have just a small sense that maybe I shouldn't do it. That is the voice of your inner guidance system. It is not necessarily God speaking to you in an audible voice, or even in plain English, but your guidance system is just that. It is absolutely infallible. There is no man who is infallible. Only God is infallible. The Bible in its present form is not infallible, God is infallible.

Here is a quote by Watchman Nee from "Sermons That Never Die", by George Hawtin. Watchman Nee wrote,

I recall a story of two brothers who cultivated paddy-fields. Their fields were half way up the hill: others were lower down. In the great heat they drew water by day and went to sleep at night. One night while they were sleeping, the farmers lower down the hill dug a hole in the irrigation channel surrounding the brothers' fields and let all the water flow down on their own fields. The next morning the brothers saw what had happened but said nothing. Again they filled the troughs with water, and again all the water was drawn off the following night. Still no word of protest was uttered when the next day dawned and they discovered what a mean trick the same farmers had played on them. Were they not Christians? Ought not Christians to be patient? This game was repeated seven nights in succession: and for seven days in succession these two brothers silently suffered the wrong. One would have thought that Christians who could allow themselves to be treated like that day after day, and never utter a word of reproach, would surely be overflowing with joy. Strange to say, they were not happy at all, and their unhappiness distressed them to such an extent that they brought the matter to a brother who was in the Lord's service. Having stated their case, they asked him: "How does it come about that having suffered this wrong for a full week, we are still unhappy?" This brother had some experience and he replied: "You're unhappy because you have not gone the full length. You should first irrigate those farmers' fields and then irrigate your own. You go back and test it out, and see whether or not your hearts find rest." They agreed to do it, and off they went. The next morning they were afoot earlier than ever, and their first business was to irrigate the fields of those farmers who had so persistently robbed their fields of water. And this amazing thing happened—the more they labored on their persecutors' land, the happier they became. By the time they had finished watering their own land, their hearts were at perfect rest. When the brothers had repeated this for two or three days, the farmers called to apologize and added: "If this is Christianity, then we want to hear more about it."

Here we see the difference between the principle of right and wrong and the principle of life. Those two brothers had been most patient: was that not right? They had labored in intense heat to irrigate their paddy-fields and without a word of complaint had suffered others to steal their water, was that not very good? What then was lacking that they had no peace of heart? They had done what was right, they had done what was good, they had done all that man could require of them. But God was not satisfied. They had no peace of heart because they had not met the demands of His life. When they conformed to His standard, joy and peace welled up in their hearts. The demands of His divine life must be met, so we dare not stop short of God's satisfaction.

God has led me in many areas since I learned to listen to my inner guidance. In 1986, my wife and I both had very good jobs. I was doing NASA's receiving inspection for the space shuttle. My wife had been at Pacific Telephone Company for 16 years, very close to a 20 year retirement, and God spoke to me and said, "Leave your job and go help a pastor who is starting a work for me." Carol and I had already discussed this, and I had told her what I felt the Lord was saying. She was scared, I also was a little bit nervous, but she said, "I know you hear God. You do what He says." This pastor had often said how wonderful it would be to have me along his side, to be able to minister to the needs of the people, and so I walked into his office one day and said, "Brother, I have good news for you. The Lord told me to leave my job and come help you." He said, "No, brother, you can't do that. Gary, there is no way that I can afford another salary." I said, "I didn't say a thing about salary, I said God spoke to me and told me that you need help. He doesn't want me to come here and take from you." I said, "You have known me for several months now. Do you think that God would tell me to do something and then leave me in any kind of lack or hurt when I obey Him?" He said, "No." I told him that if he was not in agreement that I would not do it, but "I am telling you what God told me." He said, "Gary, don't misunderstand me, I would love to have you with me." I said, "Then don't worry about the salary." He said, "Alright, we'll pray and agree." I left my job and went to work in that ministry, and as God is my witness, money started coming to me. The income of the ministry increased so that the salary that I left at NASA was given to me by the ministry.

Then the Lord spoke to my wife, and she joined me full time in that ministry. We both left excellent jobs because we learned how to hear the voice of God's anointing. Then there was a time when I had to resign that ministry. I had a salary that a lot of people would give anything to have. I had to walk away from it because the ministry had left the anointing of the inner guidance, and so God said that I must walk away from it. Once again, my wife and I fellowshipped together. She was in full agreement, and we left that ministry, not knowing where our next month's rent was coming from. However, we never missed a month's payment on our rent.

We all have this inner guidance system. We have just not been taught to practice it. Every one has times when you go to do something and you have just a small sense not to do it. You should follow that sense. Many times, you may be unwilling to do something, but you just have the sense you should do it. That is your infallible guidance system.

That is why the greatest man that ever lived went away, so that He could become a life-giving spirit to guide you from within, and become your living guidance system.

Learning to follow your inner guidance system is a simple way for you begin to walk in the reality of the Kingdom. You open yourself to God every day and become sensitive to what He is saying to you.

If you will seek the Kingdom of God first, then all things shall be added unto you. So many people put their focus and their attention on seeking after *things,* even the things of God. There are multitudes of people today who set their attention, focus and desires on the gifts of the Spirit. Having the gifts operate through you is wonderful. However, many hunger and thirst and pray and desire to have the gifts above everything else. Some of them then begin to perform mighty works, and people begin to be healed. They walk in the gifts of knowledge and wisdom, giving people words everywhere they go. There may come a day when they stand before the Judge of the Universe and say, "But Lord, we cast out demons in your name. God, we healed the sick and we raised the dead in your name." They may hear Him say, *"I never knew you. Yes, you sought after something of me, and your intent was to have something of Me, but you did not take the time to have Me infiltrate your being. You were like the foolish virgins who arose and said that there was not enough oil in their lamps. So I have to say to you that although you have raised the dead and healed the sick in my name, now you must go and pay the price to have the Spirit of the Living God infiltrate and transform your being."* It is so very important to remember that one who operates in spiritual gifts is not necessarily a spiritual person. Some of the most spiritually gifted people are the most carnal.

Everything that you could possibly desire is within you. This is why the shell of your outer man (the Adamic nature) must be broken. All of your life, you may have been taught that you must make that thing better, and you have missed the fact that He who is within you is greater than he who is in the world. You may never stop your habits and your addictions in Adam. Some who have strong natural characters and wills may be able to do so, but others are hopeless to ever make Adam better. That is why you need the glorious gospel of God that will give you the power of God to break every chain and every fetter.

Years ago, I used to sit in the assembly of the righteous, singing "Jesus breaks every fetter", with tears streaming down my face, thinking, "Oh God, I wish that this was so." I didn't know about my inner guidance system. All I knew was that I was wrong and that I was very bad. I loved God, but the law of sin and death was stronger than my desire for God, so I was a hopeless human being, like many are today. If you never get hold of the reality of He who is within you, you will die trying to become a good Christian, not understanding that you are trying to become something that you already are, not in Adam, but in Christ.

When I began to follow my inner guidance system, the voice of my spirit, one of the things that God taught me was to never go by any kind of an outward law, whether it's the law of the Bible or the law of the Ten Commandments. He said those are but shadows and types of the reality, because today He is writing His law in our hearts. So today, when people ask me whether or not they should tithe, or do any number of other things, I tell them that the only responsibility they have is to go into their closet and seek God and then do what He says. You cannot lose if you begin to hear the voice of your inner guidance.

The reason that it is so hard for you to follow your inner guidance is that you have never been taught that you can trust what you hear. In fact, you'll be taught just the opposite. If you take my message to a pastor in town and tell him that this man told me that I can hear God and just do whatever He says, the first thing he will begin to do is to caution you. He would probably be very well-meaning, but he would want you to take everything you heard and run it by him so he could discern for you whether or not you are hearing God. The moment you do that, you are violating the very words that Jesus told you. *"When He the Spirit of truth is come, He will guide you into all truth."*

The anointing that abides in you will teach you all things, and it is the truth. It won't lie to you, but what happens is that when you begin to hear it, it is so foreign to everything that is inbred into your consciousness concerning God and religion, that when your guidance system begins to talk to you, if you have the typical religious mindset, you will rebuke the devil. I've done it myself. One of the first things you will learn when God begins to speak to you and you begin to understand your inner guidance, is that you'll shut out the other voices. Now, that doesn't mean that you won't listen to someone if they have something to share with you. However, you must not let others control you. God will guide you, and you do not need another to take His place in your direction. Jesus said, *"My sheep hear my voice and the voice of a stranger they will not follow."* The reason most of you have been listening to the voice of the stranger all of your lives is that you don't know God's voice. The voice of the stranger sounds like God's voice. There isn't a pastor that I know that is intentionally leading his people astray. He just does not understand.

You will pay a very dear price for walking in the Kingdom of God. When you begin to follow your guidance system, many Christians will think you are being led astray. God will lead you out of all religions and religious practices and teach you how to follow Him. The first thing God does is stir your heart up. He has given you a pure heart. He has taken out the stony heart and has given you a heart of flesh, and you have a heart for God, so you want to please Him. You have many desires for God. But not every one of those desires and ideas come from God. You will learn to discern by His leading within you. Your pastor does not know in intricate detail God's will for your life. God's leaders have no jurisdiction and no control over your life. A leader is simply there to guide you, not control you. Please understand this. The moment a pastor, or a leader, or a shepherd, or an elder begins to control you in an outward way, and begins to tell you what to do, *run from that man.* He should only confirm to you what your inner guidance is trying to tell you. This does not mean that I never give anyone advice, but my place as a minister of the gospel is to help you to the best of my ability. So, if I see you walking into a ditch, I may caution you, but I will not tell you that you can't do that, and if you continue walking and fall into the ditch, I will be the first one there to help you up and brush you off and encourage you to keep walking. Today, if most pastors tell you something and you don't do what they say, they label you a rebellious person.

The Kingdom of God comes from within the very depths of your being, not from an outward rule. It's an absolute joke that people are being taught that when Jesus comes, they will rule and reign with Him for a thousand years. What do you think you are going to do? Do you think you are going to legislate morality? Do you think you are going to pass laws to make this a righteous nation? Do you think that Jesus is going to come back and force His rule upon humanity and make them bow the knee? If so, you don't know your Maker. He is going to come and rule and reign within a people, yet those people will not rule and reign over anything in an outward way. To walk in the Kingdom of God means that the King and Master of the Universe is ruling and reigning within my being. For me to take that and try to force it on you is an abomination unto God. He destroys His enemies from the inside out. Carnally minded men today are once again trying to reestablish the New Testament Church, and I say, for what? It didn't make it the first time. Why do we want to go back and do it again? The Kingdom of Heaven is being established in the hearts of God's people, and they will surely reign, but only over their own being. You will never rule and reign with Christ until He has full rule and reign in your life, and then you would never rule and reign over another human being. You will simply minister life to them. You will lead them by example, not rule over them.

You see, when the fullness of His life comes forth in humanity, they will run to you. They will fall at your feet. Now I'm not saying I'm there in totality. Of course I'm not. But even today, little children come to me with tears in their eyes saying how much they appreciate hearing the love of God. One little girl this year, 12 years old, after a message like this, came up to me with tears in her eyes and a dollar bill in her hand as an offering. And she said, "Everywhere I go, people have told me that I'm a bad girl and that Jesus won't love me. I'm so thankful that you have told me that God loves me." And I can guarantee you, that little girl's life will change. I have teenagers call me on the telephone, just opening their hearts to me telling me about their drug addictions, telling me about their problems, because they know there's at least one man on the earth who has nothing but love and compassion and consideration for where they are.

The Gospel Is Good News for Everyone

When the brightness and the glory of God's manifested presence in His people fills the earth, they will run to Zion in countless thousands. They will fall before the presence of God that you carry, and you will have nothing to minister to them but love and compassion and strength. You see, that's your God. Yet we've been taught to fear God in the wrong way, to fear His judgments. Christianity has this horrible teaching that there will come a day when God will hold His precious people up in the air, and then He will pour out His anger and His wrath and His horrible judgments full of tortures and boils and demons upon the whole earth to make them suffer for their sins. The people who teach this cannot possibly believe that Jesus in reality took away the sins of the world. Those who are teaching that are going to suffer more than the sinful masses of humanity when they stand before the judge of the universe and discover that they have misrepresented the love of God. They have perpetrated a wrong concept of God to the people. The people who have rejected God have only rejected the concept that Christianity has given to them. Do you think they would reject the God that I am presenting to you? There are some hardened, bitter people who would. But listen, you can't withstand this kind of love and knowledge and compassion forever, no matter how hard and bitter you are. As you understand that God's judgments are for correction and purification, no matter how hard and bitter a criminal you are, eventually your heart is going to melt. And then you will understand the scripture that says, ***"As in Adam all die, so in Christ shall all be made alive, and every man in his own order."*** The gospel is good news for everyone.

We all know what Jesus taught. He taught His followers how to live the God kind of life. If someone strikes you, if someone asks for your cloak, you give them everything. You return blessing for cursing. You say, that's impossible! Well it is, in Adam! But I could tell you many experiences I've had of horrible rejection from the Christian population. I could tell you horror stories of what people have done to me. And I can also stand here and tell you very clearly and very definitely that I have laid on my face weeping for those very people who have tried to do me the most harm, because the King lives in me. I don't just *have* the compassion of God anymore. I have *become* the compassion of God. I don't seek after His gifts anymore. I have Him! If He ever says to me, "Go pull Jason out of his wheelchair," I can guarantee that he will come out, and you'll see that day happen. But God today is pulling the plug on everything, in order to get His people centered on Him. You're not seeing a whole lot of gifts today. In Pentecost you have the gifts. But in Tabernacles, in the Most Holy Place, you have God Himself. In Pentecost we began to *hear* the voice of God. But in Tabernacles we *become* the voice of God. And again, the self-righteous Pharisees will say, "Who does this man think he is?" They can prove to you that I've never been to a Bible school. They can prove to you that I know nothing about homiletics and hermeneutics. Who does this man think he is, walking among us, declaring that He is the voice of God? Well, judge for yourself if what I say to you is truth or error. You can do that, and you have the liberty to do that. But the moment you begin to throw stones, it is very dangerous, not for me, but for you. There will come a day when every one of you will stand up in the conviction and the boldness to be able to say, "I have become the voice of my Master on the earth."

We are learning how to operate in the Kingdom. We see miracles happen every day in our publishing. We are sending thousands of books and tapes all over the world. There is no way that we could distribute thousands of books and tapes and go where we go and do what we do without God supplying our need. We never take an offering in our meetings. And if we go somewhere and we walk out without anyone giving us a dollar, God will supply our need. And that's not letting you off the hook, because you are under obligation and responsibility to do what God tells you to do. If He speaks to you to do something for someone and you don't do it, you're missing your guidance system. We don't give people the idea that they can't give to us, but we want them to understand the principle of the Kingdom is in giving and receiving. God said to me many years ago, ***"When you go somewhere, you give, give as much as you possibly can. My people need to see how I give, not how I take."***

This is such a new concept to most of God's people that we almost have to beg people to take what we give them. They feel bad walking out with a bag of books and tapes that they don't have money to pay for. *Get over it!* You don't have to feel bad. When God wants to give you something, just appreciate it. And who knows, maybe next year you might come into a million dollars and you'll remember a man who blessed you so tremendously that you'll want to bless his ministry so he can continue to bless others. You see, we're not concerned about what you can do or can't do anyway. We're concerned that you hear the message that God is in the business of saving you, *not from hell, but from Adam*, your carnal nature. And He can only do that as you go before Him and have Him teach you how to follow His anointing that is within you.

If you're in the typical Christian circles, you'll hear many messengers that will be absolutely diametrically opposed to what I'm teaching you today. But, you see, you've heard the truth, and you'll recognize the voice of the stranger. Listen! Not just to what I'm saying, but learn to sit and listen to what God says. And if you feel God wants you to do something and you're not sure if it's God, search out your heart, be honest with yourself whether this is a selfish ambition or whether you honestly feel this is a desire that may be of God. If you feel it is of God, then go do it, regardless of what anyone says. If it's wrong, you will learn by your mistakes as well as your successes how to follow your inner guidance system. You'll learn that sometimes you're absolutely convinced that this is God and you'll do it and it won't be, but it will make you very clear that you can't just follow your natural understanding. You will learn to be so sensitive to that still, small voice of your spirit. It's like a woman's intuition. That's the voice of your spirit. And most of us have never been taught or know how to follow our own spirit.

So you have an infallible guidance system. And that guidance system will lead you into every truth that has ever been known of God. Carnal religious men don't know that truth. There isn't a pastor on the face of the earth that could lead you into all truth. But Jesus said that your inner guidance system will. He said, *"He will guide you into all truth."* It's the only place you will ever find it. You have to quit looking for God out in the universe somewhere. Where is He? Is He up on another planet somewhere? God is everywhere, but you must discover that *His infallible guidance system is within you.*

Made in the USA
Middletown, DE
03 November 2016